Growing Stronger

Stewart Holloway

ISBN: 9798649881982

DEDICATION

To the churches I have been privileged to serve:

First Baptist Church, Lecompte, Louisiana
My home church that nurtured me, gave me an opportunity to serve, and taught me what it means to have big faith through a church merger and faith-filled building program.

Pine Grove Baptist Church, Ruby, Louisiana
Who gave me my first position as a youth minister and showed me how a rural church can be a strong church.

Bellevue Baptist Church, Hurst, Texas
Who showed me that church revitalization is possible.

Forestburg Baptist Church, Forestburg, Texas
My first pastorate who taught me that big vision can be realized anywhere – even in the middle of ~~nowhere~~ everywhere.

First Baptist Church Pineville, Pineville, Louisiana
Our present pastorate that is growing stronger every day for His glory.

CONTENTS

PREFACE

In 2014 our church was preparing for our first building program in twenty years. As the committees met and excited conversations occurred among our people, I felt the Lord leading me to preach through 1 Corinthians to help us grow stronger as we prepared for our future. At thirty-seven messages, the series was the longest I had preached to that point in my ministry. Still, the response was encouraging. Throughout the series, members of our congregation took notes and commented on what they were learning. We were indeed growing stronger.

While I was editing this work, my oldest son Zachary asked, "Daddy, why are you working on this book?" Good question! My prayer is that this study will help you and your church grow stronger. The book could be used in a number of ways. An individual might use the book in his or her personal devotions by reading the scripture text covered by a particular chapter, reading the chapter, and then reflecting on both the biblical text and the chapter. A pastor might use this book as the beginning nuggets of a message series on 1 Corinthians. We all need help saying old truths in new ways. Finally, a small group could use the book to guide a study of 1 Corinthians. However you choose to use *Growing Stronger*, I pray it is beneficial to you and your church.

I am grateful to many people who helped make this book possible. While a student at Southwestern Baptist Theological Seminary in Fort Worth, Texas, I had the privilege of taking an exegetical class on 1 Corinthians with Dr. Ken Hemphill, then President of Southwestern. Dr. Hemphill's class was one of the most enriching of my seminary days. I am indebted to him for some of the content of this work.

My wife Rebecca's belief in me has been my motivation. She has offered suggestions for improvement as well as "handled" our boys when I have focused on writing.

My mom is also a constant encourager in my ministry providing far more help to us in this stage of life than we do to her.

Someone has said, "The church makes the pastor." For the last twelve years, the people of First Baptist Church Pineville have been making me a better preacher. As attentive and affirming listeners, they are a great congregation to whom to preach. My additional appreciation is given to the Wednesday night group who journeyed back through this content with me during the summer of 2017. Their thoughts and insights helped make the book more helpful.

I am also grateful for my pastors and fathers in the ministry including Bob Williford, Ron Aguillard, Waynon Mott, Carl Burris, Rick Henson, and Mickey Hudnall. The foundation they laid and the examples they set have helped make me into the preacher I am. My gratitude also extends to the host of retired ministers and missionaries in First Pineville who are constant encouragers to me as their pastor.

Stewart Holloway
Pineville, Louisiana
July 2020

INTRODUCTION

Every church needs to be stronger than it is today. Our church does. Your church does. No matter the size, location, or denomination, every church needs to grow stronger.

When I speak of growing stronger as a church, I do not mean the typical measures of building and bodies or programs and ministries. I mean the people, specifically, the congregation's commitment to the Lord and to each other. While counting people and evaluating programs are important practices for growing a strong church, the greatest growth comes when members grow in both their vertical relationship with God and their horizontal relationships with others. How do we grow in those relationships? First Corinthians offers help.

Paul's Most Challenging Church

The church at Corinth was possibly Paul's most challenging church. The people of Corinth were self-absorbed. They admired themselves, did what they wanted, and indulged their every whim. Consequently, the church was a mess.

The Corinthian situation begs a question: why look at a messed up church if we want to learn how to help our church grow stronger? Simple – often the worst model provides the best example from which to learn. We can learn a lot of what *not to do* from the Church at Corinth, and we can learn a lot of what *to do* from Paul's instruction to the church.

If Paul had published 1 Corinthians as a book today, on the back cover would be a quote from some prominent pastor saying, "This book is a must read for every church leader and member." The issues Paul deals with in this letter are ones that nearly every church faces and are as pressing in the twenty-first century as they were in the first.

As we journey through Paul's letter to this messed up church, we will both laugh and cry as the Lord encourages us and convicts us through the mess of Corinth and the message of Paul. We *will* grow stronger.

Corinth: The City and Its People

Situated on a narrow neck of land that connected the Peloponnesian Peninsula with northern Greece, Corinth served as the capital of the Roman province of Achaia. Because of its unique location, the city had not one but two seaports, one on the east and one to the west. Today, these two seaports are connected with a canal which traverses the peninsula. In the first century, however, they were connected by a paved trackway known as the Diolkos. Ships would sail into one port and then be moved across land to the other. The shortcut allowed the vessels to avoid the much longer and dangerous trip around the peninsula. Aristophanes, a comic playwright of the fourth century B.C., penned a phrase "as fast as a Corinthian", indicating the trackway had acquired a reputation for swiftness.

Naturally, because of the amount of trade which flowed through the area, Corinth was a place of incredible economic prosperity. By New Testament times, the population could have been as much as one half million.

Corinth was also known for an athletic event, the Isthmian Games. This Olympic-style competition took place every two years. Huge crowds thronged the city during the games.

Heavily influenced by the Greeks, the city had a temple dedicated to the worship of Aphrodite, the Greek goddess of love, pleasure, and procreation. Ancient writers indicate that as many as one thousand sacred prostitutes offered their bodies in the temple in the service of the goddess. Whether or not there were temple prostitutes to this extent by the time of Paul is doubtful, but this *was* a sea-port town. It was a city of more than one Bourbon Street. And, like Las Vegas, what happened in Corinth, stayed in Corinth. Yes, Corinth was a sin city – so much so that Aristophanes coined another term, one built on the word for Corinthians which meant "degenerate" or "to practice fornication." Paul had his work cut out for him!

Paul's Relationship with the Corinthian Church

Luke gives us a summary of Paul's relationship with the Corinthian Church in the book of Acts:

> ***Acts 18:1-11*** *After this, Paul left Athens and went to Corinth. [2] There he met a Jew named Aquila, a native of Pontus, who had recently come from Italy with his wife Priscilla, because Claudius had ordered all the Jews to leave Rome. Paul went to see them, [3] and because he was a tentmaker as they were, he stayed and worked with them. [4] Every Sabbath he reasoned in the synagogue, trying to persuade Jews and Greeks. [5] When Silas and Timothy came from Macedonia, Paul devoted himself exclusively to preaching, testifying to the Jews that Jesus was the Christ. [6] But when the Jews opposed Paul and became abusive, he shook out his clothes in protest and said to them, "Your blood be on your own heads! I am clear of my responsibility. From now on I will go to the Gentiles." [7] Then Paul left the synagogue and went next door to the house of Titius Justus, a worshiper of God. [8] Crispus, the synagogue ruler, and his entire household believed in the Lord; and many of the Corinthians who heard him believed and were baptized. [9] One night the Lord spoke to Paul in a vision: "Do not be afraid; keep on speaking, do not be silent. [10] For I am with you, and no one is going to attack and harm you, because I have many people in this city." [11] So Paul stayed for a year and a half, teaching them the word of God.*

Arriving in Corinth during his second missionary journey (A.D. 49-52), Paul preached the gospel for eighteen months in the city. As a result, many people came to faith in Jesus Christ and were baptized. As they did, Paul established the church in the home of Titius Justus, next door to the city's synagogue from which the Jews previously had run him out. Amazingly, Crispus, the synagogue ruler, and his entire household believed in the Lord! Though Paul was somewhat apprehensive about staying in Corinth, God gave him courage to remain in the city and continue preaching.

After leaving Corinth and going on to Ephesus, Paul wrote a letter, now lost, in which he urged the Corinthians to avoid association with professing believers who were immoral (1 Cor. 5:9-11). Paul then wrote 1 Corinthians from Ephesus during his third missionary journey (A.D. 52-55) to advise the Corinthians on problems in the church.

The Corinthian Church

Though there were some people of substance who came to faith in Christ and joined the church, most members in Corinth were commoners. Still, among the congregation, there were clearly both "haves" and "have nots". Problems developed in the church because of these different classes of people, and Paul addresses these relationship clashes in his letter.

In the months following Paul's first visit, the situation in Corinth became problematic. Paul received reports about the church's condition from Chloe's household (1:11). Chloe was a merchant woman and leader in the church who knew Paul. She was likely an innocent volunteer of information with genuine concern for the church.

In the letter, Paul demonstrates that the real problem in Corinth was spiritual enthusiasm. There is nothing wrong with enthusiasm when it is channeled appropriately. Unfortunately, in Corinth, this enthusiasm was an immature zeal that resulted in an attitude of spiritual superiority.

After he sent his first letter to the Corinthians, Paul made his "sorrowful" visit, named such by his discovery that problems still existed (2 Cor. 2:1). Paul sent another letter, also lost, calling the Corinthians to repentance and urging discipline for an opponent in the church (2 Cor. 2:3-4). Titus carried the letter to Corinth. Some believe this letter is actually 2 Corinthians 10-13, but we cannot be sure. Sometime later, Titus brought encouraging news of the reception of Paul's letter (2 Cor. 7:5-16). Of course, there were still some who doubted his motives and even denied his apostleship. Paul wrote 2 Corinthians in response and in preparation for a third visit (Acts 20, 2 Cor. 12:14).

Paul enjoyed consistent, frequent, and close interaction with the city and church in Corinth for nearly a decade. His letter is written from a pastor's heart to a beloved but troubled congregation.

CHAPTER 1
Growing Stronger as a Church
1 Corinthians 1:1-3

When I was called to pastor the First Baptist Church of Pineville, Louisiana, the church was coming out of the lowest point in its history. Two years before, the church suffered a devastating split – the final blow of a slow, forty-year decline. Keeping the debt serviced and the buildings from falling apart was enough to strap the people who remained, let alone trying to do ministry. Many denominational leaders and people in the community did not think the church would survive. Some people in the church wondered as well.

On my first Sunday as pastor, Rebecca and I attended the young adult Sunday School class that met in one room of an otherwise vacant second floor of one of our education buildings. This "young adult" class encompassed everyone from twenty to fifty years old. Rebecca and I were two of eight people in the class that day. That Sunday there were only 172 people in Sunday School in a facility built for 1000. About 100 of the 172 were above fifty years old. Many of those were above seventy years old. One elder member quipped, "I hope you like doing funerals." During one of my first services, my then 85-year-old grandma attended. After the service, she said, "Stew, there sure are a lot of blue hairs in the church." I thought, "Great! If my grandma sees it, what do younger people see?" I knew what they saw – an old, dying church.

Thankfully, though the church was at an all-time low, I inherited a fairly stable situation. Director of Missions Herb Dickerson, Interim Pastor Reggie Ogea, Interim Minister of Music Randy Turner, Deacon Chair Doug Ashe, and that remnant of church members, had prayed hard and worked tirelessly to keep the ship afloat. By the time I was called as pastor, the ship was no longer taking on water. Still, for the first few months of my ministry, we continued to grant letters of transfer by the droves. While we might not have been taking on water, to shift metaphors, we were still hemorrhaging! My only solace was the fact that I did not know any of the people leaving. They had left before I even arrived. Thankfully, at least the people who had stayed to meet the new pastor stuck. (Well, at least most of them.)

I knew we had to grow. The only alternative was to die! In those early days, there was no way to grow the church other than to grow stronger slowly and trust that as we grew stronger spiritually, God would help us grow larger numerically.

It has been amazing to watch God bring about both kinds of growth over the last decade. Within the first six to eight months, we welcomed strong new members who I believe God sent to us for "such a time as this." Most of those fine people are still serving today, and several of them frequently comment how they are amazed at what God has done. As I look back to the First Baptist Pineville of 2008, I see no logical reason for those people to have joined our church other than the fact that God called them to do so. I'm both glad He called them and that they responded.

Even though we are far stronger today than we were in 2008, we are nowhere near where we need to be. Of course, I'm not sure we will ever be where we need to be. No church ever arrives at that point. We can always grow in some way. Here in Pineville, we have so much more vision to accomplish, problems to fix, attitudes to adjust, ministries to tweak, and lives to see transformed. For over a decade, we've been growing stronger, but we are not through!

Even though we have seen numerical and physical growth as a church, when I speak of growing stronger as a church, I do not mean the nickels and noses or the programs and ministries. I mean the growth of the people and our commitment to the Lord and to each other. The numerical measures are by-products of the spiritual impact upon people's lives.

At the beginning of this letter written to Paul's arguably worst church, we find the essence of what every strong church should be:

1 Corinthians 1:1-3 *Paul, called to be an apostle of Christ Jesus by the will of God, and our brother Sosthenes,* [2] *To the church of God in Corinth, to those*

> *sanctified in Christ Jesus and called to be holy, together with all those everywhere who call on the name of our Lord Jesus Christ-- their Lord and ours:* [3] *Grace and peace to you from God our Father and the Lord Jesus Christ.*

From this passage, we can glean four foundational truths that form the essence of a church.

A strong church belongs to God. (*The church of God . . .*)

As we begin to speak of a church, we need to make sure we understand to what we are referring. When we speak of a church, we are not talking about a building at a particular location. Our building is located at 901 Main Street in Pineville, Louisiana. The church campus is spacious and beautiful now that it is renovated, but the facilities are not the church. If the facilities at 901 Main were gone tomorrow, First Baptist Church of Pineville would still exist. During the COVID-19 Pandemic of 2020, our church ceased meeting at 901 Main Street for eight weeks. The church campus was a ghost town. Yet, the church still existed! That is because when we speak of a church, we are talking about the assembly of believers in a particular community. The congregation is the church. If you had traveled to Corinth in Paul's day, you would not have found a building. You couldn't even put their address in your GPS! The Church at Corinth was simply a group of people. The church is a body of believers not a building of bricks.

To whom does this body of believers, the church, belong? When we ask this question, we are talking not about ownership but about leadership or headship. Paul calls the church at Corinth, the *church of God.* Paul had founded the church, but he doesn't call it "my church." Paul knew that a lady named Chloe was concerned about the church, but he doesn't call it "Chloe's church." He knew there were people who thought they were super-spiritual in the church, but he doesn't call it "the church of the spiritually elite." He calls the Church in Corinth "the church of God" because the church belongs to no one but God. A strong church understands that it belongs to God.

"Many problems in a church revolve around a selfish possessiveness, by pastor and congregation, towards its life and activities."[1] If you will listen closely, you can hear it. In fact, you may have even said it! A pastor might say, "God has put me in charge. This is *my* church." The people might say, "Preachers come and go, but we'll always be here. This is *our* church." I'm sorry Pastor John, it's not your church, and, Mr. and Mrs. Jones, it's not the people's church either. *Your* church is actually *God's* church.

The main deficiency at Corinth was that the people's belief was "not in God, but in their own belief in God and in particular leaders."[2] Since the Corinthians saw the church as belonging to someone else other than God, they looked to whomever that owner was – whether it be Paul or Chloe or the spiritually elite or someone else. In so doing, they failed to put their belief in God.

If you put your belief in a human, you will be disappointed. I don't care who that human is or how spiritual he or she is, every human will fail. In my years as a pastor, I've made mistakes and disappointed people. Some of the mistakes I knew I made when I made them while others I didn't realize until someone pointed them out. Even though I have apologized for my mistakes, a handful of people have left the churches I have served over them. They believed I failed and could not get past that fact. While such losses hurt because I take each one personally, we all should be reminded that God never fails. Though I am a frail child of dust, God is seated high on His throne and always will be. If we put our belief in God as the leader of the church, then even when we humans make our inevitable mistakes, our church can still keep growing stronger.

A strong church has a local responsibility. (. . . *in Corinth*)

It seems to be trendy today to name a new congregation "The Church at ________." In an effort to step away from denominational baggage or over-used names like Calvary, Trinity, Emmanuel, or a number, such as "First", some church planters have simply decided to focus on the city in which they are planted.

While naming a new congregation "The Church at ________" may sound innovative and trendy, guess what? Not so much – unless a 2000-year-old practice is trendy! The same thing was happening in the first century with the first churches ever planted!

Interestingly, Paul notes that this church is "in Corinth" or "at Corinth." Paul usually prefers, for example, "the Church *of* the Thessalonians." Here, however, he uses the Greek preposition that means "in" or "at". Some scholars think Paul used this construction to show a contrast.[3] Corinth was a sin city, but in the middle of that sin city was a church shining forth the light. That light was the church of God *in* Corinth. God wants to shine His light in the midst of sin. Don't forget that.

When Hurricane Katrina hit New Orleans in 2005, one of our church members in Texas popped off, "God is judging that sin city." I replied, "Well, His aim sure was off. He destroyed New Orleans Baptist Theological Seminary and many of the churches but left Bourbon Street!" God doesn't forsake dark cities. He puts churches of light in those cities just as He did in Corinth.

Every church has a local responsibility. On top of our church is a cupola. A cupola is a "steeple thingy", as my architect friend calls it, that looks a lot like a light house. Every time I see that cupola, I am reminded of our mission. A lighthouse is a beacon of light, guiding ships around rocks and to safe harbor. If a lighthouse was removed from the seashore, ships that depended on it to guide them would miss it desperately. Therefore, I sometimes ask our people, "If our church was gone tomorrow, would Central Louisiana miss us?" We have a responsibility to our city and region. Your church has a responsibility to your community, town, city, or region. If your church was gone tomorrow, would your community, town, or city miss you?

A strong church is set apart from the world (*to those sanctified . . . and called to be His holy people*)

Paul is clear about what it means for the church to be set apart from the world. For certain, he does not mean we are to be stuck up, haughty, or snooty with a judgmental "we're better than you" attitude. Put down the pickle juice, Ethel! Paul means we are to be set apart in the sense that the world notices that something is different about us. He communicates this truth by describing Christ's followers in two ways: sanctified and called to be His holy people.

Paul says the church is made up of *those sanctified in Christ Jesus.* The word "sanctified" indicates "inclusion in the inner circle of what is holy, because of . . . association . . . with God."[4] Every person who has accepted Jesus Christ as his or her Lord and Savior has been welcomed into that circle.

Sanctification doesn't happen all at once. It is a process. The tense of the word translated "sanctified" helps us see this process. There is a past event whose consequences stretch into the present. Think about it like this – if you know Jesus as your Savior, you are being *saint-ified.* You are being made like a saint.

Now, don't think that saints are some kind of super-race with halos hovering over their heads. Saints are simply people who have been redeemed by God. In fact, every person who has been saved by Jesus Christ is a saint. Therefore, if you are a born again believer, guess what? *You* are a saint. I don't suggest you go around calling yourself Saint So-and-So, unless you want to be looked at funny, but you *are* a saint.

Obviously, if you and I are saints, we know one thing is for certain – saints aren't perfect! However, saints *are* set part. They are set apart for the purpose of serving God. When you are saved, you surrender your life to Jesus Christ and your aim in life becomes to serve God's purposes.

As we serve God's purposes, we pursue holiness. We answer God's call to be His holy people. The Church at Corinth was full of saints, but they weren't living like saints. The Church at Pineville, Louisiana, is full of saints, and we *want* to live like saints. Several times a week, I pray, "Lord, wherever our people may be scattered, help us make impact for your kingdom." In the schools, on the airplanes, in the businesses, in the stores, in the gyms, on the ball fields, in our homes – wherever we are, we have been called to be holy.

Being holy doesn't mean we eat prunes while talking in King James English! It doesn't mean we fuss about everything in society being "of the devil". It doesn't mean we come to church to hide out from the rest of the world and sing:

Amazing Grace how sweet the sound
That saved a saint like me.
They're all lost but I am found.

They're blind but I can see.

Living holy lives means we resemble Christ.

In our church we've charted out five tenets that capture what holy living looks like. The five tenets are based on the word F.I.R.S.T. We want to see our children become students who become adults who are:

Focused on God
Involved in ministry
Respected by peers
Strengthened in faith
Transformed by Christ.

All five of our F.I.R.S.T. tenets develop holiness or are the product of holiness. We have developed action points for these goals as follows:

Focused on God
I practice the privilege of worship.
I read and memorize Scripture regularly.
I pray because it matters.
I know and follow God's plan for my life.

Involved in Ministry
I practice biblical stewardship.
I know and use my spiritual gifts.
I serve in at least one ministry.
I share the Gospel with lost people.

Respected by Peers
I live with consistency and integrity.
My family relationships are growing.
I develop relationships among all generations of our church.
I participate in a D-Group.

Strengthened in Faith
I know what I believe and why I believe it.
I am personally accountable to other Christians.

I am involved in a Sunday School Class.
I can defend my faith.

Transformed by Christ
I spend time with God daily.
I obey God instantly.
I serve God selflessly outside of FBCP.
I am making disciples.

When we encourage each other to *Be F.I.R.S.T.*, we are not being elitist. Rather, we are challenging each other to live up to our high calling as the saints of God. There must be something different about the people who make up the church when compared to the people who make up the Rotary Club or Garden Club. Those groups are made up of good people, but they aren't necessarily godly people.

A strong church is part of a global movement (*together with those everywhere . . .*)

Every church has a local responsibility while also being a part of the global movement of God. The Church in Corinth was part of a developing network of churches that were taking the gospel through the Mediterranean world and the Roman Empire. Our local church is part of a network of churches that is taking the gospel to the entire world. We are committed to supporting the cooperative efforts of the Southern Baptist Convention through our gifts to the Cooperative Program. We want to work alongside sister churches in church planting, revitalization, disaster relief, and mission work. We are not alone in what we are doing, and we want to see God do great things.

In this chapter, we have described some characteristics of a strong church. There is still one thing that must happen if we are to become strong: we must focus on Christ. This truth underlies Paul's entire introduction to 1 Corinthians. Paul wishes to draw our attention away from ourselves and towards Christ.

In the 1970s, Ralph Neighbour, Jr., wrote a book called *The Seven Last Words of the Church.*[5] He identified those seven last words as "We've never tried it that way before." However, he added that the seven first words of the church should be, "I can do all things through Christ." When Christ is our focus, we can be strong. We can be everything and anything He calls us to be.

Do you believe that? I do. After more than a decade of seeing God do it in our church, I claim it. Ministry at our church has been hard. There have been trials and tests as well as attacks from the enemy that I hope to never repeat. The work of turning around an old, rusty ship has been challenging. Still, God has always given victory because His desire is to see the church grow stronger. He wants that for your church as well. Pray that it may be so. Trust God to make it so.

CHAPTER 2
We Don't Need a Thing
1 Corinthians 1:4-9

Does it seem like your church is always in need of something – especially a little more money or a few more volunteers? Well, alright, go ahead and replace "a little" and "a few" with "a lot"! That is closer to the truth! It seems that way for me too. Something is going to break. Someone is going to move away. Some ministry is going to outgrow the budget. It can easily feel like you are always playing catch up.

I want to encourage you. A church that is growing stronger can say with all honesty, "We don't need a thing." Why is that? Is it because a strong church is a rich church? No. A poor church can be a strong church, and a rich church could be a weak church. Is it because a strong church is a big church? No. A small church can be a strong church and a big church can be a weak church. Is it because in a strong church the budget is always met, and the volunteers are lining up by the droves? No. I have never heard a pastor of any size or strength of church have an Exodus 36:6 moment and restrain people from doing any more!

Why can a strong church, that may be poor and small, say, "We don't need a thing?" Is that even an appropriate statement? Isn't it arrogant? No, for the strong church, it is not an arrogant statement. Rather, it is a grateful statement. While it may sound like a statement of self-sufficiency, it is a statement of total reliance. A strong church can say, "We don't need a thing," because a strong church will add four more words: *because we have Jesus*. If a church has Jesus Christ, that church has everything it needs regardless of its finances, volunteer base, or any other popular measure of strength. If *you* have Jesus Christ, *you* have everything *you* need.

Did you just think, "Well, that is the most Sunday School statement I've ever heard! Jesus is all we need, hallelujah, whoopty-do, and

Amen!"? If you did, wait! Before you give up on this chapter, let me ask you this: Do you believe it? Do you believe Jesus is all you need? It's easy to say, "Sure!" But do you really believe it for yourself? Do you believe it for your church?

I'm not sure I have always believed that Jesus is all our church needs. When I look at resource needs or financial needs or maintenance issues or things we need to do to continue reaching our city, sometimes the needs look like Mount Everest (and I'm not into mountain climbing). I get sidetracked into discouragement and worry, both of which are sin and indicators that I do not believe that "we don't need a thing because we have Jesus Christ." Thankfully, Paul shows us that even if the needs are like Mount Everest, we have everything we need in Jesus. That goes for our church, your church, and the life of every Christian. Therefore, if you've ever grown worried or discouraged by needs or problems, hang tight and read on.

A Thanksgiving

Paul's focus in this passage is the church aspect. But many of the same truths apply for our individual lives. First Corinthians 1:4-9 is traditionally called the thanksgiving. We can see reflected in Paul's letter the typical opening for first century letters:

> The sender: Paul . . .
> The recipients: To the Church of God in Corinth . . .
> The salutation: Grace and peace . . .
> Thanksgiving: I always thank . . .

A thanksgiving was typical, but, as you read Paul's thanksgiving for the Church at Corinth, remember how messed up this church was. If I were writing this letter, I would get to the thanksgiving spot and just stare at my blank computer screen. After a few minutes, I'd skip the thanksgiving, hoping the church wouldn't notice!

Thankfully, Paul was a better man than I! He chose not to skip the thanksgiving. In fact, even though Corinth was a dysfunctional church, if you read vv. 4-9 apart from the rest of 1 Corinthians, you come away with a positive view of the church! Go ahead, try it! (Yes, get your Bible and read it again.) See! That simple exercise reminds us how important these six verses are to the letter.

Every church has warts and blemishes.

Don't think that Corinth was the only church that has ever had "issues" or that Corinth and the church you used to attend were the only ones with "issues"! I've been a part of five churches, and every one of them had "issues." Our present church has "issues." Your church has "issues." There are no perfect churches. "Even those churches which have glowing reputations are known all too well by their members and pastors to be full of weaknesses and sin."[6]

The more I connect with pastors, the more I find that all churches have warts and blemishes. Even as I have opportunity to talk with pastors of very large churches, I find all that glitters isn't gold. The larger the church, the bigger the nose, and the bigger the nose, the bigger the warts! Every church should readily admit they are not perfect. Problems come when anyone thinks the church is perfect or thinks there can be a perfect church. One writer says, "The church is a fellowship of sinners before it is a fellowship of saints."[7] That truth alone should remind us that every church has warts and blemishes.

Paul doesn't start with the warts and blemishes.

Paul starts with what is good in the church. Even a troubled church has something for which to be thankful. Anybody can look at a church and say, "Look at that wart on their nose!" It takes a loving leader to say, "What a beautiful nose! We'll work on that wart later."

Paul even gives thanks for the good things that the church has turned into warts. For example, spiritual gifts were a big issue in Corinth. Certainly, spiritual gifts are good things. Unfortunately, some people were peacocking around because they thought their spiritual gift was more special than someone else's – a good thing turned into a wart. Still, Paul gives thanks.

Paul celebrates who the Corinthians are. Notice, however, he doesn't celebrate who they are *in themselves*. That's how they got in this mess! He celebrates who they are in Christ (v. 4).

Grace is when God gives us what we do not deserve. We sing of it, "Amazing grace! How sweet the sound that saved a wretch like me." What are we saying? "I was a lost sinner, but God in His amazing grace found me and saved me." Paul begins his thanksgiving reminding the Corinthians that they have received the grace of God through Jesus Christ. The grace of God should be the first reason a believer rejoices and the best motivator for a believer's growth and correction. Therefore, Paul begins with grace. From this grace statement, Paul shares with them why they don't need a thing. They don't need a thing because they have Jesus Christ.

Since we have Jesus, we have His gifts to enrich our church (vv. 4-7).

Paul reminds us that we have gifts. Paul celebrates their gifts by saying, "You have been enriched in every way. You do not lack any spiritual gift." Paul does not doubt the gifts. He notes that they are present and should be present because spiritual gifts corroborate the truth of the gospel and its impact on our lives. Every believer has spiritual gifts and should seek to discover, develop, and use those gifts.

Just as they did, Paul highlights the spiritual gifts of word and knowledge. These were not just two gifts; rather, they were two clusters of gifts over which the Corinthians argued. The word or speaking gifts include things like prophecy, teaching, preaching, evangelism, speaking in tongues, and interpretation of tongues – any use of speech which can build up the church. The knowledge gifts include wisdom, insight, and discernment. Paul concentrates on these gift clusters because the Corinthians concentrated on them.

For Corinth, the problem was not what they had or didn't have. The problem was their attitude towards what they had. Therefore, Paul shows us something else: not only do we simply have gifts, the gifts we have are from God.

There are three statements in vv. 4-7 that speak of the lavish generosity of God: because of His grace given you in Christ Jesus (v. 4), you have been enriched in every way (v. 5), and you do not lack any spiritual gift (v. 7). Whose grace is it? Who enriches? Who gives the gifts? Cue the five-year-old Sunday School answer: God! The gift always points back to the Giver. The gift might be tailored for the gifted, but it always points back to the Giver.

Think about when you get a gift from someone. You open it up, and it is wonderful. Maybe it's a shirt you like and certainly will wear. From then on, every time you wear it, you think of the giver. When people say, "What a lovely shirt," you reply, "Thank you. My best friend gave this to me." The gift always points back to the giver.

Unfortunately, the Corinthian's were focusing on the gifted instead of the Giver. It would be like someone complementing you on a shirt your best friend gave you and instead of responding with, "Thank you, my best friend gave this to me," you say, "Oh, I know! Don't I look great?" There's something messed up about that! But that's what the Corinthians were doing with their spiritual gifts.

"You have the gift of tongues!"

"Oh, yes, I am super holy."

"You have the gift of preaching!"

"Yes, I am immensely eloquent."

The Corinthians were ridiculous and conceited.

Could our problem be sometimes like Corinth – not what we have or don't have, but our attitude towards what we do have? Whether that be thinking our gift is more important than someone else's or that our gift is less important than someone else's? Get the focus off of yourself! Gifts say nothing about the gifted but everything about the Giver. "Precisely because they are 'given' by God and are 'grace' (unmerited by the recipients), there can be no grounds for boasting on [our] part."[8]

These gifts enrich the church. The point of spiritual gifts is not for the gifted to be puffed up; it is for the church to be built up. Every local church potentially possesses every spiritual gift and should prayerfully expect God to bring those gifts into mature expression.[9] If the church doesn't bring the gifts to mature expression, it will get sidetracked. Likewise, if a believer is not using his or her gift within the church, he will get sidetracked. No individual has all the gifts. He must join with the body of Christ so that his gift might fit and be used.

Sometimes we are tempted to look at other people or other churches and say, "Look what they have." But they have nothing we don't have. Perhaps they've just put what they have to better use.

At a community singing during our later years serving Forestburg Baptist Church in Forestburg, Texas, I overheard a lady from a sister church say, "We're not a *big* church like Forestburg Baptist." For context, our church was far from "big". We were running about 100 in worship at the time. However, the other church was running around 20. So, comparatively, yes, we were "big."

This lady looked at us and thought her church couldn't do the kind of ministry our church did. But about seven years before we were called to Forestburg, every church in the community was about the same size (forty or less people in attendance), no matter the denominational label. However, one Saturday at the weekly men's breakfast, the men of Forestburg Baptist said, "If we don't do something, we're not going to have a church in a few years."

It wasn't long before the church added a five-room addition for Sunday School classes even though they didn't have the people to put in them. The gifted laborers in the church built much of that building. Next, they hired a youth director even though they didn't have any youth! Members stepped up to run van routes and teach. By the time I was called as pastor, a new sanctuary was under construction because the church had outgrown its original building! Again, members did much of the work. We benefited from such vision and application of spiritual gifts during my years as pastor. To be running about 100 in Sunday School and be called a "big" church seemed funny to me, but the comparison of the Forestburg Baptist Church's vision and application of spiritual gifts was markedly different from some of her sister churches. We had nothing they didn't have. The difference came down to vision and the application of the gifts we did have. Everyone has gifts. These gifts are from God and are meant to enrich the church.

Since we have Jesus, we have His faithfulness to sustain our church (vv. 8-9).

Not only can we be confident that we have the resources we need, but we can also be confident that God will be with us no matter what. He will never fail us. He will sustain us. He will keep us strong until the end. He seals us as His own.

Whatever ups and downs a church might face, we can be confident that God will be faithful. As we look back at a church's history, God's faithfulness in both good times and struggling times stands out.

One of my favorite pictures from our church is one taken at the fiftieth anniversary celebration of our sanctuary in 2009. The picture captures nearly the entire congregation at worship. On the screen you can clearly read the words to a hymn: "For I know whate'er befall me." The first time I saw the picture I gave praise to God thinking, "How true! God, You have been faithful no matter what this church has been through." I often use that picture in our new member classes because it captures this truth. That line is from the first stanza of the hymn "All the Way My Savior Leads Me." There are ups and downs, but all the way my Savior leads me.

All the way my Savior leads me;
What have I to ask beside?
Can I doubt His tender mercy.
Who through life has been my guide?
Heavenly peace divinest comfort,
Here by faith in Him to dwell!
For I know whate'er befall me,
Jesus doeth all things well.[10]

We can depend on God. If He has called us and enriched us, He will never abandon us. He will never disappoint. People will disappoint; people will fail – from pastors to deacons to church members – but God will never fail. If you have God's faithfulness, you don't need a thing. If you have His gifts, you don't need a thing. If you have Jesus Christ, you don't need a thing.

What does all this mean for us?

First, your gifts are needed. Every church is enriched with every gift. Therefore, every member needs to discover, develop, and use his or her gifts. The weakest part of a church is the member who is not using his or her gifts.

Pay attention to this: if you see a need in your church, the need has *already* been met by Christ. The question is, "Where is it? Who has it?" If you see a need, the person or people who can meet that need are either already in your church or will be there before you know it. Your church has everything right now to do whatever God is calling your church to do right now.

Second, remain confident that God will strengthen your church. No matter what we face, He will be faithful to strengthen us and bring us forward.

I had to be reminded of this truth while preaching the original series on this epistle. One afternoon I was discouraged after running into a ministry roadblock. It wasn't a huge deal, but it sucked the joy out of me. I left my office and walked into the sanctuary. I walked around talking to God, "Here's where we are. Here's where we need to be. Here's why we can't get from where we are to where we need to be." I unloaded! "God, you know all the stuff that is before us. You know what we have. You know what we don't have. You know the potential. You know the pressures." That afternoon, God put three words into my spirit, "I will provide." That's all I heard. I kept griping. God said it again, "I will provide." Finally, I got right in front of the pulpit and looked back across the sanctuary and said, "O.K. You will provide." Since that day, I've seen Him do it time and time again (and He has had to remind me time and time again!). It was just one more reminder:

We don't need a thing because we have Jesus Christ.

CHAPTER 3
We Must Be United
1 Corinthians 1:10-17

A phone call was my first clue that something was wrong. "Stewart, can I talk to you for a moment?" The person on the other end of the line was a member of a former church. For the next thirty minutes or more, this friend shared with me frustrations over some things happening in the church. I did my best to give counsel as a former pastor and encourage the person in her work. A few weeks later a call came from a different family, "Stewart, can we get your advice on something?" I listened, gave counsel, and encouraged them as best I could. A couple of months later, friends from the church visited our home. We had been talking in our living room for an hour or so when I asked, "How are things going at the church?" The look on their faces told me something was up. "We said we wouldn't talk about it," they replied. However, we did talk about it, and things were not good.

Within a matter of months, the church split and over half the church scattered to other churches or nowhere. Rebecca and I never would have thought a split would happen at that church. They had such a sweet spirit of unity while we were there. What we saw happen over a period of months broke our hearts. Years later, heartbreak remains for both those who stayed and those who left. However, I am happy to say the church is rebuilding.

Church conflict is one of the nastiest tools in the enemy's arsenal against the work of God. Go to nearly any city and you will find signs of it. In towns where the population would be better served by one strong church, you may find two or more struggling churches. (Oddly enough, their names are often Harmony, Unity, or Friendship.) When you ask why there are so many churches in such a small town, people will tell you splits occurred. They remember the stories. In many cities, you will find once great churches now empty. When you ask what happened, you will be told that a split occurred, and the church never recovered.

Sadly, in every town and city where a church has split, there are once faithful people who are no longer in church because of the scars they received or because the split became an excuse to depart and never return. In addition, there are scores of people who could have been won to the Lord if the church had remained unified. How many people have been turned off to the gospel by the poor witness of a split church? How many lost people have said, "I told you Christians are hypocrites!"

First Corinthians 1:10-17 is the first of several passages in this letter that deals with church conflict and the need for church unity. We must learn to protect the unity of the church so the church's witness may remain strong. The local church must be unified because disunity not only hurts our testimony, it nullifies our testimony.

Paul found out about the problems in Corinth much like I found out about the problems in my former church: someone contacted him. Specifically, Chloe's people informed Paul of what was happening in Corinth. We don't know a lot about Chloe. We think she may have been a wealthy member of the church. In fact, the church may have even met in her home. As these struggles in the church developed, Chloe thought of Paul and then either sent messengers to Paul to inform him of the issues or sent him a letter by messenger in which she outlined the problems in the church.

Let's be clear: Chloe wasn't a gossiping bitty gripping that the preacher preached too long or that the drums were too loud. In fact, Chloe wasn't gossiping or griping; she was genuinely concerned: "Paul, we have problems in our church. Can you help?" Chloe was crying out for assistance. We know the information came as genuine concern because the issues are outlined clearly. Also, Paul uses Chloe's name, which gave credence to the source of information. If Chloe had been the church gossip, people would have rolled their eyes and said, "There goes Chloe again." Instead, Paul mentions her name so the people will sit up and listen.

Every church has men and women who are Chloe's. They are respected, godly, level-headed men and women who can see what's happening and cut through the mess to the real issue. They are often the true leaders of the church even though they may not hold the leadership titles. Sometimes they don't speak until others have had their say, but when the respected leader speaks, everyone listens.

Here is a conflict principle: *the Chloe's of a church can save the church from destruction.* They are wise enough to see problems and find help. They are wise enough to handle issues appropriately before they get out of hand. At this point, the church is still united enough for Paul to expect that the letter will be heard by the people. If correctives can be given and heeded, the church can survive.

Here is another conflict principle: *most churches facing conflict have the opportunity to hear and heed advice.* Whether the advice comes from people within the church, denominational leaders, or former pastors, the advice is generally good and objective. Still, many churches end up splitting because they fail to heed the advice they receive. With Paul's letter, the Church at Corinth had the opportunity to prevent disaster.

The report from Chloe's people clarified the quarrels in the church. Here is another principle: *To deal with church conflict appropriately, you need to know the real issue.* Often, the surface issue is not the real issue. Desire for a position of service masks personal pride. Requests for multiplication of leadership can mask personality conflicts. Theological debates mask power struggles. Concerns over "cultural compromise" mask personal preferences. To deal with the real issue, you must take off the masks. Otherwise, you have perpetual Mardi Gras in the church – it may be fun for a day, but it doesn't make for a godly lifestyle.

What was the real issue in Corinth? The real issue was spiritual pride masquerading in various forms. Some Corinthians felt themselves more spiritual than others because of the leader they were connected to or the certain spiritual gifts they possessed. The first form of spiritual pride Paul deals with is the kind that was masking itself in divisions over leadership preferences (vv. 11-12).

Chloe's people identified four groups within the church: the Paul group, the Apollos group, the Cephas or Peter group, and the Jesus group. Nothing suggests that the leaders named were responsible for the discord. Nor did these differences have anything to do with true or false doctrine. Each of these leaders taught the same thing but in different ways. Though we do not know a lot about the groups, we can glean some things from the larger context of 1 Corinthians and even the New Testament that help us understand these groups.

The Paul Group

Paul had planted the church, and some members felt a personal loyalty to him. Because Paul started the church and they had a personal connection to him, everyone else in the church and every other leader that came to the church was considered second-rate.

We see this kind of thing in the church today. People say, "Pastor Perfect was the best pastor we ever had. He *never* made a mistake. *Every* sermon was interesting. People joined *every* Sunday." While this pastor has never existed, every minister who leaves a church in good standing becomes a saint. If the new minister has a chip on his shoulder, conflict will begin to brew with the Paul group. If the new pastor will remember he too may be a saint if he ever leaves, he can make it through.

The Apollos Group

Apollos came upon the scene after Paul and was a gifted communicator. People rallied to Apollos. By his own admission, Paul was better in writing than he was in person. But Apollos was eloquent, and people loved to listen to him.

Yes, the Apollos Group is still in the church today. While the Paul group is talking about the former pastors, the Apollos Group is printing t-shirts for the new pastor! They say, "That old guy was so boring. I thought he'd never leave (or retire or die!). But new Pastor Preacherama is the best pastor we've ever had! Our church will be running 50,000 in two years!" Such amazing growth will never happen, of course. Therefore if this group keeps it up, they'll come into conflict with the Paul group in a matter of months.

The Peter Group

"Though there is no evidence that Peter was in Corinth or had visited the city before this letter was written, some leaned toward him as the appointed leader of the Jerusalem apostles." [11] Therefore, a group in the church looked back to this elder churchman. This group was made up of the traditionalists of the Corinthian Church. They may have even been legalists. Paul was reaching the Gentiles, and Peter clashed with him over Jewish food laws. "From the very beginning, there had been among Corinthian Jews significant conversions to Jesus as the Christ and the temptation to return to legalism must have been very strong."[12]

The Peter Group is also in today's church. They look back to a blessed day gone by "when church was done right." Though those methods of the days-gone-by church probably came out of a fresh move of God, they soon became the "safe" way or the "right" way – the letter of the law without the Spirit.[13] When a renewal of the Spirit slides into legalism, people begin emphasizing particular outward forms of behavior or dress, strict duties toward the church, particular church methods, and specific structures for the church. Some "Christians feel secure in such strait-jackets. It even reaches the state where real spirituality is assessed by such outward evidence."[14] Conflict is always around the corner because everything new is deemed wrong.

The Jesus Group

Scholars debate the nature of the Jesus group. It was probably a group that felt they would be more spiritual than everyone by going back beyond Apollos, Paul, and Peter to Jesus Christ Himself. Unfortunately, though they exalted Christ, they may have been the most spiritually-elitist in their thinking.

Today, the Jesus Group is composed of people who think they have a hotline to God and carry an air about them that they are above the fray of "normal" church people. Consequently, they make other people feel spiritually inadequate.[15] If they persist, they may begin to feel that the average local church is not spiritual enough and form their own church, home group, or even feel they do not need the fellowship of the "lowly brethren." Conflict comes as they pull away.

Paul notes four distinct groups with four different attitudes, but they all had the same problem: spiritual pride masking itself in divisions over church leadership. Chloe identified them clearly. Paul understood them perfectly. He calls for unity to prevent schism. Paul appeals to the church based on two things: their common relationship in Christ and their common message of the gospel (v. 10).

Here we find another lesson for conflict: *When facing church conflict, begin where everyone can agree – with everyone's common relationship with Jesus Christ and the common message they share because of Christ.* A church may agree on nothing else, but they can agree on these two matters. Unity is not based on the fact that we belong to the same organization or have the same gifts. Unity is based on the fact that we have the same Lord!

Here is the next conflict lesson: *With a common relationship in mind, call people to the common message they share.* In v. 10 Paul's key words stick out – *agree / no divisions / unites.* These words give us a picture of what Paul means when he calls for unity. He does not mean uniformity or unison. He means that they say the same thing with true harmony.

Think of music. While unison singing is nice, harmony is much richer. In harmony each part of the group is singing different notes – maybe even different words or sounds – but they are still *saying* the same thing with no division as a perfectly united group. Men, women, boys, girls, sopranos, altos, tenors, basses, join to say the same thing in harmony. But harmony can never be achieved unless there is perfect unity in mind and thought. If one person in a choir is singing "Amazing Grace" while another is singing "How Great Thou Art," you will have a mess! But if everyone is singing the same thing and is focused on the same thing, then you have a thing of beauty. A church is united by their shared relationship with Jesus Christ and their common message.

In v. 13 there are three questions stated. Each question is centered on Christ – and for good reason. Factions develop in churches when men and women "take their eyes off Christ and focus them upon men. Factions dissolve when they take their eyes off men and focus them once more upon Christ."[16] There's another lesson about church conflict: *distraction from the gospel underlies all disunity.* To remove disunity, remove the distraction and get your focus back on the gospel of Christ.

These probing questions are meant to shame and shatter all the misplaced loyalty evidenced in the partisan cries at Corinth.[17] The obvious answer to every question is NO! But for the Corinthians, the answer to at least the first was YES!

The folks in Corinth were so distracted that they were more interested in who baptized them than the gospel that their baptism celebrated (vv. 14-16). No person should emphasize the importance of the baptizer. The baptizer is of no count. The thing that matters is the power of Christ in the gospel. When we put the focus on man, we take the power away from Christ. Don't miss the warning found in v. 17, "For Christ did not send me to baptize, but to preach the gospel-- not with words of human wisdom, lest the cross of Christ be emptied of its power."

How can you share a gospel that has had the power emptied from it? You can't. How can you minister to a watching world when you are divided? You can't.

Here we come to the main question: why must we be united? We must be united because disunity not only hurts our testimony, it nullifies our testimony. Jack MacGorman, explained it this way:

> Above all else the gospel is a love story. It describes God's love for a sinful, human race that led Jesus Christ, His Son, all the way to the cross. Only love can tell this story well. Unlove may use the right words, but the vibrations will be wrong. And people feel vibrations while hearing words. Thus the church whose fellowship is broken by divisions gives the lie to the message of God's reconciling love that it is charged to proclaim and live. . . . [T]he church that reflects more of a sinful world's power to divide than of Christ's power to unite has lost its right to address it.[18]

Disunity not only hurts our testimony, it nullifies our testimony. Only love can tell the love story of the gospel. Therefore, the people who call quarreling churches hypocrites . . . well, they're right. Why should people listen to us talk of God's love when we can't show love to one another?

We *must* be united. People's eternities are at stake. Conflict in our church today could prevent us from reaching hundreds of people tomorrow.

We *must* be unified. Everyone will not always agree on everything, but, at the end of the day, we must come back to our relationship as brothers and sisters in Christ and stand before the cross and its message of the gospel and say, "Lest the cross be emptied of its power, we will be united."

CHAPTER 4
The Cross is Powerful
1 Corinthians 1:18-25

The Gospel is foolishness.

Wait! Don't throw this book in the trash! Just stop and think about the gospel story.

A baby was born among barn animals to common, everyday people. The townsfolk said the child was illegitimate. This boy grew up the son of a carpenter. He didn't have great schooling. He didn't have political power. He was a nobody from nowhere. He became a small town carpenter. He lived a simple life. He didn't own a home. He just drifted from place to place preaching. He preached against the religious leaders of the day. He hung out with the dredge of society – thieving tax collectors, cheating adulterers, nasty lepers, stinky fishermen, and sinful harlots. He loved these people. Then he was killed. He wouldn't stand up for Himself. He just took it.

Why in the world would the all-powerful God choose to go through all of that? It just doesn't make sense. It seems rather foolish. Doesn't it? But . . . is it?

When I was a boy, my dad received an invitation to the grand opening of a Mexican restaurant. Mom, Dad, and I had a great time as waiters brought around all kinds of food from nachos to enchiladas. At the end of the meal, a waitress asked, "Would you like to try our fried ice cream?" I had never heard of such a thing! How in the world do you fry ice cream? Wouldn't it melt as soon as it hit the grease? My own wisdom said it was foolishness. However, when the fried ice cream came to the table, it was delicious! My wisdom was shattered.

To say, "Christ crucified," sounds about as ludicrous as "fried ice cream," but those who experience the cross are blown away. They realize it is not foolishness; it is powerful wisdom!

Paul addresses this fact in 1 Corinthians 1:18-25 by admitting that the cross is foolishness to some people but showing that it is power to others. Into which group do you fall?

Paul identifies two groups of people: Group One is composed of those who are perishing; Group Two is composed of those who are being saved. For all the diversity in the world based upon nationality, language, culture, and economics, there are basically only two groups of people. Both groups are made up of people like you and me. In both groups are husbands, fathers, wives, mothers, teenagers, and children. There are different nationalities, languages, and cultures in both groups. In fact, to look at the groups on the outside, you might think there was no difference in the people. However, when you ask them what they think about the cross, the difference becomes evident.

Group One would say, "The cross? That's foolishness!"

Many of the Corinthians were in this group. They regarded the Christian message as a philosophy to be discussed.[19] The attitude was, "Surely we can come up with a better plan." This group gives two options. Paul identifies the options in v. 22.

Part of the group says, "The cross is just too violent and gory. Let's find something less bloody and more amazing." This was the suggestion of the Jews in Corinth. Jews demand miraculous signs.

For the Jews, a crucified Messiah was a ludicrous thought. For them, God is the One Who shows up and makes 100-year-old people have a baby, like He did Abraham and Sarah. He is the One Who parts the Red Sea, like He did in the Exodus. He is the One Who makes the walls of Jericho collapse with a trumpet blast and a shout. He doesn't show up and get killed by the enemy! He shows up and slaughters the enemy! Therefore, the Jews looked for signs.

The world likes that idea. Some might say, "If God would just do something spectacular, everyone would believe." But wasn't that a lie at the temptation of Christ? Satan said, "Jesus, just jump off the pinnacle of the temple. God will save you and then everyone will believe!" (See Matt. 4:5-7). Jesus refused Satan's suggestion.

Wasn't it also the question of the rich man who said, "Surely if someone rose from the dead, my family would believe." But Jesus' reply was, "They would not believe even if someone rose from the dead" (Luke 16:30-31).

The Jews had so experienced the miraculous evidences of God's existence that they demanded that He continue to produce such evidences. But "such a demand was a refusal to take God on trust, for it called on Him to present His credentials in a visible, identifiable act."[20] He shouldn't have to do that for a people who should have known Him better than anyone else.

The other part of Group One would say, "Oh, that fancy stuff is great, but what we really need is to get smarter." This was the suggestion of the Greeks in Corinth. Greeks search for wisdom. "Let's have some societal advances – make a plan to get rid of poverty, solve the problems of pollution, end racism, and answer the political and ethical questions of the age.

For the Greeks, a crucified Messiah didn't make sense. How could a pure God become so involved in a sinful world that He would end up getting killed? "Let's think about this a little bit," they would say. The Greeks thought they could reason their way to God.

The world likes the idea of the Greeks because it says, "We can figure this out." For some reason, people always think they can come up with a better plan than God. But isn't that the lie of Babel? The people in Genesis 11 said, "Let's get together and build a city with a tower that reaches to heaven. We'll make a name for ourselves and won't have to scatter over the earth like God has told us to do. We know better!" But they didn't. And neither did the Greeks.

The Jews and Greeks in Corinth would have suggested a plan that would mix the brawn of Arnold Schwarzenegger with the brain of Albert Einstein. Picture a guy with the head of Einstein on the body of Schwarzenegger! We might call him Arnbert Swartzenstein. He would be powerful and wise. He wouldn't seem foolish at all! Really? Can you conjure up that mental image? Just because a plan seems wise and powerful by human standards, that doesn't mean it will work.

The results of the suggestions from Group One are no good. Our human intelligence can't come up with something better than God's plan (vv. 19-20). Paul quotes from Isaiah 29:14: "I will destroy the wisdom of the wise; and the intelligence of the intelligent I will frustrate." All the people listed in v. 20 – the wise man, the scholar, the philosopher – belong to this present age that has been judged by God and is on its way out. The question is: where are they? The answer is: nowhere! Why? God has made foolish the wisdom of the world. Compared to Him there is no wise man, no scholar, and no philosopher of this age. Sure, brilliant people help find answers to worldly problems every day, but when human wisdom tries to find answers to spiritual problems, its suggestions come out looking like Arnbert Swartzenstein every time.

What is true foolishness? It is defined in Psalm 14:1, "The fool says in his heart, 'There is no God.'" Foolishness is saying there is no God or acting like there is no God.

Group One does not know God. They are trying to be God. They demand things of God that He will not do. Consequently, they are passing away. "For the message of the cross is foolishness to those who are perishing, but to us who are being saved, it is the power of God."

Group Two would say, "The cross? That's power!"

Instead of viewing the gospel as a human philosophy to be discussed, the second group, which included Paul, saw the gospel as good news to be believed and proclaimed (v. 21).[21]

"For since in the wisdom of God the world *through its wisdom* did not know him" – God knows that, left on its own, mankind creates gods in the likeness of created things or in their own distorted likeness. Therefore, since we don't do too well finding God on our own, God reveals himself to us. True knowledge of God comes only through revelation.

Paul tells us in Romans that man has had every opportunity to encounter God. Romans 1:20 speaks of God's revelation to us through nature, a revelation so clear that we are without excuse. Yet, we still miss it. Romans 2:14-16 describes God's revelation through our conscience. It too is an obvious revelation. Yet, we miss it. And then Romans 3:1-2 refers to God's revelation through scripture. Again, as the very words of God, scripture is a clear revelation, so clear that we should not miss it. But we do.[22] All this revelation, yet the world through its wisdom has not known God. Therefore, Paul continues, because of that, "God was pleased through the foolishness of what was preached to save those who believe."

What was the foolishness that was preached? Christ crucified. Gordon Fee says, "Only God is so wise to be so foolish."[23] We miss God in creation, our conscience, and the Scriptures. Therefore, God came to us in Christ.

Paul admits it seems like foolishness, but it is powerful. Christ crucified blows up the wisdom of the world (vv. 22-24). The word used there for power is the word from which we get our word dynamite.

So here is the picture Paul gives us: you have the philosophies of the world which contain all the Swartzensteins and alternate theories of how to be saved. Placed all under these philosophies is God's dynamite. It's ready to ignite, and God has the igniter in His hand. When this world passes away and the true power and wisdom of God is completely understood and every knee in heaven and on earth and under the earth bows, the dynamite will detonate and the philosophies and intelligences of this world will be shown for what they are – powerless compared to the power of God. "God does not argue with those who argue with Him."[24] He simply acts in power.

The apparent weakness of God in allowing His Son to die on a cross is stronger and more effective than any human effort. It has achieved what human wisdom and power have never accomplished – releasing mankind from the bondage from sin.

Have you experienced that release, that freedom? If you've been in Group One, would you move to Group Two? It's really a rather simple step. There are no fancy words, no magic formulas – just simple faith based in wise foolishness.

CHAPTER 5
We Are Unworthy
1 Corinthians 1:26-31

"Brothers, think of what you were when you were called" (1:26a). What *was* I when God called me to salvation?

- I was an 11-year-old, sixth grade boy.
- I was a Baptist kid attending a Catholic school.
- That year I got sent to the principal's office for the first time. I was sent there because I was counting the Hail Mary's on my fingers during a Rosary. (Lesson: don't make fun of the Hail Mary's when your teacher is a nun!)
- That year I also drew a picture of one teacher making fun of her. When another student tattled on me, I lied and told her it was a complement. She thanked me and kept the picture.
- I was a pretty good student. I made A-B Honor Roll and did well in the school social studies fair.
- I enjoyed church. I was close to my church friends.

So what was I when God called me to salvation? A typical, sinful sixth grade boy. Nothing special.

While leading a devotional at an assisted living facility, I shared some scripture and my testimony of coming to faith in Christ. I then asked those senior saints to share about when they trusted Christ:

- One lady shared about coming under conviction at a revival she attended as a young girl. She talked about making her way to the mourner's bench and her dad coming down and kneeling by her.

- Another remembered going down the aisle with her friends as a child but then later realizing she truly needed the Lord when she was a teenager.
- Another talked about how she and her mom made professions of faith on the same day. She wept as she told the story especially as she shared that her dad came to faith later.

If we were to ask the question, "What were these senior saints when they were called?" The answer might be "small children or teens", but, when you get right down to it, they were nothing special in and of themselves. They were sinners.

If God has called you to salvation, what were you when you faced the decision to trust Christ? Was there anything special about you? Probably not – at least not in the world's eyes.

Most of the Corinthian Christians were "plain ole", nothing special people. Most of the Corinthian church was composed of the simplest and humblest of people. That does not mean there were not some among them who were of the upper classes. Paul says, "Not many of you were . . ." which implies some of them were. In fact, we glean from the letter that men like Crispus, Gaius, Erastus, and Stephanas must have been well off by human standards. Chloe was likely well off as well. Further, there were enough well-to-do people in Corinth for Paul to address the way some of them were abusing the have-nots at the Lord's Table (1 Cor. 11). Still, the majority of Corinthian Christians were simple and humble people.

In the first century, Christianity spread more rapidly among the lower classes. Most Christians were of such low means that the movement became a bit of a laughingstock to some of the Roman elites. For example, about a century after Paul, an opponent of Christianity named Celsus described Christians in this way (178 AD):

> Their injunctions are like this: "Let no one educated, no one wise, no one sensible draw near. For these abilities are thought by us to be evils. But as for anyone ignorant, anyone stupid, anyone

> uneducated, anyone who is a child, let him come boldly." By the fact that they themselves admit that these people are worthy of their God, they show that they want and are able to convince only the foolish, dishonorable, and stupid, and only slaves, women, and children.[25]

Celsus wasn't correct, of course. The church didn't encourage ignorance and stupidity! However, most of the people in the church then and always have been what we might call "plain ole people." They didn't fit the world's standard. They didn't have the trifecta of importance Paul describes: education, influence, and the right family.

Isn't that what the world still respects? Paul nailed it 2000 years ago and not much has changed. Education, influence, and being of the right family (or knowing the right people) can skyrocket you to the top.

Paul tells the Corinthians that not many of them were what the world would call "special people." Even more, some of the people in Corinth weren't even good when God called them! (consider 6:9-11.) Apparently, "God took some who were morally worthless and made them into a church."[26] Isn't that true of what God does all the time? He doesn't wait for us to get perfect because He knows we could never be perfect on our own! He calls us in our imperfection. He calls us when we are far away and offers to bring us near. So, "think of what you were when you were called. Not many of you were wise by human standards; not many were influential; not many were of noble birth."

Why does God call people in such a nothing special state? The answer is found in vv. 27-29. God likes to overthrow the world's false standards of education, influence, and pedigree, and welcome the person who has none of that. You see, God didn't say:

> "That girl is so pretty, she needs to be saved because pretty girls get saved."
> "That boy is a star athlete. He deserves to be saved."
> "That guy is rich. He needs to be saved and pay for missions."
> "That lady is a socialite. She'll look good on the church rolls."

God will welcome the pretty girl, the athletic boy, the rich man, and the socialite woman, but He welcomes them just as He welcomes the homely girl, the clumsy boy, the poor man, and the maid at the socialite's party. God is not a respecter of persons. He knows it is not more holy to reach the down and out than it is to reach the up and out. Nor is it more beneficial to the kingdom to reach the up and out than it is the down and out. Both the up and out and the down and out come to the cross on the same level.

To come to the cross, everyone must bow the knee. Perhaps that is why the educated, the influential, and the well-bred find it so hard to come to Christ. It is hard to come to Jesus Christ in repentance, admitting you have done wrong, and to come in faith trusting in something far beyond yourself.

I think of the story of the rich man and Lazarus from Luke 16. The rich man had everything available to him that Lazarus had in order to hear the call of God and accept that call. But the rich man was so self-absorbed in himself and his wealth that he missed it. In deliberating with Abraham and requesting that someone go tell his family about eternity, he was really trying to justify himself. But he had the scriptures, and he had witnesses. However, he refused to listen to them because he was self-absorbed. It's hard to bow the knee when your nose is in the clouds. It's hard to get excited about being lifted by the king when you think yourself a king.

Nothing special people don't have quite as hard a time. They find it easier to bow before the one they discover is the King of Kings and the Lord or Lords. They know they have sinned. They know they need something greater beyond themselves. The prospect of being lifted up by the King is a wonderful thought. As William Barclay wrote, "Christianity was, and still is, literally the most uplifting thing in the whole universe."[27]

In these few verses, God reminds everyone of who they were in their fallenness before He transformed them. They were plain ole, nothing special people. They were sinners. Now that God has raised them up, they have no reason to boast in themselves.

God has always been taking "stuff" and making something incredible out of it. He took nothing and made the universe. He took dirt and made a man. He took a man's rib and made a woman. And he takes a "plain ole", nothing special, sinful person and makes a saint.

When you consider that amazing re-creation, every worldly standard is nullified, and no one can boast before Christ.

Everyone comes to the cross on the same level. "God loves all men regardless of their achievements, positions, or identities. His love does not take its cue from what we are; rather, it is an expression of who He is."[28] All that matters before God is who you are in Christ. "God only gives special attention, position, and honor to His Son, Jesus Christ."[29]

Sometimes in the church, insignificant and "plain ole" people bother the wealthy and influential. The well-to-do look down their noses at the down-and-out. Oh, the wealthy will give money to help out the down-and-out as long as their money can also keep them out. When such judgmental attitudes creep into a church, the death of the church is around the corner. How dare we stand before Christ and expect to be welcomed into His presence in heaven when we have not welcomed His people into His presence in our church! At the cross, all the worldly standards are nullified. The Ph.D. stands beside the G.E.D. The mayor stands with the mechanic. The Rockefeller stands with the Holloway. No one can boast before the Lord.

The world says those who have it all have it all together. But the truth is you can have it all and be falling apart. While I was working on the sermon series that preceded this book, acclaimed actor Philip Seymour Hoffman died of a drug overdose. As far as anyone could tell, Hoffman had everything – a great career, lots of money, fame, and more. I was interested to know of his faith background. A day or so after his death, a newsletter reported that Hoffman:

> . . . was turned off by his religious experiences as a child, but his perspective changed when one of his sisters became an evangelical Christian. He went to meetings with her, which he described as "so heartfelt and emotional. Nothing about it felt crazy at all. And my sister was certainly the sanest person you could ever meet. It all felt very real, very guttural, even rebellious." Hoffman described himself as a believer and someone who prayed occasionally, but he resisted the total commitment to Christ his sister made.[30]

Only the Lord really knows Hoffman's heart, but it would seem he had a hard time making that final bow before the Lord. Just because you have it all doesn't mean you have it all together. In the end, fame, fortune, name recognition, and earthly achievements didn't matter. Hoffman was still looking for something more and missing it.

As Paul says, "No one can boast in himself before the Lord." But in whom can he boast? He can only boast in the Lord. Why can we only boast in the Lord (v. 29)? Because everything else is nullified. If everything else is nullified, then all that is left is God's grace. His grace can make a nothing special person into a something special person. Grace takes a nobody and makes them a somebody. If that has happened, how can you boast in yourself? You didn't do it. He did it.

How did He do it? By coming to live in us and giving us the things we so desperately need. We read in v.29 that Jesus is:

- Our *wisdom* through whom we come to know God. He gives us the right path to follow and the right truth to believe.
- Our *righteousness* who puts us right with God. "Of our own efforts we can never achieve that. That comes only through Jesus Christ when we realize that it comes not from what we can do for God, but from what God has done for us."[31]
- Our *holiness* who sets us apart for God.[32] Only in walking close to Christ guided by the Spirit can we walk in holiness.
- Our *redemption* who "sets us free from the power of sin and death to serve God."[33] He has rescued us from darkness and brought us into light.

Now, that's good stuff! In fact, it is far better than education, influence, and upbringing. So what should you do? You should do what Paul says paraphrasing Jeremiah 9:23-24. You should boast in the Lord!

When I stand before the Lord, I cannot boast in anything about me. I can only boast that in 1987 God called a nothing special sixth grade boy to trust Him. I accepted that call, and, ever since, God has been working on me to transform me into His likeness. My boasting can only be in Him. He made a nothing special kid into something special.

What does it mean to boast in the Lord? It means you are grateful and committed. If you are grateful for Him then you can't help but be committed to Him.

CHAPTER 6
Preaching Has Power
1 Corinthians 2:1-5

God works in ways that do not seem wise to us and yet are remarkably powerful. He takes nothing special people and turns them into something special saints. He also takes something like preaching and accomplishes great things through it.

I preached my first sermon the summer after I graduated from high school. The sermon lasted about fifteen minutes and sounded more like a high school speech than it did a sermon. I was nervous going into the event, but empowered during it because of the number of people I knew who were praying for me. That day I fell in love with preaching. After my first class in preaching at seminary, I determined that homiletics would be the focus of my doctoral work.

I enjoy preaching. I enjoy helping others preach. Therefore, a text like 1 Corinthians 2:1-5 resonates with me. In this passage, Paul continues his instruction about the power of the gospel by talking about the method by which it is conveyed – preaching. Paul gives us a picture of what every preacher should be.

It doesn't take long for someone to realize there are all types of preachers. What we don't always realize is that some preachers are distortions of what a true preacher should be. Some years ago, H.C. Brown, Jr., identified five common preacher distortions. They are as true today as they were then:

- **The Pulpit Coach** – This preacher says¡ "Do More! Go More! Attend more! Give more!" A comedian once said, "The government builds roads and church folks wear them out going to meetings." This preacher spends little time in the study and lots of time attending activities, doing ministry, and going to meetings. He may work hard, but he doesn't work much at his main task of preaching.

- **The Gospel Falsifier** – "What I'm against and don't like, God is against and doesn't like." This preacher preaches his own conjured up doctrine week after week with little biblical connection. Anything and everything becomes gospel if it fits his intentions.
- **The Clown Prince** – His motto is "leave 'em laughing." Whereas humor is effective in preaching just as seasoning is to food, this preacher is addicted to laughter and applause. "Instead of sprinkling a little salt on steak, he sprinkles hamburger meat on blocks of salt."
- **The Madison Avenue Con Artist** – Taking his cues from the public relations experts, he is as flashy as possible. Some find the flash in clothes; others find it in elaborate sets for their sermons; others find it in special effects or sensational sermon titles.
- **"How to" Guru** (Brown calls this the "Psychological Pump-Primer") – This preacher wants to help people be better, but he puts Band-Aids on problems instead of dealing with the problems. The plethora of "How To" sermons coming from his pulpit sound helpful but fall flat. "Seven Simple Ways to Save Your Marriage" do not work if you never deal with the sins that the husband and wife are committing that are tearing their marriage apart.[34]

Many Christians have become so accustomed to these distorted preachers, that they do not know what true preaching is. Some who are pastored by such preachers may sense that something is missing in their church, but they do not know what that something is.

Thankfully, Paul gives us here what every preacher should be. As we look at these principles for a true preacher, consider them carefully. These are things to which you should hold your pastor accountable.

In Paul's day, there were a lot of wandering preachers and philosophers. You never knew when the next *preacherama* would stroll into town, stand on a corner, and draw a crowd. Most of these preachers gained their hearing by their eloquence or wisdom. They could wax eloquent and everyone would be amazed. Each preacher had his own technique, and, when he found what worked, he worked it to his advantage.

Then came Paul. We do not have a sermon from Paul. We can only imagine his presence, voice, and mannerisms as a preacher. But we can conclude a good deal about his style from his letters and the way he argued in them.[35] Paul may not have been a great speaker. He granted that he was bolder in writing than in person. He may not have demonstrated either the eloquence of Roman and Greek orators or the wisdom of the Greek philosophers. What he did demonstrate, however, were essential qualities every preacher should possess. Let's note the characteristics of a true preacher as outlined by Paul.

The preacher's message must be Christ Crucified (vv. 1-2).

"I resolved to know nothing while I was with you except Jesus Christ and him crucified." What does this mean? Does Paul mean that he spoke about nothing else but Jesus' crucifixion?

In a preaching class I taught a few years ago, a student proudly said, "Whenever I pastor, I'm just going to preach the gospel every week. That's all they need." I responded, "Yes, but your congregation sure is going to get bored. What about discipleship, evangelism, worship, not to mention marriage, parenthood, etc.? Are you going to edify the Christians at all?" Did Paul mean he preached nothing but the gospel? Of course not. So, what does Paul mean? We actually find our answer in Colossians 1. In that chapter, Paul centers all of kingdom history in the cross. When Paul says he knew nothing but Jesus Christ crucified, he means that everything finds its center at the cross. The cross is literally "the crux, the heart and center, of this kingdom history which encompasses all things."[36] The cross is what everything in the Old Testament anticipated and from which everything in the New Testament proceeds. "Whatever point Paul raises . . . or whatever advice he gives, is related to the death and resurrection of Jesus Christ. As Paul sees it, everything in the world has to do with Jesus Christ."[37]

Is this not true? When a preacher speaks on sin, grace, mercy, forgiveness, redemption, or reconciliation, it all goes back to the cross.

When he speaks on supporting the work of the church, praying for the missionaries, or giving of your resources and time, it all goes back to the cross. When he speaks about raising your kids in a godly home, making God's priorities your priorities, and using your gifts and talents for his work, it all goes back to the cross.[38] Charles Spurgeon wasn't that far off when he supposedly said, "I take my text and make a bee-line for the cross."

The original goal of "preaching was the proclamation of good news to those who had not heard it."[39] We call that evangelism. But the disciples quickly learned that the public declaration of the gospel proved just as effective for edification.[40] The disciples came to understand that preaching has a dual purpose to evangelize the lost and to edify the saved.

Therefore, when Paul said, "I resolved to know nothing while I was with you except Jesus Christ and Him crucified," he didn't mean that's all he preached. He didn't just evangelize. He edified as well. What Paul meant was his ministry was Christocentric, Christ-centered. Every Christian preacher must be Christocentric as well. If a preacher does not preach Christ, he does not preach anything.

Some time ago, an edition of our state Baptist paper contained a letter to the editor discussing the importance of the pulpit. I expected the article to use "pulpit" as a synonym for preaching and to talk about the importance of preaching. Instead, the writer talked about the actual piece of furniture. As I read the article, I laughed when I read, "The pulpit is much more than a piece of furniture; it should be the focal point of the worship service." Really? What happened to Jesus? I like a pulpit as much as the next guy, but it is just a piece of furniture. The focus of the church in worship is not a piece of furniture. The focus is not even preaching. The focus is Christ. When our focus is anything else in the church or in preaching, we have no focus.

The preacher's manner must be humility (v. 3).

Paul did not come with prideful eloquence or wisdom. He arrived in fear and trembling. Paul was hardly some hick preacher from the backside of nowhere. He was well educated. He knew rhetoric and philosophy. He may not have been as exciting as Apollos, but all you have to do is read his epistles to know that Paul could communicate as beautifully or powerfully as the next guy. However, Paul didn't wear his education on his cloak sleeve like some of the preachers. Some of them entered town or a room like they were the most important thing to ever grace the face of the earth. In contrast, Paul diligently sought to avoid any stylistic artistry that might obstruct the proclamation of Jesus.[41] He wanted all of the attention to go to Jesus, not to him.

Paul came in humility. Some of that humility involved fear and trembling. In Acts we get a glimpse of what it was like when Paul first came to the Corinthians. It was a difficult trip. Apparently, Paul was dealing with some anxiety over speaking there. In Acts we read:

> ***Acts 18:9-11*** *[9] One night the Lord spoke to Paul in a vision: "Do not be afraid; keep on speaking, do not be silent. [10] For I am with you, and no one is going to attack and harm you, because I have many people in this city." [11] So Paul stayed for a year and a half, teaching them the word of God.*

It was not an easy time, and it was not without opposition. Nevertheless, Paul kept on preaching and did so with humility.

Paul's ministry in Corinth was unlike the other preachers. They were proud. He was humble. The Corinthians noticed the difference. Therefore, Paul calls it to their memory here.

Humility is always needed in preaching. There should be a tinge of nervousness each time a preacher prepares to preach. The ministry of preaching is a sacred office and a scary task. God has entrusted a preacher with being His under-shepherd to guide a congregation in their spiritual journey. Each pastor will have to give an accounting for that someday. That's scary. It should bring about humility every time a preacher steps behind a pulpit. A preacher's hands should always tremble a bit when he holds up the word before his people.

The preacher's method must depend upon the Spirit's power (vv. 4-5).

Fred Luter serves as pastor of Franklin Avenue Baptist Church in New Orleans. He is the only preacher I know who has grown a church into a mega-church twice. Franklin Avenue was devastated and scattered after Hurricane Katrina in 2005, but they have recovered and rebuilt into a vibrant church once again.

No doubt, much of that rebuilding came from Fred's powerful ability at preaching. Fred starts low, goes slow, aims high, and then catches fire. By the end of the message, everyone is on their feet smiling, clapping, and wanting to get right with Jesus.

Apparently, though, Paul was no Fred Luter. No one jumped up clapping when he was through preaching. He wasn't even a Billy Graham who could have hundreds of people streaming through the stadium aisles coming to receive Christ. However, Paul did have something that Fred Luter and Billy Graham both have – the power of the Holy Spirit in his preaching.

Even though Paul preached with humility, he expected his message to go forth with power. This speaks to the divine-human mix that takes place in preaching. In *The Moment of Truth,* Wayne McDill says, "The preacher, in all his weakness, boldly declares the Word of God in the power of the Spirit."[42] Paul "felt the weight of responsibility that rested upon him as God's messenger. Thus he depended upon the Spirit of God for power."[43] Every preacher, regardless of his personal talents and abilities, must depend on the power of the Holy Spirit to make his preaching effective. David Allen writes, "When individuals make conclusions about a preacher's eloquence rather than the glory of God . . . , they fail to see the power of the gospel."[44]

The power is not in delivery. "The tradition of Greek and Roman oratory gave great weight to a dramatic presentation for effective public speech."[45] In contrast, preaching is not great speaking; it is bearing witness to what God has done in Christ. The difference between a religious speech and a biblical sermon is the Spirit's empowering. Great preachers deliver their messages well, but there is always that "something extra" that you notice. That "something extra" is the Holy Spirit. The Spirit gives the message power.

Neither is the power in arguments. Persuasion is important to preaching, but the power is not in finely crafted arguments. The power is in the Spirit. Apparently, Paul could have crafted fine sounding arguments, but he chose not to do so. Paul knew that no human power can bring salvation. Only the grace of God in the cross of Jesus Christ can save, and the preacher must make that known.[46] Paul also knew that if people's faith was built on his convincing them, someone else could convince them otherwise. However, if God himself did the convincing, no one would ever turn the people away from their faith.

These verses are not a free pass for the preacher on study or working on crafting his sermons. Paul is not condoning sloppiness or lack of preparation or ignorance. Preaching should be creative and assertive. It should be persuasive. It should be well done. But the preacher must realize that the power is not in all of that. The Holy Spirit takes all we do and makes it powerful. Neither should a preacher think that volume is indicative of Spirit power. Sometimes passion invokes intensity of volume, but not always. I've heard preachers who yelled everything. If you yell everything, you emphasize nothing.

When I first accepted a call to ministry, I was concerned about my future preaching ministry. I had sat through enough sermons to know that some sermons were engaging and some were not. Some preachers had "it" and some did not. I figured you got "it" in a preaching class. I learned a little about preaching in college, but when I got to seminary, I was amazed at everything we covered. I also realized something: I didn't get "it" in class. However, I did learn in class what "it" is – unction. Unction is an old word that refers to the Holy Spirit's power at work in the preacher during the preaching event. You can't teach unction. You can't conjure it up. Unction must come out of the overflow of the preacher's spiritual life, the expectation of the congregation's spiritual life, and the anointing of the Spirit upon the preacher. When a preacher has unction, he will be dependent on the Spirit's power. A sermon can be well studied, beautifully written, and professionally delivered but fall flat without the Spirit's power.

The preacher's motivation must be for people to find faith in God's power (v. 5).

Paul's preaching was simple, but it had astounding results. Those results demonstrated convincingly the power of God.[47] Perhaps no one has done so much for the expansion of the church as Paul did, especially when you consider that he did it in about thirty years. That expansion came because Paul was motivated to see people find faith in God's power. Every church planted, every believer who started a church, every letter written, every visitor that came and went – all of it helped people find faith in God's power. Every shipwreck, every beating, and every imprisonment was worth it because Paul could see more people find faith in God's power.

Today, we preachers can be motivated by all kinds of things – ego, success, numbers, money, facilities, recognition, sermon downloads, likes, followers, etc. However, the greatest motivation for us must be to see people come to faith in Christ through the power of God. That motivation must be the same whether a man stands before ten people in a white frame church or ten thousand people in a mega-church.

I enjoy handshakes after messages that say, "Great sermon, Pastor," or "That really spoke to me." But the greatest thing is when I stand down front during the invitation and someone comes to follow God's call on their life or when I open my email and find a heartfelt note from someone who was touched and grew as a result of the message. That's what it's all about. It's not about entertaining people or motivating people or even encouraging people. It's not about growing the church or putting people in the pews. It's about helping people find faith in God's power. When that happens, true preaching has happened.

God has chosen this bizarre thing called preaching as His vehicle for sharing His message. It has endured for 2000 years and will endure until He returns. It has been accomplished on street corners and in cathedrals, in government halls and in wood-frame meeting houses. It has been done by people with much education and people with no education. But it has only been accomplished with effectiveness when it was accomplished as Paul says it should be here.

Since I was called as pastor of First Baptist Church Pineville, my prayer has been that our church would be known for its pulpit – not the piece of furniture, as nice and unique as it is, but the ministry of the word that takes place each Sunday and continues through the week as we live and share the message in our daily lives. May that be so in our church and may it be so in every Bible-preaching church.

CHAPTER 7
Do You Know the Secret?
1 Corinthians 2:6-10

One night at the supper table, when my oldest son Zachary was about five, he said, "Daddy, I want to tell you a secret." I leaned over, and Zach whispered in my ear. Then he went to Rebecca, "Mommy, I want to tell *you* a secret." He then whispered in Rebecca' ear. Then he went to our youngest son Evan and said, "Evan, I want to tell *you* a secret," and whispered in Evan's ear. He told us all the same thing. Do you want to know what he said?

Sorry, it's a secret.

The idea of a secret intrigues us. The secret can be a simple, goofy thing, but if we know the secret and no one else knows it, we think we possess something great. Likewise, if someone else knows a secret and we don't, we feel like we're missing out. The Corinthians were enamored by false teachers in their midst who were claiming that they had deeper truths, secret spiritual knowledge, that no one else had. If you followed the false teachers, it was believed you could go deeper than anyone else and discover hidden mysteries that only the spiritually elite knew. Therefore, Paul does something interesting in this passage. He uses the language of the false teachers but applies his own theology.[48] He uses their words like "mystery" and "secret" and "hidden" and "Spirit" but applies true biblical theology to those words.

What is the secret? (vv. 6-8)

In 2006 a self-help book known as *The Secret* became a best-seller as people rushed to discover what the secret was. The book was based on the law of attraction and claimed that if you think positively you will attract positive things, but if you think negatively you will attract negative things. There are theological problems with the book, but there are two lessons you can get from the book even without reading it. The first lesson: the book's philosophy works about as well as carrying around a rabbit's foot. The second lesson: write your own book, call it something like *The Secret*, and you'll find a secret alright – the secret to becoming wealthy because people want to know secrets!

What is the secret that Paul has for us? As you consider vv. 6-8, notice that v. 6 drives vv. 7 and 8. The first part of v. 6 is expounded in v. 7, and the second part of v. 6 is expounded in v. 8. In the midst of all of this, we discover what the secret is.

First, the secret is a message of wisdom spoken among the mature (v. 6a). Who are the mature? For the false teachers, the mature were those who had been initiated into their systems of philosophy. In contrast, Paul says the mature are those who have received Jesus Christ as their Savior and Lord, in other words, the Church.

Maturity is a believer's ultimate goal. All Christians are potentially mature in Christ, unfortunately, only some of us are actually what all of us should be.[49] We should be continually maturing from the time we trust Christ to the day we die, even if there are 100 years in between.

Second, the secret is not the wisdom of this age or of its rulers (v. 6b). Every generation of humanity has its own wisdom and its own arrogance to go along with it. "We know better than those before us" is a constant mantra for nearly any field. But Paul says God's wisdom is not a wisdom of this age or its rulers.

Who are the rulers of this age? Scholars have debated this concerning everything from demons to humans, but it seems most natural that Paul had in mind the Jewish and Roman leaders of his day, though they certainly may have been influenced by the realm of darkness. These rulers and their philosophies are on their way out. Their philosophies cannot last, so the secret cannot be the wisdom of this age or its rulers.

Third, only certain people have access to the secret (vv. 6-7). If the mature can get the secret, but the rulers of this world cannot, that means only certain people have access to the secret. The word "secret" here has a double meaning. First, it is a hidden secret. No person can discover the secret on his own because it has been hidden by God. Second, it is an accessible secret. How can it be hidden and accessible at the same time? The secret can be known if God unlocks it. God unlocks the secret out of love for those who humble themselves before Him, the ones Paul calls the "mature."

Interestingly, while only certain people currently have access to the secret, it is accessible to anyone! Anyone who will do what the mature have done can have the secret revealed. What have the mature done? They have humbled themselves before Jesus Christ.

Fourth, the secret was unveiled at the right time (v. 7). God's secret wisdom was hidden until such a time as He was ready to reveal it. Before the beginning of time, God had a plan. The statement in v. 7 is a glimpse from God's perspective of eternity past to eternity future. God can see it all.

God had a predetermined plan. Some translations say He predestined that plan. A word like "predestined" causes many people to get nervous. If that's you, let me ease your nerves a bit. Predestination is not about *who*; predestination is about *how*. It is not about who will be saved or who will not be saved. Predestination is about how *anyone* can be saved. Before the world ever was, God knew everything that was to come. He knew He would create the world. He knew He would give man free will to obey Him or to disobey Him. He knew man would use that free will to rebel and allow sin to enter the world. In His wisdom, God decided on Jesus Christ and Him crucified as the way of salvation to bring His people back to share in His glory.[50] God would still give man the free will to decide to accept the salvation offered in Jesus or to reject it. But God predestined the plan. It was not so much a plan of who would be saved and who would not be saved as it was a plan of how anyone could be saved. Then, at the right time, God revealed His plan.

God started revealing His predetermined plan immediately after the fall. In Genesis 3:15, when God is cursing the serpent after the fall, we read, "And I will put enmity between you and the woman, and between your offspring and hers; he will crush your head, and you will strike his heel." That passage is known as the *protoevangelium* – a foreshadowing of the gospel. And what is the gospel? The plan! The death, burial, and resurrection of Jesus Christ! So guess what the secret wisdom of God is? Jesus Christ and Him crucified! The secret is "revealed, embodied, and made available in Jesus Christ."[51]

We confirm that in v. 8. The crucifixion is the greatest evidence of the failure of the world's wisdom because it is the crux of God's wisdom. "The very ones who were trying to do away with Jesus by crucifying Him were in fact carrying out God's . . . will." Instead of crucifying a religious nuisance, "they killed 'the Lord of glory himself.'"[52] Instead of bowing to the One who could have given them a much higher glory, they chose to maintain their earthly power and destroyed the One at whose feet they should have bowed. This makes the statement in v. 8 powerful.

Christians in liturgical traditions repeat the Memorial Acclamation in their services. The priest or minister will say, "Let us proclaim the mystery of our faith." The congregation responds, "Christ has died. Christ is risen. Christ will come again." The gospel is the mystery. The gospel is the secret.

The mystery is not something extra. It's not something you find under a rock or locked in a secret room or in some dusty old book. It's not even something you get by praying in a particular place in a particular manner using particular words. The mystery is Christ crucified – foolishness to the world but to those whom God has called the power of God and wisdom of God (1:22-24).

Why is the Secret Hidden? (v. 9)

After being closed for about fifteen years, the historic Hotel Bentley reopened a few years ago in our sister city of Alexandria, Louisiana. The hotel has historical significance because it was used during the Louisiana Maneuvers in World War II. Dwight Eisenhower and George S. Patton resided for long periods of time at the hotel, and were sometimes joined by Henry Kissinger, Omar Bradley, and other notables of the time. At a business luncheon, the hotel's owner told a story of when the hotel was first restored back in the 1980s. During that restoration, the contractor discovered a hallway that was shorter in the hotel than it was on the plans. The curious construction crew cut through the wall and found a room that had been sealed up. In the room they found a collection of door hardware from the hotel – all German made. Apparently, the hotel had been stripped of that hardware around the time of WWII when people weren't so into

German things! Thankfully, someone had hidden the hardware instead of disposing of it. It was like the person knew the wisdom of the world couldn't handle the German items in the 1940s, but they knew if they were revealed at the right time by the right person, they would be appreciated. They certainly were!

In a similar way the secret of Christ is hidden from plain sight because of what Paul says in v. 9.

> ***1 Corinthians 2:9*** *[9] However, as it is written: "No eye has seen, no ear has heard, no mind has conceived what God has prepared for those who love him" –*

Here, Paul turns to his Bible for support, using a free citation of Isaiah 64:4 with some parallels to two other passages in Isaiah (65:17 and 52:15). Paul shows that the secret is hidden because our three great sources of knowledge (seeing, hearing, thinking) are handicapped when it comes to the things of God. We cannot grasp the truth of God with our own natural processes.

First, our eyes have not seen. There is the problem of our personal perspective. Our understanding is limited by what we have seen for ourselves. If we have never seen it, we have a hard time believing it. But Jesus said, "Blessed are they who have not seen and have believed" (John 20:29). We need help to see and believe.

Second, our ears have not heard. There is the problem of our experience. If we have never heard of someone else experiencing it, we have a hard time believing it. One day while talking about the unfolding of God's plan, Jesus said, "He who has ears, let him hear" (Matthew 11:5). We need help to hear and believe.

Third, our mind has never thought of it. There is the problem of our perception. If we have never thought of it before, we have a hard time believing it. Jesus rebuked Peter one day saying, "You do not have in mind the things of God but the things of men" (Mark 8:33). We need help to train our minds on the things of God and believe.

If we need help to see, hear, and think of the things of God, then we are at a loss. The secret is hidden and will remain hidden as long as we try to grasp it on our own. Since God's secret wisdom does not originate in this world, it cannot be obtained through the normal processes of this world.[53]

How Can You Discover the Secret? (v. 10)

In the 1960s The Beatles asked, "Do You Want to Know a Secret?" Of course, everyone did. So they said:

Closer,
Let me whisper in your ear,
Say the words you long to hear,
I'm in love with you.

The girls all swooned as everyone discovered the secret.

All you had to do to discover The Beatles secret was turn on your record player or listen to the radio. But how can you discover the secret of the cross?

As v. 9 says, it is for "those who love Him." First and foremost, you need to love the Lord. The Corinthians were in love with knowledge and wisdom because they thought that was where the secret was found. Paul said the key to finding the secret was in loving God.

What does it mean to love God? Does it mean what the Beatles meant – a love that surely faded and left? Certainly not. It means to love God with the same kind of love He has for us – an unstopping, never giving up love. It is agape love, committed love, going-the-distance love, totally surrendered love. When you experience that love, the secret is revealed by the Spirit.

The secret is not found by human discovery. It comes only by divine disclosure through the Holy Spirit.[54] Why the Holy Spirit? Because the Spirit has access to the deep things of God. The Spirit also lays out the deep things for every believer to see. Jesus told His disciples in John 14:26, "[T]he Counselor, the Holy Spirit, whom the Father will send in my name, will teach you all things and will remind you of everything I have said to you."

The Holy Spirit is at work from the moment you first hear the gospel. He puts people in your path to share with you the truths of Christ. He convicts you of sin. He shows you your need for Jesus. He helps you see, hear, and understand. Then He asks, "Will you trust?" He doesn't force you to believe. As with Adam and Eve in the Garden of Eden, you can choose to follow God or reject God. He wants you to believe because God's greatest desire is for you to trust Him. But He does not force His love and transformation on anyone. The beautiful thing about the secret wisdom of God found in Christ is it's not just for a select few spiritually elite people. It is for anyone who will believe.

What would happen if you saw a folder on a desk with big red words stamped across it that read "Top Secret." No one is around. There are no hidden cameras. It's just you and that folder. Wouldn't you want to know what was in it?

Before all of us is the secret wisdom of God. Across it we read "Top Secret", but the Spirit is with us. He says, "I'll open it, if you'd like. Inside is a wonderful story of a God Who loves you and gave Himself for you. If you will repent of your sin and trust Him, He will save you. Would you like to see for yourself?"

What is your answer to the Spirit's question?

CHAPTER 8
Is the Spirit Working in Your Life?
1 Corinthians 2:10-13

For some reason, when we start talking about the Holy Spirit, we get nervous. We have no problem talking about Jesus Christ or God the Father, but, for many Christians, the Spirit is like a weird uncle no one wants to bring up. We Baptists used to be more into the Spirit's work, but the rise of the Charismatic Movement caused many of us to stick the Spirit into the Church's theological junk closet. As a result, we've often missed out on what all the Spirit has to offer.

There are several reasons we need to talk about the Spirit. For one, when you take out the Spirit, you remove the Church's power supply. In Acts 1:8 Jesus told his followers, "[Y]ou will receive power when the Holy Spirit comes on you; and you will be my witnesses in Jerusalem, and in all Judea and Samaria, and to the ends of the earth." The Spirit is the individual believer's power supply for living the Christian life and He is the Church's power supply for being an effective part of the advance of God's kingdom. Why would you want to stick the Spirit in the junk closet? It's like ripping the engine out of your car! It still might look nice, but it won't "go no mo"!

Second, if you remove the power supply of the Spirit, you must rely completely on your own abilities as a human. What did Paul say about that? In the last chapter, we saw that we are at a great loss without the Spirit: "No eye has seen, no ear has heard, no mind has conceived what God has prepared for those who love him but God has revealed it to us by His Spirit" (1 Cor. 2:9-10). If you take out the Spirit, you miss out on the greatest things of God and are limited to the things of humanity. The things of humanity get you nowhere. No individual Christian or church needs to live like that. Why would you want to stick the Spirit in the closet?

The question for each of us is this: is the Spirit working in your life? The Corinthians would have quickly said, "Oh yes!" One of them would have said, "I speak in tongues! Have you heard? *Yabadabadoo!* Don't I sound holy?" Another would say, "I can prophesy! Isn't that great?" Another would say, "I had a mysterious dream last night where the Spirit revealed to me some secret things. He told *me* because I'm more holy than *you*." These folks were so proud of their spirituality – or at least what they thought was their spirituality.

The Corinthians were into the Spirit. They loved the outward manifestation gifts like prophecy and tongues. They liked "mysterious" and "spiritual" things. They were the opposite of some of us. Whereas we effectively cram the Spirit in a junk closet, they made Him into something He wasn't – a showpiece, and that was the problem. Though they thought the Spirit was at work in their life, sometimes He was, but often He wasn't. Sometimes it was just them hyping up themselves or trying to be what they were not.

When Paul talks about the Spirit, he deals with the mysterious and spiritual things by using the Corinthians' words but also carefully applying accurate theology to those words. He wanted them to have a right understanding of the Spirit's work in their lives.

The Spirit knows the things of God and reveals them to us (vv. 10-11).

The things of God are mysterious and locked up. In Psalm 92:5-6 we read, "How great are your works, O LORD, how profound your thoughts! The senseless man does not know, fools do not understand." Unfortunately, the problem is everyone is in that fool camp! Psalm 14:2-3 and Psalm 53:3 say essentially the same thing, something Paul picks up in Romans 3 as well, "The LORD looks down from heaven on the sons of men to see if there are any who understand, any who seek God. All have turned aside, they have together become corrupt; there is no one who does good, not even one." Everyone is in the camp where no eye has seen, no ear has heard, and no mind has conceived. Therefore, we need the Spirit to reveal the great and wonderful things of God to us.

Why can the Spirit reveal the things of God to us? Because the Spirit *is* the Spirit of God. Earth shattering, I know. But it's true!

No one knows me as well as I know me. My wife Rebecca and I have been married for almost twenty years. We have no secrets between us, but she doesn't know me as well as I know me. Why? Because only I know all of my thoughts. Rebecca would say, "No, I know your thoughts. They're church, church, church." But they are not *all* about church. There are some mysterious thoughts! And she can only know them if I reveal them. (And I'll be asked to reveal them when she reads this!)

In a similar way, only the Spirit knows God's thoughts and can reveal God's thoughts. He searches out those things and reveals the things God wants revealed.

What does the Spirit reveal? Jesus said in John 16:13, "But when He, the Spirit of truth, comes, He will guide you into all truth." The Spirit reveals truth. Whatever is revealed apart from Jesus is the responsibility of the Spirit.[55] The things we know of God in general revelation through nature are pointed out by the Spirit. The things of God we discover through biblical revelation are revealed by the Spirit. The Spirit reveals the truth of God so we can know God.

How does He reveal? By pointing us to God. Why does the Spirit have no name, or, if He does, why has it not been revealed? Because the Spirit's task is not to be known Himself. His task is to point us beyond Himself. He says, "Look! There is Jesus. Look! There is the Father." The Spirit never draws attention to Himself. His goal is to point people to the truth of God the Son so people may have a restored relationship with God the Father. If we neglect the work of the Spirit, we miss out on getting to know the Father and Son. Likewise, if we overemphasize the Spirit, we can miss out on the Father and the Son.

The Spirit helps us understand what God has given (v. 12).

Jesus often asked His followers, "Do you understand this?" After asking that question in John 14:26, Jesus says, "[T]he Counselor, the Holy Spirit, whom the Father will send in my name, will teach you all things and will remind you of everything I have said to you." On their own, the disciples couldn't understand, but when the Holy Spirit was given, things started clicking because the Spirit made them click.

Truth is useless if you can't understand it. The greatest source of truth is God's word. Since the greatest source of truth is God's word, God made sure His followers could understand it. Whenever a person trusts Jesus as his or her Savior and Lord, God gives that believer the Holy Spirit to help him understand His truth.

When we encounter God's word, God doesn't send a second-hand messenger. He sends the One who helped write it. The Holy Spirit was the agent of inspiration for the biblical writers (2 Peter 1:21). "The Bible wasn't written by a secondhand angel. It was written by God Himself through the Holy Spirit's inspiration of godly men. God didn't trust the transmission of scripture to anyone outside the Trinity."[56] Because the Holy Spirit helped write the Bible, He is the perfect one to help us understand the Bible. When we study God's word, we get the privilege of having the author sitting beside us. The Holy Spirit helps us understand what God has given us.

One of the Spirit's chief jobs is illumination. He turns on the light for us to see and understand. Without the Spirit, we remain in the dark. We could know a lot about God's word, but we will never experience the true power of God's word without the Spirit. This is the difference between secular scholars who study the Bible but are never changed by it and those of us who know the Lord and are changed by God's word. Because the scholars are not open to the Spirit's work in their lives, they remain in the dark. But when a person comes to the word, desiring to understand, God turns on the light through His Spirit, and that believer comes to understand God's word.

I was an English minor in college. I primarily chose that minor because I liked my professor. I didn't choose that minor because I was the best at pulling out insights from literature. In fact, my knee jerk answer to the question, "What is the author trying to do here?" was "Um, tell a good story?" I improved at figuring out better answers to that question (or at least making them up!), but sometimes I wondered if we were making too much of what the author had written. I simply wish we could have had the author sit in class with us and explain what he or she was doing – if he or she was doing anything at all!

When we study God's word, we get that privilege! We have the Author sitting beside us! The Holy Spirit helps us understand what God has given us. Have you ever had a time when you were reading the Bible and thought, "I've never seen that before!" For some reason on that day, the Spirit made it click for you so that you never read that passage the same way again. The Spirit helps us understand what God has given.

The Spirit teaches and empowers us to share spiritual truths (v. 13)

The Spirit not only helps us understand the truth, he also helps us share the truth through preaching or teaching or witnessing. You do not have to be a preacher or a teacher to share spiritual truths. You can share spiritual truth in your own home, office, or business – and you should!

Truth is no good if you hold it for yourself. We are not to be repositories of truth. We are to be fountains of truth, sharing what God reveals to us with the world. We are to be distributors not libraries!

Jesus said that when the Spirit came we would receive power to be His witnesses. We would be His witnesses wherever and whenever. That might be in our home to our unbelieving family members. That might be at school to unbelieving friends. It might be in the public square where we have to give a witness for Christ. Wherever we share that faith, we need power.

Any time a preacher steps into a pulpit, he needs the Spirit's power. Any time a Sunday School teacher tells a Bible story to four-year-olds or facilitates discussion among forty-year-olds, she needs the Spirit's power. Any time a boy is alone with his girlfriend and has to cling to biblical principles of purity, he needs the Spirit's power. Any time a businessman is asked to compromise his convictions to make a little more money, he needs the Spirit's power. Any time the truth must go forth from our mouth or be applied by our minds or our hands, we need the Spirit's power.

Allow the Spirit to work in your life. Pray today the words of the old gospel song:

Spirit of the Living God, fall fresh on me.
Sprit of the Living God, fall fresh on me.
Break me, melt me, mold me, fill me.
Spirit of the Living God, fall fresh on me.[57]

CHAPTER 9
Do You Have the Mind of Christ?
1 Corinthians 2:14-16

What distinguishes a spiritual person from an unspiritual person? Unfortunately, we typically focus on the outside of a person for our answer. We look at a person's appearance, and, if they are clean-cut and dressed "nice", we think they must be spiritual. However, if they are a bit "grungy", they must be unspiritual. Where does a person's choice of clothes figure into the spiritual life? Nowhere. In fact, there weren't all that many different styles back in biblical days! Further, if you think about it, John the Baptist was grungy while Pontius Pilate was dressed nice!

At other times, we look at a person's socio-economic level to try to distinguish the spiritual from the unspiritual. For some reason, we tend to think that those below us or above us on the socio-economic level are not spiritual. We think those below us must not work hard, and God teaches us to work hard. But we think those above us are not spiritual because they "obviously" are greedy and focused only on possessions. Do you see how ridiculous this is?

We look at a lot of things to size up someone as "spiritual" or "unspiritual". But the things we look for are typically not the things that truly indicate a person's spirituality. The distinguishing mark of spirituality is actually something that cannot be seen. However, it is something that is lived out every day. The distinguishing mark of spirituality is the transformed mind, what we call the mind of Christ.

The human mind is amazing. Did you know your brain uses enough energy to power a 25 watt light bulb? There are more electrical impulses generated in one day by a single human brain than by all the telephones in the world! With all those electrical impulses going on, the brain ponders 70,000 thoughts in an average day!

Yes, the human mind is amazing! It is limited, however, if it is not spiritually focused. Let me ask you, "Do you have the mind of Christ?" Paul helps you determine if you do.

The spiritual and the unspiritual person are different (vv. 14-15).

Paul makes it clear that there is a difference between the spiritual and the unspiritual person. Consider the person without the Spirit. Paul says this person "does not accept the things that come from the Spirit of God, for they are foolishness to him, and he cannot understand them, because they are spiritually discerned."

Think of the natural man as stuck in a box. The box represents this physical world. Therefore, when he tries to consider the things of God through his own human abilities, they don't make sense to him. He concludes, then, that if he cannot understand something with his mind, it must be foolishness and he rationalizes it away.

Think about the questions that we raise of scripture that can plague the unspiritual person: How could the Red Sea part and the ground become dry? How can someone dying on a cross pay for sins? Why does a good God allow evil? If you are living for God, why do bad things happen to you?

Every person meets these questions and a thousand more in his or her life. But the person without the Spirit can never find satisfactory answers or allow his question to go unanswered as he trusts the sovereignty of God. Instead, he uses his questions as bullets to try to shoot holes in the faith. Since he cannot understand these things with his mind, they must be foolishness. Therefore, his earthly mind guides the way he lives. He lives as if there is nothing beyond the box and that the most important needs are physical and material.

Furthermore, the unspiritual person has a hard time understanding spiritual standards. Therefore, he rationalizes them away. For example, since God's standard for relationships and marriage do not make sense to him, he rationalizes that it is reasonable for a couple to live together before they are married or that homosexual relationships are fine or that a little bit of pornography is o.k. Since he cannot understand the Bible's teachings that everything belongs to God, if anyone speaks of stewardship, he says the church is just trying to get his money.

That kind of earthly mind continues in all areas of life. This person focuses on this life – his career, his money, his hobbies, his family, his personal desires. His focus may not always be necessarily bad, but it is always earthly. This person may even go to church, but his relationship with God isn't important to him. If you looked at his calendar, you would see far more Sundays with other stuff than you would a commitment to being in the Lord's house. You would see him living in a way that is contrary to the teachings of Christ while rationalizing his decision to live that way.

Compare the earthly minded person to the person with the Spirit. Paul says the person with the Spirit makes judgments about all things, but he himself is not subject to any man's judgment: "For who has known the mind of the Lord that he may instruct him?" Whereas the person without the Spirit cannot understand the things of God, the spiritual man is willing to look beyond the box and realize there is far more to life and eternity than can ever be captured with one earthly mind. "The spiritual man accurately discerns and evaluates all things, both secular and spiritual. Because he has received the Spirit, he is able to appraise all things, for he both understands them and is furnished with a moral standard for proper measurement of them."[58] He comes to the same questions as anyone else, faces the same challenges as anyone else, but addresses those questions and challenges with a different mind-set than the person without the Spirit. His spiritual mind guides the way he lives, and he seeks the Lord's guidance so he might understand and live by spiritual standards.

Let's take the same examples as above. God's standard for relationships and marriage makes sense to the spiritually minded person because she understands that God established marriage to be between one man and one woman. She understands that God set forth a clear process for the marriage relationship found in Genesis 2:23-24 whereby a person receives the person God has for them, leaves their father and mother, cleaves to their spouse in holy matrimony, and then becomes one flesh through sexual union. Further, the spiritually minded person understands God's teaching on stewardship and allows it to totally transform his worldview. Instead of viewing everything as belonging to him, he views everything as belonging to God. He cheerfully gives back to God a portion of his income as a way of saying thanks to God and as a means of investing in God's kingdom. Further, his calendar reveals his interest in the things of God as well. He is committed to his local church and makes sure his family is as well. Each of them attends worship, is growing through a Bible study, and is serving in a ministry. They are involved in plenty of things outside of church, but their service to the Lord is first. This type of mindset continues in all areas of life.

The world doesn't understand true believers; therefore, it has a hard time evaluating them. People may try to judge the person with the spiritual mind, but the person can't be judged by them. Ultimately, the man or woman of God is answerable to God alone.

To support his statement about the person with the spiritual mind, Paul quotes Isaiah 40:13 in verse 16. Much of Isaiah 40 talks about the greatness of God, but it also describes the Spirit-guided life. In Isaiah 40:28-31, we read:

> *Do you not know? Have you not heard? The LORD is the everlasting God, the Creator of the ends of the earth. He will not grow tired or weary, and his understanding no one can fathom. He gives strength to the weary and increases the power of the weak. Even youths grow tired and weary, and young men stumble and fall; but those who hope in the LORD will renew their strength. They will soar on wings like eagles; they will run and not grow weary, they will walk and not be faint.*

Is that not a great place to be? There is something unique about those who hope in the Lord, those with the spiritual mind as opposed to those without the spiritual mind.

The difference: the spiritual man has the mind of Christ (v. 16b).

Have you ever known someone and thought, "Man, I wish I had their mind!" Well, you can't. We haven't come up with a way to do brain transplants or even downloads! But you can have your mind transformed into the mind of Christ.

What does it mean to have the mind of Christ? Paul doesn't say, so we must construct it from other places. In his study *The Mind of Christ,* T.W. Hunt outlines six characteristics of the Christ-like mind.[59]

First, the mind of Christ is alive. In Romans 8:6 we read, "The mind of sinful man is death, but the mind controlled by the Spirit is life and peace." This mind of Christ is active. It is not lazy. It is active in prayer. It is active in learning the things of God. What is actively thought guides what is actively lived.

Second, the mind of Christ is focused. Hunt says it is "single-minded". You can hear the focus in Philippians 4:8, "Finally, brothers, whatever is true, whatever is noble, whatever is right, whatever is pure, whatever is lovely, whatever is admirable-- if anything is excellent or praiseworthy – think about such things." Throughout the New Testament, we are challenged to be devoted to Christ. Often the expression is "set your minds on Christ" or "consider Christ." Instead of being distracted by the things of the world, we are focused on Christ – His commands, His person, His ways. Our direction of focus guides our direction of living.

Third, the mind of Christ is humble. Hunt describes it as lowly. Notice the humility of Romans 12:3, "For by the grace given me I say to every one of you: Do not think of yourself more highly than you ought, but rather think of yourself with sober judgment, in accordance with the measure of faith God has given you." When you see yourself in relation to God, you cannot help but come to a more reasonable view of yourself. We do not compare ourselves to the imperfections of others; we compare ourselves to the perfection of Christ. Our attitude of humility guides our attitude of living.

Fourth, the mind of Christ is pure. Paul reminds us in Titus 1:15-16, "To the pure, all things are pure, but to those who are corrupted and do not believe, nothing is pure. In fact, both their minds and consciences are corrupted. They claim to know God, but by their actions they deny him." The pure-minded person works to keep his focus on the right things. As the psalmist, he covets to "set no wicked thing before my eyes" (Psalm 101:3). Because he knows if he does, his mind can be quickly corrupted. Pure thoughts lead to a pure life.

Fifth, the mind of Christ is responsive. We see the activity of Jesus in Luke 24:45, "Then he opened their minds so they could understand the Scriptures." The disciples did not always get what Jesus taught them, but they were teachable. Once God opened their minds and gave them the Holy Spirit, they became responsive. Immediately, on the day of Pentecost, they began actively living out the faith. Responsiveness to God's teaching will lead to responsible living.

Sixth, the mind of Christ is peaceful. Romans 8:6-7 reminds us, "The mind of sinful man is death, but the mind controlled by the Spirit is life and peace; the sinful mind is hostile to God. It does not submit to God's law, nor can it do so." Isaiah 26:3 encourages, "You will keep in perfect peace him whose mind is steadfast, because he trusts in you." Peace is a fruit of the Spirit that is given to the person who has Christ. A peaceful mind leads to a peaceful life.

Active, focused, humble, pure, responsive, peaceful – this is the mind of Christ.

How can I have the mind of Christ?

It might sound mysterious or difficult but attaining the mind of Christ is not all that difficult. However, it does require total commitment. We might say the mind of Christ is easy to get from God but potentially difficult to receive from God. God freely offers it, but it is difficult for us to give the total commitment needed to receive it. There are essentially three things you need to do to receive and develop the mind of Christ.

First, commit your life to Jesus Christ. In this first step, you repent of your sins and trust Jesus Christ as your Lord and Savior. Without this step, you cannot receive the mind of Christ because you will not have the Spirit of God in your life.

Second, ask for the mind of Christ. Sometimes we have not because we ask not. We "must pray to have the mind of Christ, for only when Christ dwells within us are we safe from the encroaching invasion of the demands of material things."[60]

Third, develop the mind of Christ. If you don't use it, you lose it. Just as the physical mind needs to be used and developed, so the spiritual mind must be used and developed as well.

I hope you will seek the mind of Christ for yourself. It distinguishes the spiritual person from the unspiritual person. It guides your life. It directs your actions.

CHAPTER 10
Can You Be Divided and Spiritual?
1 Corinthians 3:1-4

Can Christians be both divided and spiritual at the same time? For the church at Corinth, that was a pressing question. The church was threatening to break up from the factions within it. The people who made up each faction thought themselves to be spiritual. But can you be both divided and spiritual?

This is an important question. When a church's members take sides over an issue, can the members of that church be both divided and spiritual? When the bonds of a denomination are threatened by issues within, can the group be both divided and spiritual? When division comes to a family and members stop talking to one another, can the family be both divided and spiritual? When spouses find their marriage bond being challenged, can they be both divided and spiritual?

Can Christians be both divided and spiritual? Paul is as direct in this passage about conflict as he was previously. Paul's answer to the question is a resounding, "No!" Why? Because division reveals immaturity and worldliness.

For most of the last chapter, Paul has been demonstrating what it means to be spiritual. He's taught us about the Spirit's work and he's instructed us that the spiritual person has the mind of Christ. Now he says, "You're not that!" Though they are believers, they are thinking and behaving like unspiritual people. [61] These people aren't lost, but they are acting like they are!

Unfortunately, this happens far too often in Christian circles. It's what happens when pastors act like autocratic dictators or when deacons practice deceit. It's what happens when believing husbands and wives treat each other like dirt or when Christian siblings write off one another. It's what happens when denominational brothers slam each other or keep only their personal interests in mind. It is all Christians acting like nonChristians.

Are they saved? Yes. Are they walking in the Spirit? No. Paul says their reason for acting this way centers on two things: immaturity and worldliness. For the Corinthians, it was both. For some of us, it could be both. For others, it may be one or the other.

Immaturity (vv. 1-2)

Because of their false sense of spirituality, the Corinthians were saying, "Paul, we want something deep spiritually." Paul says, "I'd love to give you more. There *is* so much more, but you're still babies in Christ. I gave you milk because that's what babies drink, but you're still sucking on a bottle. I can't even move you to smashed peas!" A bottle is fine for a baby, but when a grown up is sucking on a bottle, something is desperately wrong.

Every Christian, regardless of age, starts out spiritually sucking on a bottle. When you are a baby, you can't handle any more than that. But you shouldn't stay that way. You should learn more, hunger for more, and progress to more. Unfortunately, so many Christians do not. There are many Christians who, though they have been believers for decades, are still spiritually babies.

When you are a spiritual baby, you tend to live out your faith as an infant. Preschoolers get the basics but not much else. Most of them are more interested in boogers and bugs than they are the things of God. But just as we grow beyond the silly things of preschool, we should also grow in our knowledge of the faith.

Unfortunately, many Christians never grow beyond the basics of preschool. They know the Bible stories and the simple truths, but the rest of their theology is controlled by what they hear in the world. In terms of their interest in church, they go little beyond what they get from it and what they like about it. Babies want *their* way, and they cry to get it. Spiritual babies do the same thing in the church, in their marriages, and in their relationships. The result is a bunch of crying babies with no pacifier big enough to make them hush!

So what does Paul say? He says he would love to give them more. In fact, he should be giving them more, but they can't handle it. He'd love to address them as mature, spiritually-minded people, but they are immature, earthly-minded people.

Spiritual immaturity is at the root of why some churches deal with multiple splits in their history. These churches have remained in the baby stage for decades. Spiritual immaturity is also why many marriages end in divorce. When a husband and wife are immature in their faith, they deal with life like babies. Every marriage has conflict. The key to success is how you deal with it so you don't end up with division. It is easy to get sucked back into infancy: "I want that toy. It's mine;" "I want my way;" "You're not my friend anymore!" To infant attitudes, Paul says, "Grow up! Stop behaving like kids! Just stop! You can't be spiritual and divided. You are immature."

Worldliness (vv. 3-4)

Not only are the Corinthians still babies, they are worldly as well! All of us are made of flesh. That is not bad because we have no control over the substance of our being. But the Corinthians were not only made of flesh, they were characterized by the flesh. In fact, Paul points to the jealousy and quarreling among them as Exhibits A and B for their worldliness. They were acting as "mere men" – not spiritual men, not church men, not godly men – *mere* men.

What do you do with a statement like that when you have jealousy or quarreling in your church (or anywhere for that matter)? You sit up straight and listen, that's what you do! When we allow jealousy and quarreling to come into any of our relationships, our tendency, even as believers, is to do what the world does.

Anytime there is conflict in the world, all kinds of things are done – sanctions are imposed, assets are frozen, trade is stopped, military conflict is threatened. We tend to do the same kinds of things when we operate from the flesh in our relationships. We threaten. We form unholy alliances. We deceive. We lie. We cheat. We slander. We fight for our good instead of the good of the whole. We demand our way. We withhold our giving when we don't like what is happening in the church. We enter a cold war of silence in our family to try to show how serious we are in our stance. We stop the trade of intimacy in marriage as a way of controlling our spouse.

Do you know what all of that is? Worldliness. It is mere men and mere women operating in mere flesh. Such activity has no place in the church or in the Christian home.

Jealousy and quarreling lead to terrible things among us as believers. Jealousy leads to pride, unforgiveness, self-promotion, being easily offended, jockeying for control or power or recognition, and more. Quarrelling leads to factions, slander, gossip, arrogance, disorder, anger, and more. Those things do not belong in the church or any relationship between believers.

The Corinthians were arguing about their favorite teachers. Paul basically says, "Who cares? It doesn't matter!"

You can stick almost anything that churches argue about today in the place of Paul or Apollos and come up with the same conclusion: "It doesn't matter!" Whether it's an argument over hymns or praise songs, pews or chairs, premillinialism or amillennialism, red or green carpet, the conclusion is the same, "It doesn't matter." None of these are areas of breaking fellowship – neither were Paul and Apollos. Any time you allow peripheral matters to become the central matter, you walk into the dangerous waters of worldliness.

For some reason we tend to be friends with people until we find the one area out of a 100 where we disagree and then we condemn them to hell. My Baptist history professor, Dr. Karen Bullock, gave us a humorous anecdote. You may not know all of the types of Baptists mentioned in this conversation, but you'll get the gist:

I met a man the other day. We started talking about religion.

I said, "Are you Protestant or Catholic?"
He said, "Protestant."
I said, "Me too! What kind?"
He says, "Baptist."
I said, "Me too! Northern Baptist or Southern Baptist?"
He says, "Southern Baptist."
I said, "Me too! Charleston Southern Baptist or Sandy Creek Southern Baptist."
He says, "Sandy Creek Southern Baptist."

> I said, "Me too! Sandy Creek Georgia Tradition Southern Baptist or Sandy Creek Landmark Tradition Southern Baptist?"
> He says, "Sand Creek Landmark Tradition Southern Baptist."
> I said, "Me too! Sandy Creek Landmark Tradition Southern Baptist fundamentalist or Sandy Creek Landmark Tradition Southern Baptist moderate?"
> And he says, "Sandy Creek Landmark Tradition Southern Baptist moderate."
> And I said, "Die! Heretic!"
> And he said, "Double death on you, you ignorant redneck!"[62]

That would be a lot funnier if it weren't so true. It seems that every time we divide, we divide again.

Whenever and wherever there is jealousy and quarreling among believers, we need to stop and go to our knees. For we have walked away from a close relationship with God and into worldliness. William Barclay challenges, "You can tell what a man's relations with God are by looking at his relations with his fellow men. If a man is at variance with his fellow men, if he is a quarrelsome, competitive, argumentative, trouble-making creature, he may be a diligent church attender, he may even be a church office-bearer, but he is not a man of God."[63] Oh my! The simple test case is this: If you are distant from your fellow man, you are distant from God. If you are divided from your fellow man, you are divided from God.[64]

To the Corinthians whose church was threatening to rip apart because of conflict, Paul said, "Stop it! Just stop it! People of the Spirit simply must stop behaving the way you are."[65] The gospel was being stripped of its power and their vain pursuits were leading to divisions.[66] They had to stop. They could not be both divided and spiritual.

If you are involved in a conflict today, stop it. If the conflict is in your marriage, sit down with your spouse and say, "I love you. We've got to stop this. Let's seek the Lord and help together." If the conflict is in your family, stop it. Call the person from whom you are disconnect and express a desire to reconnect. Wherever the conflict in your life, find a way to stop it as far as it depends on you. Do away with your worldly nature and follow the Spirit. You cannot be both divided and spiritual.

CHAPTER 11
A Proper View of the Church
1 Corinthians 3:5-17

The church I pastor has had fourteen pastors in its more than 100 year history. Each pastor was called to the church for a purpose and left his mark on the church by accomplishing positive things that still remain as part of our church today. Here's a brief summary:

1. Railey helped the church get started.
2. Wallace helped the church grow through a visitation ministry.
3. Franks led the church to move to its present site and build the first sanctuary.
4. Gwatkin began the church newsletter.
5. Gayer grew a love for the pastor while helping the church be strong in evangelism.
6. Price built a fantastic preaching ministry and preached to five different groups on the church campus each Sunday (he was doing multi-venue worship before anyone had thought of that). He also embraced the mass media by using radio to promote the gospel and the church.
7. Knight led the church to purchase land for building expansion.
8. Wright led the church to build a three-story education building and reach the soldiers training in the area during World War II.
9. Smith reached the post-war generation and constructed what is now the preschool and children's building, the present sanctuary, and the activities building.
10. Richards helped the church begin reaching a new generation and began the process of building a second education building. He brought the church to regional prominence through a daily television program.

11. Debord helped the church focus on the five purposes of worship, evangelism, discipleship, fellowship, and ministry before anyone had ever heard of Rick Warren.
12. Baker helped the church begin modernizing the campus.
13. Baldwin established the intercessory prayer room.
14. Holloway – well, we're still waiting to see what that guy accomplishes.

Every pastor was called to the church for a specific season and left his own mark.

While each pastor labored, dozens of staff members served, and thousands of people across the years formed the membership. But above all of these pastors, there has been one chief shepherd, the Senior Pastor, the Lord Jesus Christ.

In 1 Corinthians 3:5-17, Paul helps us capture a view of the church where we find Jesus Christ in the primary leadership role. Here we find a proper view of church leaders and members.

Leaders are servants with a purpose (vv. 5-10a).

As we have seen, the Corinthians were divided over their leaders. Some grouped themselves under the old leader, Paul; while others grouped themselves under a newer leader, Apollos. To this conflict, Paul basically says, "Who cares? It doesn't matter!" Interestingly, he does this with a single word.

When talking about people, you normally use the word "who." But here Paul uses the word "what." He doesn't ask, "Who is Apollos? Who is Paul?" He asks, "*What* is Apollos? *What* is Paul?" If he had asked the question, "Who?", people would have focused on the person. Since he asks "What?", Paul helps the Corinthians focus on the purpose of the person. What is Apollos? What is Paul? They are only servants through whom the Corinthians came to believe. Paul essentially says, "The Lord used Apollos and me to help you come to faith. Some of you came to faith while the Lord used me; others of you have come to faith while the Lord has used Apollos." I had my task. Apollos has his.

Paul next moves to an image from farming. He pictures the city of Corinth as a huge cultivated field. Paul identifies himself as the first "farmer." He was called to plant the seed. Next, Apollos was called to water the seeds. Paul and Apollos were not competitors in purpose; they were co-laborers in purpose. "Both Paul and Apollos are gifts from God to the church at Corinth and are to be received as such."[67] Planting and watering are both after the same purpose. Both are vital. Both are dependent on each other.

Further, both of those men were completely dependent on God.[68] It was God who caused the planted and watered seeds to grow. Whereas their work was contained to a period of time, God's work was continuous. Paul doesn't dismiss his and Apollos' roles as leaders, but he certainly diminishes their roles. They had but a small part when compared to God's big part. "The roles of servant and Lord must never be confused."[69]

During seminary, I served as a part-time Associate Pastor at a church. One day as I sat in my office reflecting on my role, the Lord taught me an important lesson: no matter what the title on my desk or stationary, I would always be an Associate Pastor because Jesus is the Senior Pastor. That lesson helped me a great deal when I later became "the" pastor of a church. Twenty years later, numerous times a year, I still think about the lesson the Lord taught me that day. I also refuse to use the title Senior Pastor because that's not my title. Jesus Christ is the Senior Pastor of our church and every church.

The earthly pastors who have planted or watered have had one purpose and each will be rewarded according to his own labor (v. 8). As Jack MacGorman writes, "It is always possible for one to plant well and another to water poorly, or vice versa. When this happens, the harvest is less, but the faithful worker is not penalized for the faithless performance of his fellow servant."[70] Each is rewarded according to his own labor. Even among the fourteen pastors of our church, some have planted or watered more effectively than others. Still the follies or foibles of one do not reflect on the whole; they reflect on the one. God will reward each pastor according to his own labor in fulfilling his purpose in his time.

In v. 9, Paul identifies the people as the field or building. God is the owner. Leaders are just servants God hires to accomplish specific tasks. Someone is called to lay the foundation. And, even though he may be an expert in his field, God moves him along and someone else is called to build the house. That's because it is God's house, not the pastor's house.

Viewing leaders as servants with a purpose helps us gain a proper perspective of the church. Most importantly, we eliminate the tendency to establish personality cults. We come to realize that leadership transitions are fine as long as the purpose is maintained. We remember that God is our Senior Pastor, and we stay focused on our purpose.

I learned this principle during my first pastorate. I followed my friend Kris Barnett as pastor to Forestburg Baptist Church in Forestburg, Texas. On the day Kris preached in view of a call at his new church, I supplied for him at Forestburg. After the worship service, Rebecca and I enjoyed lunch in the home of the Hudspeths, one of the only families that knew where Kris was that day. After lunch, Dale Hudspeth asked, "So, if Kris leaves, are you interested in being our pastor?" I nearly fell out of my chair. But two months later, I was pastoring those wonderful people.

God soon showed me something as I began understanding the history of that church. I realized what God had been doing! The pastor before Kris, Bill Smith, was nearing retirement. Wisely, he had led the church to prepare for growth. With around forty people in attendance, the church built additional Sunday School space, tripling their capacity.

The day they dedicated the building, Bill resigned, and Kris began. It was Bill's last pastorate and Kris' first. Kris came from being a youth minister to that pastorate. Therefore, Kris both pastored the church and built the youth ministry until the church could hire their first part-time youth minister. The church saw immediate growth.

About four years later, the church began building a new sanctuary. I arrived in the middle of that process. At that point, music and organization were the church's greatest needs. I was coming to my first pastorate after being a music minister and an associate pastor. I worked to organize the church as well as led the music and preached for about a year and a half until we hired our first part-time minister of music. Soon we also made one of our volunteers our part-time children's minister. We enjoyed a new sanctuary, the most staff the church had ever had (even though they were all part-time), a growing budget, more baptisms and new members than ever before in the history of the church, and we had momentum. At some point during all of that, I remembered this text in 1 Corinthians and realized that I was reaping the benefits of the labors of both Kris and Bill. Bill had laid the foundation for growth. Kris had started building upon it. I was able to continue. Together, we were part of almost 15 years of consistent growth for Forestburg Baptist Church. I realized I was part of a mighty plan of God for that church in that time. Lesson in a nutshell: leaders are simply servants with a purpose.

Do you believe God is involved in the work of your church? Do you believe He has a plan? I certainly believe that for our church. Your attitude of God's work in the church will be incredible if you take this view. Every staff member added; every person who is saved; every person who joins; every ministry added; every special gift that is made; every building that is updated or constructed; every church planted – all of it is part of the plan of God in building His Church.

Today, I get the distinct privilege of standing at our church's pulpit – a place of leadership, a place of direction. It is somewhat the helm of the ship. But that helm was built by thirteen pastors before me and thousands of members before our present congregation. Our church is not owned by me or our people, it is owned by God. Preachers move, retire, or die. Church members move away, move on, or die. But God never moves away, moves on, retires, or dies. If the church is built on a preacher or even on a generation of members, the church will die. If the church is built on Christ, the church will thrive.

Whereas Paul's first principle for a proper view of the church dealt with the church's leadership, his next principle relates to the members.

We must build the church with care (vv. 10b-15).

Alongside the pastors are the members of the church. These precious people must be careful what they build upon the foundation.

We must build the church with care because of the foundation we have. The foundation is Jesus Christ. Scripture is clear that Jesus is the chief cornerstone of the church. This foundation of Christ is expensive. The foundation actually costs more than the building itself because it cost Jesus His life! If the foundation is that costly, shouldn't we build something great upon it? The quality of the building must match the foundation!

Too often in our churches and with our lives we build something shabby on the expensive foundation. Paul reminds us that *we must build the church with care because judgment is coming.* The imagery in this passage shows a person running though fire clutching the work of his life. This is not a picture of hell. It is an image of a refining process. The fire has no effect on the person, the fire only affects the treasure. As the person runs through the fire, the treasure is tested and shown for what it is.

The first person who runs through the fire is one who has built a treasure of straw. He has worked throughout his life to do everything he could on his own to build this treasure. It is beautiful – nicely woven, with a variety of grasses combined together. But, as he runs into the fire, the treasure of hay burns up. No matter how good it looks; no matter how beautifully woven together it is; it is still just straw and burns up. When this person falls at the feet of Jesus, all that will be left is ashes.

The second person who runs through the fire is one who has built a treasure of wood. The master carpenter, she has worked hard throughout her life to build something beautiful. This person is self-made, just like the builder of the straw treasure. This person does quite well, building a beautiful work for God. But this treasure of wood, while better than straw, still burns up, no matter how expensive the wood or elaborate the carvings. This person too, when she falls at the feet of Jesus, will be able to offer only ashes.

The third person who runs though the fire does so clutching a work of gold, silver, and precious stones. This person realized early on that God wanted him to build something great with his life. He knew that God laid a strong and sure foundation. He knew that God would provide all the resources needed. Therefore, he built what God wanted. He built what mattered. As he runs through the fire, his treasure is not burned up. In fact, it is refined! This person is able to offer Jesus a treasure that is even better than when he entered the fiery test. The Master says with joy, "Well done, good and faithful servant!"

I pray you are not building a treasure of wood, hay, or straw, because, no matter how good it looks, it's just going to burn up. I pray that our church and your church is not just a pile of wood or straw that will not endure the flames. We must build the church with care. We must stay grounded in Christ and the truths of His word.

Do not be a part of destroying God's church (vv. 16-17).

Jack MacGorman said this is "one of the severest pronouncements in Paul's writings."[71] This goes for church members, staff members, and pastors. Do not be a part of destroying God's church! The universal church cannot be destroyed, but local churches can be destroyed. Every day local churches are destroyed by autocratic pastors, gossiping staff members, devilish deacons, and conniving congregants. Paul says, "You better not be one of those."

God is passionate about His church. He knows well that nothing destroys a church more quickly or completely than dissension and strife. God "is prepared to destroy anyone who uses his God-given talents to suck the life out of His church."[72] How will He destroy them? Paul doesn't say. I think the point is you don't want to find out! This warning goes for the pastor and the members.

When I have taught pastoral ministry or mentored those going in the pastorate, I have instructed, "If the issue in the church is ever you, get out and move on graciously. Don't burn bridges. Don't set a fire on your way out. Leave graciously." Splitting the church is never the answer. Mac Brunson says, "The pastor who allows the church to split over his leadership is teaching the group who stays with him how to split again if they ever disagree with his leadership."[73] How true! A pastor should never be a part of destroying God's church. Why? Because it is God's church, not the pastor's church.

The same is true for members. Never allow yourself to cause a church split. You may need to move on graciously. Don't start a fire or burn bridges, move on graciously. I have known fine Christian people who have had to do that. They didn't throw gasoline and a match at the church before they left; they just left, usually telling their pastor in a gracious meeting why and leaving on good terms. Sometimes the pastor was the issue, sometimes it was other members, sometimes it was just a change brought by a season of life. But it was a gracious parting. That's how it ought to be. A church member must not be a part of destroying God's church. Why? Because it is God's church, not the member's church.

One of my constant prayers as a pastor is, "Lord, help me to not do something stupid that will mess up what You are doing." Every church member should pray a similar prayer. I don't know about you, but I don't want to be destroyed because I destroyed God's church!

If your church is not experiencing conflict at this time, spend some time thanking the Lord. Consider this chapter preventative maintenance. Do everything you can to help your church stay united.

CHAPTER 12
Are You of Christ?
1 Corinthians 3:18-23

Optical illusions fascinate me. From the work of illusionists to drawings and photographs, I am intrigued by how easy it is to trick the eye. Optical illusions work because of the deception of perception. One article states, "Seeing is not an objective, clearly defined experience. Vision is a construction of the mind. . . . Perception involves interpretation, and our thoughts, memories and emotions determine how we interpret what we see. Yet we readily accept what we see as 'real.'" Perception becomes reality. "Magicians figured this out long ago. By directing the audience's attention, magicians perform their tricks in full view. . . . This means that we can easily deceive ourselves and yet be convinced that our judgments are exact and correct."[74] It is the deception of perception. We can be tricked in two ways: we can be tricked into seeing what is not there or we can be tricked into missing all that is there.

If the deception of perception can happen so easily when we look at a photograph or watch a magician, what could happen in our spiritual lives? Could we be tricked into seeing what is not there or tricked into missing all that is there?

These dual tricks of the deception of perception are addressed in 1 Corinthians 3:18-23. In this last paragraph of chapter 3, Paul brings his arguments about godly wisdom and divisions in the church together to ask, "Are you of Christ?" He expects the church to answer, "Sure we are!" So, then he says, "Well, if you are, then don't fall victim to the deception of perception."

Are you of Christ? "Sure we are, Paul!" Then do not deceive yourselves. Turn things upside down to get full perception (vv. 18-20).

While we can be deceived by others, we can also deceive ourselves to see what is not there. Since the Corinthians thought they were far more superior than they really were, Paul tells them, "Do not deceive yourselves. You think you are wise, but you need to be a fool."

What? Yes, in order to be wise, you need to become a fool. That's because the world's wisdom is a deception of perception. When you become a fool to the world's perception, you become wise to God's perception.

The wisdom of this world is foolishness in God's sight. Worldly wisdom gives a tragic deception of perception. For the Corinthians, worldly wisdom was the root of church division. It was leading them to assess the worth of their leaders, creating a deception of perception by which they focused on what they *wanted* to see instead of what they *needed* to see. For example, instead of hearing the content of Paul or Apollos' message, they criticized everything that was supposed to carry the message – the way in which the message was delivered, the correctness of the language, the strength of the argument, probably even the dress of the preacher.[75] They never heard the truth because they couldn't get past the deception of perception. Therefore, Paul tells them to turn things upside down – to focus on the spiritual content instead of the physical externals.

They needed to do this because worldly wisdom falls flat on its face before God. To illustrate his point, Paul quotes two Old Testament texts in v. 19. The first is Job 5:13, "He catches the wise in their craftiness, and the schemes of the wily are swept away." God will catch the crafty in their schemes.

When I was growing up, if I was frustrated about a wrong someone did, my dad would say something like, "Son, he'll eventually hang himself." Dad was saying that the person would eventually get caught in his own wrongs.

The second text is from Psalm 94:11, "The LORD knows the thoughts of man; He knows that they are futile." There is ultimate futility in the thoughts of the wise. They think they are so smart that they are actually ignorant. The person parading around like a prince of worldly wisdom can't see the snares all around him. Neither can he see that he is really not a prince at all! He is actually a sorry excuse for a clown! Why is that? Pride. And pride is dangerous!

What's so dangerous about pride? Pride is dangerous because if you are a prince in your own eyes, you'll never see that you are a clown in God's eyes. You'll be closed to the gospel, closed to the truth of God's word, and closed to the spiritual wisdom God wants to give you. And you'll be doing evil when you think it is good.

Princes of worldly wisdom "are crafty in the ways of the world. They know how to maneuver and manipulate to secure their selfish advantage. They do not hesitate to destroy others in order to advance themselves." They are dangerous to a church! When they "bring their know-how to the affairs of the kingdom of God, they cause grave calamities."[76]

The problem with pride doesn't stop there, though. A prince of worldly wisdom will not repent, apologize, or resign. He believes he has done no wrong. He is wise in his own eyes. Therefore, he is a dangerous person. In fact, Barclay writes, "Intellectual pride will . . . always seek to justify itself. It will not learn. It always lays down the law. It honestly believes that whoever disagrees with it is wrong. It tends to cut men off from each other rather than unite them."[77] Therefore, Paul says that stuff has no place in the church! Instead of seeing yourself as wise, you need to see yourself as a fool.

Now, we might take offense at that. What does he mean to become a fool? Paul means you need to be humble enough to repent, admit you don't know everything, learn, and listen to others. Only then can you begin to walk a path towards true wisdom.

Are you of Christ? Sure we are, Paul! Then stop focusing on just a few things and enjoy all Christ has given you (vv. 21-23).

The deception of perception not only causes us to see things that aren't there, it can also cause us to miss all that *is* there. We can actually focus on one thing and miss out on everything!

The Corinthians were focusing on Apollos or Paul or Cephas. But when they focused on one, they missed out on the fullness of what

God was doing. Apollos, Cephas, and Paul were all gifts of God to the church, servants who were called at a time for a purpose. By focusing on just one of them, the factions in the church were missing out on the whole. Paul says, "You are cheating yourself by limiting yourself to only one of God's servants. All are yours! More than that, the world or life or death or the present or the future – those all are yours too!" There are some major implications of this shift of thought.

First, *all are yours*! They were saying, "I am of Apollos" or "I belong to Paul." But Paul says, "You don't belong to me or Apollos or Cephas. If anything, *we* belong to *you*! Why are you limiting yourself? Why are you subjecting yourself to one of us when you are supposed to enjoy all of us?"

We do not need to subject ourselves to one person or one part of the gospel or one season or one moment or even one life, whether present or eternal. We are to enjoy it all because all of it is ours in Christ. When you claim one faction or one servant as leader, you are enslaving yourself. Vaughan and Lea write:

> The man who gives his life, his strength, his energy, his heart to some little splinter of a party has surrendered everything to a petty thing, when he could have entered into possession of a fellowship and a love which is as wide as the universe. He has confined into narrow limits a life which should be limitless in its outlook.[78]

Paul seems to say, "If you'd just back up, you'd see that you are all heading in the same direction. You all live; you all will die. You all have a present; you all have a future. Don't be so divisive. Stop focusing on one thing while missing everything. All are yours!"

Second, *you are of Christ*. If all belongs to us as gifts, then there has to be someone who has given those gifts, right? There must be someone who is above us. There is. That person is Christ. You can only make sense of things when you are submitted to Christ. When Christians lose the concept of the lordship of Christ, they essentially lose their freedom. We gain ultimate freedom only in submission to Christ. For when there is submission, there is union. We move with Christ, gain the mind of Christ, can see things through the eyes of Christ, and act according to Christ.

Christ becomes our example as Paul says, "Christ is of God." God is one. There is so much unity among the Trinity that to see the Son is to see the Father. That is how unified we should be. One purpose. One direction. One calling.

If you are of Christ, stop focusing on just a few things and enjoy all Christ has given you. Don't miss all that God has given.

Paul points out the deception of perception that was wrecking the Corinthians' spiritual lives and threatening to destroy their church. There is still another deception of perception that lurks in the church, and it may be the greatest of all. The greatest illusion for many people is their salvation. Some people think they are saved when they really aren't. Their minds are tricked. Their eyes are deceived. For years they have thought if they are a part of the church, they are saved. Or if they do good things, they are saved. Or if they aren't like that "bad" person they know, they are saved. But the Bible says that it is by grace we have been saved, not of ourselves, not of works (Ephesians 2:5). The message is – don't be deceived. Good people don't get into heaven. Only perfect people get into heaven, and our very best is like filthy rags when compared to the perfection of God (Isaiah 64:6). The only way we can be perfect is if we are declared perfect by God himself. We are declared perfect when we repent of our sins and trust Jesus Christ as our Lord and Savior.

You can chance it and bring your rags to God, or you can ask, "God, help me to turn things upside down and see my rags as they are in your sight." You can turn things upside down by coming to God in humility saying, "God, I know I am not perfect. I know I sin, and I know I need something to take away my sin. I now realize that nothing I do is good enough. Therefore, God, I need you to help me."

If you have never given your life to Jesus Christ, please stop reading now and do that. Repent of your sins and allow Jesus to become the Lord and Savior of your life.

CHAPTER 13
A Proper View of the Pastor
1 Corinthians 4:1-21

Some years ago, some friends in a former church gave me a copy of *God's Front Porch* by Gerald Eugene Nathan Stone. The narrator of the story is a deacon in a little church called Blacksburg Baptist Church. The story opens with a chapter called "Preacherless Again." The deacon writes:

> Most preachers leave a church because the Lord has called them elsewhere. I understand that in the business world the expression they use is "tender their resignation," but that may be just a face-saving way of not getting fired, so you can get hired somewhere else. At Blacksburg Baptist Church, we cut through that mustard. We didn't ask for a resignation, we didn't have a going-away pounding, and we didn't hug everybody when we got rid of a preacher – we fired him. Like Millard Doss said, "Pray that your firing may not be in wintertime nor on the Sabbath, but pray that you've got some friends or family to take you in." That may be in the Bible.[79]

The story continues from there with the search for a new preacher, finding a new preacher, and the deacon connecting with the rookie preacher in a special way as he learns the ropes of the challenging Blacksburg Baptist Church.

When I first read this book, I laughed out loud on many pages. The story is funny because I've experienced or heard stories just like it – including the churches being known for firing their preachers.

Churches sometimes struggle with a proper view of their pastor. There are those that celebrate former pastors to the demise of current pastors while others celebrate the current pastor like a super saint. Still others wear out their pastor through overwork. Many churches change pastors like the members change clothes. Thankfully, there are also strong churches that have a proper view of their pastor.

The Corinthian's problem was not a lack of regard for their pastors; it was misplaced regard for their pastors. Their regard was misplaced in two ways: they regarded one minister over another, and they regarded the wrong things about their ministers. In Chapter 4, Paul helps the church learn proper regard for pastors.

Pastors should be regarded as servants of Christ (v. 1a).

Some Corinthians viewed their pastors as their servants who are meant to inspire them or entertain them. In response, Paul says pastors should be regarded as servants of Christ. No matter how gifted a pastor is and no matter the size of his ministry, every pastor should be a servant of Christ and should be regarded as such by his congregation.

Over the last several years, our church has had the opportunity to host some "big name" preachers of our denomination for various conferences. These men have more members in their churches than there are residents of our city. To hear these guys talk about all their church's ministries makes my head spin!

I have noticed, however, that these men are servants of Christ. They have a heart for pastors and churches and get just as excited about something new in their church as any pastor. They have a heart to reach people and get just as frustrated when they preach and no one responds and just as excited when someone does respond as any pastor. It is obvious they love their church and their staff and that their church and staff love them. They are servants of Christ.

Do you know what else I have observed? My friends who pastor small churches in places no one has ever heard of are servants of Christ as well. These churches run less people than most Sunday School classes at the mega churches, but these small church pastors are just as faithful as any of the big names. These smaller church pastors have a heart for people, and many have big vision. Some of them are juggling pastoring with going to school, being a husband and father, and working a second job. They do it all through a servant's heart.

The Corinthians would have celebrated the pastors with big ministries and dismissed the pastors of the other churches because of their smaller ministries, but Paul says, "Both are to be regarded as servants." The Corinthians were in awe of the big shots, but God is not impressed by the big shots. He looks at the servant heart. Paul Powell writes, "Nowhere in the Bible does the Lord ever speak of 'Moses, my leader' or 'Joshua, my leader.' It is always, 'Moses, my servant' and 'Joshua, my servant.'"[80]

When Jesus finished washing His disciples' feet at the Last Supper, He asked them, "Do you realize what happened here tonight?" They, of course, hadn't a clue because they were still the "duh-ciples." Therefore, Jesus said, "You call me Master and Lord: and rightly so, for I am. If I then, your Lord and Master, have washed your feet; you also ought to wash one another's feet. For I have given you an example that you should do as I have done to you" (John 13:13-15). Powell points out that "this is the only place in the Bible where Jesus said, 'I have given you an example.'"[81]

Pastors should follow Christ's example. We must be servants of Christ so that we might be regarded as servants. "Leaders who follow [Christ's] example will have followers who trust and serve because they see Christ in their pastor."[82] That is a scary calling, but it is the pastor's calling. Pastors are to be regarded as servants of Christ.

Pastors should be regarded as stewards of the things of God (vv. 1b-2).

What is a steward? We probably think of a steward or stewardess on an airplane. While the idea was slightly different in Paul's day, our modern idea is still helpful.

There are basically three types of people on an airplane: pilot, steward, and passenger. If we take this as a spiritual analogy, God is the pilot. He is also the owner of the plane! Let the plane represent God's plan for His people. God is taking His people somewhere. The passengers on the plane represent the church. The pastor is the steward. The steward is responsible for the passengers during flight. He is responsible for the passengers care and well-being and for helping them get where they are going. Ultimately, a steward has responsibility to care for that which belongs to another. He cares for the passengers who belong to numerous families. He cares for the airplane which belongs to the airline. Therefore, the steward must be completely trustworthy.

Paul emphasizes trustworthy stewardship in v. 2. Whereas the Corinthians would put emphasis on things like looks, education, and spell-binding speech when it came to their pastors, Paul says the emphasis should be on their being trustworthy of the responsibility of a steward. The pastor has been entrusted with the gospel and sharing it with the people of God. He must be completely trustworthy.

Do you know the top four things that ruin pastors? Power, money, women, and laziness. Notice how being trustworthy and responsible can help a pastor avoid all four of those pitfalls! Notice also, though, how neglecting trust and responsibility can lead the pastor right into them! That's why the number one qualification of a steward is that he be trustworthy.

Since pastors are entrusted by God, they are accountable to God (vv. 3-5).

With high responsibility comes high accountability. To whom is the steward accountable? The Corinthians would say, "Us!" But is the steward of the airplane accountable to the passengers? No. Who holds the pastor accountable then? Paul identifies three courts of judgment that pastors could be subject to: human courts, the pastor's own court, God's court.

Human courts. The Corinthians were setting themselves up as the judges of the pastors, saying the pastors were accountable to them. Paul says, "I care little if I am judged by you or by any human court." That is how it should be. Of course, every pastor knows that human courts can be tough! Unfortunately, we also remember the bad courts more than the good ones! Further, if we're honest, most of us want the approval of men. But Paul says, "I'm not concerned about them."

His Own Court. Paul says, "I do not even judge myself." Frankly, some of us are harder on ourselves than others are on us. We can beat ourselves up. Sometimes when I've ended a message and saw no response, I've thought, "What did I do wrong?" At other times, I've watched people get their feelings hurt in the church, but when I tried to do something about it, it was too little too late. I've racked my brain about what I could have done different, sooner, or better. Every subtraction from the church membership hurts me personally. But Paul could honestly say, "I don't even judge myself."

When Paul speaks of these two courts, he isn't prohibiting evaluation. He's not saying pastors shouldn't be held accountable. Accountabilty is a good thing. Neither is he saying that a pastor shouldn't do self-evaluation. Keeping yourself in check is a good thing. But Paul *is* warning against making a decisive "judgment that will justify or condemn a person on account of his works."[83] The reason for this warning is any present judgment will be partial, premature, and incompetent (v. 5). That's rather funny to me! Why are our judgments partial, premature, and incompetent? Because only God can see everything we do and the motive behind what we do! Therefore, Paul says, "I don't worry about the human courts or my own court, I only worry about God's court." (But I wouldn't recommend responding to that complaining church member, "Well, your criticisms are just partial, premature, and incompetent!")

God's court. Now, don't think the court of God is easy. In fact, as hard as the human courts are or as hard as your own court is, being accountable to God is much harder. You and I might miss something that needs correcting, but God will not. God knows everything! There is a blessing to the court of God that doesn't come in the court of humans or our own court – you and I might miss something to praise, but God will not! God can find grounds for reward when skeptical human beings might find none.[84] If the Master is pleased, that's all that matters. The pastor's constant question must not be, "Are *they* pleased?" or "Am *I* pleased?" It must be, "Is *God* pleased?" If He is, carry on!

There is only room in grace for humble gratitude of pastors (vv. 6-13).

The Corinthians' church traditions and expectations of their spiritual leaders had come to be as important, maybe even more important, than the Bible and its expectations of spiritual leaders. Paul says, "I have applied these things to us so you may benefit by not exceeding what is written." If the Corinthians can keep the main thing the main thing, then they will be able to have a proper view of their pastors.

Besides, Paul says, where does any difference in giftedness or anything we have received come from? God! What we have and what we can do have nothing to do with us or our abilities. They have everything to do with God's grace in our lives. Don't lift up one preacher because he has some particular gifts and downgrade another preacher because he doesn't have those gifts. Instead, celebrate the grace of God in each preacher's life and the varying gifts God has given. There is no room in grace for conceit. There is no room in grace for preferential treatment. There is only room in grace for humble gratitude. That is the attitude any church should have for its pastor.

The Corinthians thought they had achieved everything God could give them. They were wrong. The fancy word for their problem is "over-realized eschatology." The simple word is "jumping the gun." The Corinthians thought they had everything now that believers will actually get later. The apostles were the exact opposite. While the Corinthians thought themselves super spiritual, Paul says the preachers are just fools for Christ!

Paul is strong in verses 8-13. But his "strong words were inspired by an indignation that saw the state of spiritual life in Corinth as a mortal danger in the life and future of the church."[85] Paul realized if this wrong view of the pastors was not corrected, the church could be ripped apart and the members would continue to have such issues for years to come – potentially destroying other churches as well. If they could fix their view, however, the church could be unified and the ministry effective. Isn't that what every church needs?

Thankfully, it's basically what happened at Blacksburg Baptist Church:

> Finally, the day came when Preacher and Sara did what few preachers at Blacksburg Baptist Church have had the opportunity to do: They resigned withour benefit of a proper firing. They asked the congregation to bless them as they answered the Lord's call to

> the foreign mission field. It was a surprise to everyone but me, but it still warn't easy to hear.[86]

I'll not share the rest of the story in case you want to pick up Mr. Stone's book. But let me ask you, "How do you view your pastor?" Are you showing him appreciation? Or are you listing out condemnations? Are you holding him too high? Or are you holding him too low?

CHAPTER 14
Father Pastor
1 Corinthians 4:14-21

I am intrigued by job titles. An internet search revealed the following real job titles:

- Five a Day Collection Operative – Fruit picker
- Media Distribution Officer – Paper boy
- Highway Environmental Hygienist – Road sweeper
- Transparency Enhancement Facilitator – Window cleaner
- Public Waste Technician – Toilet cleaner

There are interesting titles in the church as well. In high school, I went to an Episcopal Church for the first time. The pastor was a "Most Right Reverend Doctor." I thought, "Man, that'll make you stand up and straighten your collar." Not long after that I was in a Catholic church. Their pastor was a "Monsignor." What a cool title! If I were Catholic, I would rather be Monsignor than Pope!

We Baptists tend to stick to "pastor" or "preacher." Every now and then you'll hear "Brother Pastor" or "Doctor Pastor," but that's about it. Of course, one teenager did call me "Mister Brother Reverend Doctor" for a spell. There is the rare occasion in Baptist circles, however, when members borrow titles from elsewhere to give us – sometimes joking, sometimes serious – or maybe a little of both.

A year or so after I was called to pastor in Forestburg, Texas, I was invited to ride with one of our members to his daughter's surgery in Dallas. David said he wanted to ask me about some things. We left early the morning of the surgery, had breakfast at a place near the hospital, and then headed over for the surgery. David talked almost the entire hour of our drive to Dallas, all during the breakfast, and all the way home. Jokingly, he said, "I guess I needed to have some confession time. I'll have to call you 'Father Stewart' from now on." He did and still does. Here in Pineville, an elder member picked up the same title for me. In response, I began calling him "Rabbi".

In this passage of Corinthians, we find the idea of fatherhood connected with the role of a pastor. The Catholic Church uses this passage to justify the title "Father" for their priests. However, there is nothing in this passage to suggest that Paul is advocating a title for pastors. Catholicism has attempted to justify a title that started being used several centuries after Paul with a biblical text written by Paul. That's going in the wrong direction. You don't justify what you do with the Bible. You learn what to do from the Bible. While Paul does not advocate a title for pastors, he does exemplify a model for pastors and their ministry.

Paul knows his words have been hard, so in v. 14 he makes sure the Corinthians hear his heart. He is clear that his words come from the heart of a father.

> ***1 Corinthians 4:14*** *[14] I am not writing this to shame you, but to warn you, as my dear children.*

When a child is heading into danger, a parent might yell, "Stop!" When that child comes to his parents, the parent might scold, "What do you think you're doing?" The words are strong, even harsh, but they are not meant to shame the child; they are meant to warn the child. This is the goal of Paul's words. The original word translated "warn" means something like "admonish." Paul is trying to correct the people while not provoking them or embittering them. Some have translated v. 14 to read, "I do not write this to make you blush with shame but to give you counsel as my dear children."[87]

This is a spiritual father's heart being poured out for his spiritual children. Paul calls them his children because he didn't have followers or disciples. But he did have spiritual children. Since he had brought them into the family of God, he was their father in the faith. Just as a minister might have an elder pastor who mentored and encouraged him as he was getting started and calls that man his "Father in

Ministry", so the Corinthians could look to Paul as their father in the faith because he had helped them meet Christ and be reborn into the faith. Though they have 10,000 guardians in Christ, they need a father.

The use of "guardian" in v. 15 is in reference to the many other teachers that could come to the Corinthians. They are most certainly available and do a good job. Paul's point, however, is that while guardians are great, every child with a guardian wishes for a father. Paul says, "I am your father through the gospel." Because the Corinthians are Paul's children, he feels a personal responsibility for them and pours out his heart to them.

Paul's relationship with Corinth demonstrates why "Father Pastor" is a good model for pastoral leadership. Over the course of ministry in a church, a pastor has the opportunity to see dozens if not hundreds of people come to faith in Christ under his ministry. He welcomes new converts. He embraces new individuals and families to the church. All of these people should "grow up" in the faith under the pastor's ministry. Just as a father must meet the physical needs of his children by nourishing, instructing, challenging, correcting, and listening to them as they mature, so the pastor must meet the spiritual needs of those entrusted to his care in the same ways. Paul does not see his role as spiritual father as a position of higher authority or higher status. Rather, he sees his role as one of higher responsibility.

Therefore, assuming this role of spiritual father to the Corinthians, Paul gives them a challenge and a reminder. In Paul's instruction, we find some principles for how a Father Pastor should lead.

First, Paul challenges the people to follow his example (vv. 16-17).

A Father Pastor should lead by example. Paul encourages the people, "Imitate me." His implication is "imitate me as I imitate Christ." He is not interested in recruiting personal followers, but Paul does want to set the Corinthians an example so they too can follow Christ. When Paul says, "Imitate me", he does not convey any sense of spiritual arrogance. He is simply conveying a confidence in his obedience to Christ. Paul walks so closely to Christ that he feels if the Corinthians will do what he does, they will be doing great.

Pastors should lead by example. That is a scary challenge, but isn't it a bit scary to be a parent? Children naturally imitate their parents – the good and the bad! They are sponges watching our every move and doing what we do, saying what we say, and acting like we act. Sometimes we learn about ourselves by watching our children. Have you ever seen your child do something or heard them say something and think, "Where did he get that?" You decide it must have come from someone at school. Then a few minutes later, you catch yourself saying the same thing! Just as children naturally imitate their parents so members of a church will naturally imitate their pastor in time. They don't even have to be told to do so. They just do.

That's scary, but numerous pastoral ministry books tell us that is true. They tell us simple truths like the following:

A church will take on the personality of its pastor. Just as you see things about yourself mirrored back at you in your children, in time, a pastor sees things about himself mirrored back by his congregation. The way a pastor greets people, ministers to people, worships, leads, or handles conflict will be mirrored by his people. His passions will become their passions. I don't understand how that happens, but it does. Therefore, a pastor must be careful!

A church will never move beyond the vision of its pastor. Pastors cast the vision and lead towards the vision. He has to see the vision before anyone else. When faced with a "We can't" challenge, the pastor must be the one who can say, "No, maybe we can't, but God can!" If the pastor says, "We can't," the church never will. If he can lead the church to understand that God can, they will with God's help.

A church will never rise above the spiritual level of its pastor. This one is especially scary. There will be some in the church who grow farther than the pastor, but most people will never grow beyond the spiritual level of the pastor. If the pastor models prayer, the people will pray. If the pastor models giving, the people will give. If the pastor has a quiet time, the people will have a quiet time. If he shares the gospel, they will share the gospel. On and on it goes.

Have you ever heard a dad say, "Don't do what I do. Do what I say"? It doesn't work, does it? It definitely doesn't work for a pastor. Just as our kids will do what we do, a congregation will do what its pastor does. What we do speaks louder than what we say. Pastors must lead by example. (No pressure, Rev!)

After challenging the Corinthians to imitate him, Paul reminds the people that he will hold them accountable (vv. 18-21).

A Father Pastor should hold his people accountable. Did your mom ever tell you, "Wait until your Daddy gets home"? If she did, you knew that meant accountability was coming, didn't you? There were those things you did that Momma took care of, but there were certain things you did that Daddy handled.

Paul says, "Daddy is coming home." Well, not exactly, but he does tell them, "Don't be so arrogant as to think I'm not coming to visit you." It's like saying, "Some of you are acting like I'm not coming home." Perhaps you've known teens who were trusted to stay at home while the parents went out. Sometimes those teens act as if their parents aren't coming home. When it suddenly dawns on them that their parents are coming, there is a mad scramble to clean up and get ready for the parents' return. A day of accountability is at hand!

All those people who think they have it all together will be held accountable. The language is that of the courtroom. The word we translate "find out" is the language of a judge who makes an examination.[88] Paul is saying, "I'll find out whether these men are just big talk or whether they really have God's power."[89] It will be evident. Truth is evident.

Paul ends his instruction as a Father Pastor saying, "Kids, I can bring home a spanking or a hug. It's your choice." The question is not whether he will come, but how he will come. He will hold them accountable.

I like what one commentator says, "When the father has been absent from his family for some time, he wants to come home *with love in a spirit of gentleness* (21), not *with a rod*."[90] Isn't that true? Dads really don't like to come home to the "wait until your Daddy gets home" situation. It is a total beat down to walk in the door and for a wife to say, "You've got to deal with *your* son. He has . . . ." The best days are when dad can come home and everyone is happy!

Just as a dad has to hold his children accountable, so a pastor has to hold his people accountable, as difficult as that may be. It's a bit trickier with a congregation! The pastor can't spank or punish his people (though he might like to sometimes!). The pastor can't take their toys away in punishment or give them toys as rewards. The pastor simply has to hold up the standard and remind his people of it. Holding their people accountable may be the greatest challenge for church leaders. People are flippant about their faith, but they need to be true in their faith and live out their faith.

An Example of a Father Pastor

One of my pastor heroes is Dr. Waylon Bailey, Pastor of First Baptist Church Covington, Louisiana. At this writing, Dr. Bailey has pastored the same church for over thirty years and has led First Covington to experience tremendous growth and impact for the kingdom of God. In a conference several years ago, Dr. Bailey said that, after all these years, any problems his church has are his problems. Dr. Bailey says that since most of First Covington's people have come in and been trained under his pastoral tenure, he takes responsibility for any problems they have in their church. "If we have problems," he said, "I haven't trained them right." That is a Father Pastor speaking from the heart as he looks over his children to see how he's been doing. Not only does Dr. Bailey hold his people accountable and challenge his people to imitate him, he also has the high standard of imitating Christ and being held accountable by Christ himself. Oh that every pastor can live up to such a calling. (Again, no pressure, Rev!)

CHAPTER 15
What to Do When Morality is Low
1 Corinthians 5:1-13

The issue was severe: a man had his father's wife. This lady was probably not his mother but his unbelieving step mother who was probably considerably younger than his father. To further complicate the situation, the father and the step-mom were likely still married though she was living with her step-son. This was a messed up situation!

The tone of Paul's first sentence indicates his shock that this would even be happening. Paul essentially says, "Are you kidding me? Who does this? Not even the pagans do this!" First, the Corinthians should have known better. Such a relationship is forbidden expressly in the Old Testament Law in Leviticus (18:7-8; 20:11). Second, even the pagans wouldn't do such a thing. To make such a statement about the pagans was strong. The pagans worshiped the fertility goddess Aphrodite through priestess prostitutes at her temple in Corinth. But even the pagans who did that did not have this kind of relationship with their step mom! In fact, Roman law prohibited such unions, even after the death of the father.[91] Paul was understandably exasperated. The question is, "What do you do in the church when morality is low?"

Raise the expectations of the church (vv. 1-2).

Paul was shocked that this would be happening, but the church accepted the sin. Some members were even proud of the "inclusiveness" such a situation demonstrated. The Corinthians were calling evil good. The prophet Isaiah (5:20) said, "Woe to those who call evil good and good evil, who put darkness for light and light for darkness, who put bitter for sweet and sweet for bitter." Sin is sin no matter how you package it. Sin is sin no matter how much you celebrate it.

The issue wasn't just that one man sinned, though that was bad enough! The bigger issue was that the church was approving of it, and rationalizing away the sin!

We are good at finding ways to rationalize our sin.

The liar says he had to stretch the truth.
The overeater says she was just hungry.
The alcoholic says he only drinks socially.
The thief says she was in need.
The adulterer says his spouse just didn't understand.
The prideful person says she is just blessed.
The pornography viewer says he is just curious.
The coveter says she deserves more for her work.

However, sin is sin no matter how you package it. If we rationalize away sin, the church becomes ineffective and irrelevant. The church is a hospital where sinners might be healed of their sin. It is not a country club where sinners might celebrate their sin. Grace is cheapened if we rationalize sin. The church at Corinth was "insensitive to the moral outrage in their midst."[92] The sinful world had invaded the church, and the church celebrated it!

Immorality in the church should bring us to shocking disappointment. In my pastoral ministry in two churches, I've dealt with a handful of adulterous relationships, drug and alcohol abuse problems, lying, contentious attitudes, prideful and divisive persons, and more. I stopped being surprised by the sins long ago, but every time I see a failure, my heart breaks. There is shocking disappointment. There should be.

Why should moral failings in the church shock us? Because that is not what we should be! The integrity of the Christian witness to an immoral society is at stake. Consider the implications. How can we call for politicians to be truthful if we are not truthful? How can we teach our children to remain pure until marriage when we can't stay pure within marriage? How can we stand for the truth if we do not tell the truth to one another? How can we tell people how to handle conflict in a biblical way when we have a bad business meeting followed by a church split instead of working through our differences as loving brothers?

Do you see the problem? So, what do you do when morality is low? You raise the expectations! Instead of saying, "Oh well." You say, "Oh no!" You know that's not how it is supposed to be. You are shocked, appalled, even embarrassed by the sin. But it doesn't stop there. When morality is low, you can't just raise the expectations. You also have to deal with the immorality because it shocks you.

Carry out discipline for the good of the member and the church (vv. 3-8).

Paul calls upon the church to deal with the issue. Why is that? Probably two reasons: First, the man himself is unrepentant of his sin. His attitude is, "What's the problem?" He is not listening to counsel, so the church as a whole needs to deal with the issue. But there is a second reason the whole church needs to meet. The whole church is guilty. The man may be unrepentant and engaged in flagrant sin, but the church is sinning by celebrating it. Therefore, they need to come together to repent and deal with the issue.

In v. 4 Paul tells them that they are to meet in a specific way, in the name of Jesus Christ and with His power. This is not to be a lynch mob. Too often, church discipline has been conducted by an angry mob. Discipline is to be done in the name of Christ and in His power. There should be tears instead of anger.

Neither should a pharisaical council carry out church discipline A pharisaical council is a self-righteous group of church members overlooking their own sin while calling down judgment on a member who has sinned (or been accused of sin). Church discipline should be done in the name of Christ and in His power. There should be humility instead of haughtiness.

Paul demonstrates that this discipline is beneficial for both the immoral member and the church. Consider the member first (v. 5). The man is to be excluded from the church and given to the world outside the church. The world within represents Christ's domain, while the world outside represents Satan's domain. Since the man is insistent on living in Satan's domain, the church releases him to that domain.

It's almost like saying, "See how that works out for you!" The hope is that when the man finds no friends on the outside, he will repent and want to be back inside. It is like the prodigal son who the father allowed to leave and have his life fall apart but then was welcomed back with grace as he approached with brokenness and repentance. This is redemptive action not merely a punitive action.[93] The man would benefit from the discipline because he would return.

What about the church? How does the church benefit? In vv. 6-8 Paul brings the Feast of Unleavened Bread and Passover to mind. In preparation for Passover, Jewish families cleaned their home from top to bottom to make sure there was absolutely no leaven in the house. Their diligence in cleaning their home of leaven demonstrated their sincerity in preparation for celebrating Passover. The church needs to purify itself by removing the leaven. If they celebrate the sin of this man, then they will celebrate the sin of the next man. "No church can celebrate the deliverance from sin that Christ makes possible while sheltering sin in its members."[94]

We do not talk about church discipline much in the church today. It is often neglected. Why is that? Findley Edge in an older book called *A Quest for Vitality in Religion* shares four reasons:

1) Sin is so prevalent in the lives of church members that the church does not know where to start.
2) The practice of church discipline would disrupt the life of the church. We fear that people would draw sides, get mad, etc.
3) There has been a revolt against the flagrant abuses of past practices of church discipline. Yes, church discipline has been abused. But an overcorrection is not a correction.
4) Christians have a low view of what it means to be a church.[95] We don't value the purity of the church. Therefore, church members do not hold each other accountable. If members were to hold each other accountable in private relationships, seldom would issues come to the whole church. Unfortunately, few members hold each other accountable. They then look at the church leaders and ask, "What are *you* going to do about this?" The question from church leaders to the congregation

> should be, "Why didn't *you* do something weeks, months, or even years ago before the issue grew into this?"[96]

Even though many churches do not practice church discipline, there are times when church discipline needs to happen. In these cases, what should be done? Jesus gave three clear steps in Matthew 18:15-17:

Step One: One on one.

Most issues can and should be handled right here. For the sake of integrity and grace, you must begin here. The offense you hear about may or may not be true. I have handled many issues at this level. Some turned out to be true allegations. Some turned out to be false. However, they never went any further because they were handled at this step.

When the issue turns out to be true, there is a private conversation about the issue. It is dealt with and settled. I have been criticized before by people saying, "Pastor did nothing about that." Actually, I did. It just wasn't everyone's business.

This is the level where member to member accountability goes to work. When a colleague sees a fellow colleague not being honest at work, she can pull the other aside. When an older man sees a younger man going down a slippery slope, he can warn the younger and call him back.

When we deal with the issue one on one, we can usually deal with things at step one. The key is to go personally, confidentially, and humbly. Then, if the issue is dealt with, leave it there. Going beyond step one when anything more is needed is to stir up dissension or damage reputation. However, if there is no resolution with step one, proceed to step two.

Step Two: Two by two.

If the person refuses to listen to you, take someone else with you. Perhaps you bring a pastor along or a deacon or another Christian friend. Again, go personally, confidentially, and humbly. If step one doesn't work, step two usually will. If the issue is resolved, it goes no further than the three people involved. Again, if the issue is resolved, it stops here. If not, move to step three.

Step Three: Where all agree.

Step Three occurs when there is complete unrepentance and no regard for the truth of God's word and disregard for the loving correction offered by fellow church members. Therefore, the church is brought into the mix. If the person does not listen to the church, then they are expelled just as this man in Corinth is to be expelled. This step will seldom have to happen if steps one and two are followed.

The goal from step one to three is restoration. It is never to kick out the offending person. For an unrepentant member to leave the church is a heartbreaking loss. It is not a victory to celebrate.

Become transformational in your relationships inside and outside the church (vv. 9-13).

Paul did not want the people to think that the church was to have nothing to do with the world. If the church completely pulled out of the world, the church would be neglecting its calling from God! "The problem in Corinth was not that the church was living in the midst of an immoral society." The problem was the immoral society was living in the church![97] We must have interaction with the world, but we must not allow worldliness to be in the church.

The only church that can impact the world is a church that is real in its faith and consistent in its walk. I believe the world eagerly looks for such a church. Sadly, often the world knows more about what we are supposed to be than we do. The world is waiting to see a church that takes sin seriously but enjoys forgiveness fully.[98] When the world sees that kind of church, the members of the world come to the members of the church and ask, "Excuse me, can you tell me how I can have what you have?" When that happens, the church will have the kind of impact on its community that Jesus expects.

CHAPTER 16
Advice for Litigious Christians
1 Corinthians 6:1-8

I grew up wanting to be a lawyer. That all changed my junior year of high school. Some of us interested in being attorneys put together a mock trial team where we learned a case and competed against other schools in mock trials. While our team had a good time together, mock trial helped me decide law was not for me. However, the experience provided me with respect for the mountains of minutiae that goes into good legal work – not to mention the long sentences, words no one knows except lawyers, and their own size of paper on which to print everything.

No matter the number of lawyers in the world, there's apparently plenty of legal work to go around. The National Center for State Courts reveals that we Americans, across all states, file about sixteen million civil lawsuits each year. That works out to about one new lawsuit every two seconds. That's also about one lawsuit for every twelve adults in America.

A lot of those lawsuits are silly – like the teacher in Ohio who sued the school district because she was afraid of children, or the guy who sued Subway because their sandwiches are only eleven inches and not a foot long.

Of course, a lot of lawsuits are serious as well. There are injustices and disputes everywhere which need to be worked out properly. What happens, though, when a dispute arises between two Christians? Is that lawsuit silly or serious? In 1 Corinthians 6:1-8, Paul comes down on the issue saying it is both silly and serious. It is silly because these disputes should never have to make it to court. It is serious because to do so is to be defeated already.

The Church at Corinth had numerous issues. One of the issues was that some of the members were rather litigious. They were getting in disputes and then taking those disputes to the city's court. In addressing this issue, Paul wastes no time setting forth some abiding principles. These principles should guide us today when we are faced with a dispute with a Christian brother or sister.

Principle #1: Settle your dispute as Christian brothers (vv. 1-5).

Paul's use of "dare" in v. 1 expresses his shock over anyone even considering taking another believer to court. His use of the words "has a dispute with" is a technical expression for a lawsuit in the original language so we know Paul indeed has in mind legal proceedings. Paul basically says, "Why would you ever even consider taking a dispute between two brothers to an ungodly court when you could instead take the dispute before the church?"

Let's be clear about what Paul is *not* saying. He is not saying that there should never be disputes within the church. Paul recognizes that such disputes will occur. It is perfectly natural, normal, and expected for people to disagree. Disagreements will occur, and, sometimes, we might need some help reaching a resolution. Paul's point is that if there is a dispute and you need help reaching a resolution, the issue should be settled within the fellowship not in the secular courts.

Without mentioning it specifically, Paul encourages the people to remember the Jewish practice as a pattern. "Jews enjoyed a large measure of autonomy in the ancient world. Disputes that arose within the Jewish communities were settled among themselves. Indeed, the rabbis taught that it was unlawful for a Jew to seek a judge's decision in pagan courts."[99] In fact, it was sometimes even seen as blasphemous against God's law.[100] Paul encourages the church to borrow this practice from the Jews – hold your own court, settle your dispute as brothers.

The Jews were the pattern, but the real reason they should do this is because of the Christian's perspective. Paul reminds the Corinthians that all believers will have opportunity to sit as judges at the end of time. Jesus talked about His twelve apostles sitting as judges in Luke 22:30 and Matthew 19:28. Most likely, though, Paul is remembering the words of the prophet Daniel (7:9-27). Recalling this prophesied scene, Paul says, "Guys, if you will judge heavenly matters, you are certainly competent to judge earthly matters."

We think everything we deal with is a big deal, but it is not. To check your perspective, just have a loved one get sick or be facing death. You figure out rather quickly what matters and what doesn't in your life. You start saying, "No" to things you used to *have* to do. People may still get upset when you don't do something, but you let it go because you've figured out what really matters. That's Paul's point here: Get perspective; remember your destiny! If you will judge such momentous eternal matters, surely you can handle trivial temporal matters! Compared to eternity, every matter we deal with is trivial and temporal.

Paul continues to give reasons for settling the disputes as Christian brothers as he continues in vv. 4-5. Paul's point? Better justice should come from the church. The Corinthians had been bragging about how wise and super spiritual they were, so Paul jabs them, "Are you saying there is no one wise enough to judge between two brothers?" His point is clear: to go outside the church is to admit the church can't handle it. A member of a church is in a sad state when he thinks he will receive more justice from a secular court than a brother. Even more, the church itself is in a sad state when this is the case. Better justice should come from the church. If the church is functioning properly and if the people of God are walking in his ways, disputes should be able to be settled.

Principle #2: Do not flaunt your failures (vv. 6-7).

Instead of following the Jewish plan, the Corinthians were following the Greek's plan. The Greeks were extremely litigious and carried out legal matters for entertainment. Their cases could be drawn out just as cases are today – in fact the expression "goes to law" reflects the lengthy developments of a tangled lawsuit.[101] Further, these cases were held at the city square at a place called the Bema. Therefore, the litigation drew everyone out of the marketplace to see it.

It was natural for the Corinthians, when they had a dispute, to get the matter settled before these enormous gatherings. This was detrimental to the gospel's advance in the region because it was like airing your dirty laundry in public.

Christians are to be loving and forgiving. Taking a brother to court misrepresents the emphasis on love that is at the heart of the Christian message. It confesses to the world that the disputes that shatter our fellowship are greater than our common bond in Christ.[102] When our witness is consistently inconsistent, it may as well be nonexistent.

In teaching the Corinthians to settle their disputes as Christian brothers, Paul does not intend to say that there is no place for the secular courts. Nor is he saying that there is never a time when a Christian might need the secular courts. This passage also has nothing to do with Christians serving in the secular courts. In fact, that is a good thing. We need Christian lawyers and judges. Who else is better able to try and hear cases with true ethics and justice than those people who trust in the Lord from Whom ethics and justice come? Paul is not taking on the legal system. He has one issue in mind: a Christian brother suing a Christian brother. This, he says, is shameful and hurts the church's witness.

Paul's thought was this: if you're going to court against a Christian brother, you've already lost. Isn't it better to be wronged than to destroy your witness and the witness of the church? To answer, "No!", is to reveal arrogance and a complete disregard for the gospel. To answer, "Yes!", is to understand Paul's point. Admittedly, it is hard to say, "Yes." When we are self-absorbed and worried about what we deserve, we completely forget the gospel. To that, Paul says, "Shame on you." We need to get to yes.

Principle #3: Do not defraud one another (v. 8).

As with so many legal matters, the Corinthians were taking each other to the cleaners. This should not be in the church!

Don't betray who you are in Christ by acting like an unconverted pagan. When you settle a dispute in the church, seek no more than you deserve and do so without cheating the other person. Do not defraud one another. Simply settle the matter and move on.

Application for Today

How do we apply this in our day? First, since we live in a litigious society, we need to pray for a Christian spirit among believers. If we wrong one another, we need to settle it as brothers in the church instead of as enemies in the court. Second, Christian lawyers within the church might consider serving as mediators for disputes among members of the church. Third, we should pray for Christian attorneys. These men and women face challenges every day. They deal with arguments all day every day. They need our prayers, encouragement, and support. While lawyer jokes may be fun, these men and women need our prayers more than they need our jokes. Finally, as far as it depends on you, practice these truths. Don't allow an issue that involved you and another Christian brother or sister to get to the point where you have to go to court. Work for forgiveness. Seek right. Love one another. If you can so freely accept Christ's forgiveness of your sins, you certainly should be able to give forgiveness when your brother sins.

CHAPTER 17
The Root of the Problem
1 Corinthians 6:9-20

Sexuality is a subject we need to discuss in a proper way in the church because it is discussed in an improper way outside of the church. Since God created human sexuality, the church should be the authority on this subject, not secular society.

Sexual immorality is growing in our culture. For one, premarital sex is all too common. I ask every couple with whom I do premarital counseling to make a purity covenant. They all make the covenant even though some have not been sexually pure before that moment. I've discovered that some of them have never been taught what a greater blessing it would have been to wait until marriage. Some of them have told me that, had they understood the importance of purity, they would have committed to purity earlier.

Extramarital sex is more common than we want to admit. I received a text from a pastor friend asking me to pray for him. One of his church members had called him weeping and confessing that he had sex with a woman that was not his wife. He asked my friend to go with him to share this news with his wife. It was shocking and devastating, but, thankfully, the couple made it through. That does not always happen.

Pornography is rampant. It is too easy to see and to become addicted. A website called Covenant Eyes reports that after an analysis of 400 million web searches, researchers concluded that one in eight of all searches online are for erotic content. More than seven out of ten teens hide their online behavior from their parents in some way. More than half of boys and nearly a third of girls see their first pornographic images before they turn thirteen.

Homosexuality is gaining a foothold. Currently, national surveys indicate that somewhere between 3-5% of Americans claim to be lesbian, gay, or bisexual. Though that is a relatively small percentage, the way the gay agenda pushes the issue, you would think a far greater percentage of Americans fall into these categories. As they push the normalcy of their sin, more people will fall into the sin.

A disturbing problem with sexual immorality is that it is present among church members. The world is going to act like the world. Sexual immorality is expected in the world. But sexual immorality should not be expected among us in the church. 1 Corinthians 6:9-20 is "the most important passage in Paul's letters on the subject of sexual immorality."[103] Here Paul points out the inconsistencies and immoralities among the people who claimed to follow Christ.

When we look at all the sexual immorality that is happening, even within the church, we need to ask a question, "What is the root of the trouble?" Paul helps us understand that the root of the trouble is ignorance.

Ignorance? Yes, we may know more about sex today than ever, but we're not talking about ignorance of sexuality. It is ignorance of who we are in Christ. What does that have to do with sexuality? A lot!

If you are in Christ, are you unrighteous or righteous? (vv. 9-11)

Paul gives a clear description of unrighteousness by including numerous forms of it. He paints a picture of what people without Christ might be like. Notice the ten descriptors of the wicked or unrighteous in these verses. By listing these sins, Paul is not saying that anyone who has ever committed such sins will not be allowed into heaven. He is saying that those who continually live in sin will not inherit heaven. That is why the terms are descriptors of the person – "idolaters, adulterers . . . the greedy, drunkards." These people are living an unrepentant lifestyle of sin and unrighteousness. You can't live as a member of the world's kingdom and expect to enter into God's kingdom.

Sometimes people convince themselves that God will not hold them responsible for their sins. They think they can live however they want, and God, because He is loving, will forgive them no matter what.

God is loving, but He is also just. Therefore, He will not allow sin to go unpunished. Further, God doesn't forgive sins "just because." He forgives sins because we repent of them. Repentance is not just saying, "Oops, I'm sorry for getting drunk, Lord," and then going out and doing it again next weekend. Repentance is falling on your face before God when you sin, confessing that sin, and then getting up and never going back to it – not because you just don't want to do it again but because you want to walk with Jesus, and He doesn't walk in that sin.

The wicked and the unrighteous will not inherit the kingdom of God because they have chosen not to do so. They have chosen the world's kingdom over God's kingdom. They are damned by their own choice. That is not how it should be for those who know Christ! Instead of being described with ten different sins, they are described by three powerful words of transformation. Paul says believers have been washed, sanctified, and justified.

Big change takes place when you follow Jesus! You leave sexual immorality and turn to Christ because you are no longer counted among the unrighteous where those sins are expected. You are among the righteous where those sins are not expected. You no longer want to engage in that stuff because you know the power of Jesus.

If we really grasp the joy of Jesus Christ and the power of His Spirit living within us, the things of the world will have little interest. The endorphin high from a look at pornography will not be as good as Jesus. The buzz from drinking will not be as good as walking in the power of the Spirit. The pride from buying something newer and bigger will not be as powerful as seeing the power of Christ working in our life.

You may wonder, "How can Jesus be better?" Good question! If you've never experienced the answer, that is an indicator that you are operating in a surface faith and you know little of what it means to walk with God. That's why your relationship with God is not substantial. You know the church words and you do the church thing sometimes, but the rest of your life isn't much different from a non-Christian. But it should be. If it's not, there is a big question mark over your walk with Christ. Therefore, you need to turn to Jesus Christ in repentance and faith today.

If you are in Christ, does your body belong to you or to the Lord? (vv. 12-17)

The Corinthians had religious slogans they threw around. One of those was "all things are lawful for me." Because of the freedom that Christ brings, dietary restrictions were lifted. If someone wanted to go eat a bacon sandwich, they could go right ahead! However, the Corinthians were using this statement to justify their overindulgence in things. It'd be like sitting down to eat a whole pound of fried bacon, and saying, "All things are permissible to me!" So Paul adds, "But not everything is beneficial." Yes, you're right, you *can* but *should* you?

The second slogan was "food is for the stomach and the stomach for food." The Corinthians used this to say that the appetite needed to be fed. If you are hungry, eat. Add this slogan to the other slogan and you have permission to get one of those motorized wheelchairs and scoot along the buffet at Golden Corral all day every day.

The Corinthians took these ideas and applied them to other areas of life, especially their sexuality. Satisfying sexual hunger was no more wrong than satisfying physical hunger. "Just feed the need," they would say. The Corinthians saw their spiritual self as separate from their physical self. They figured since the physical body would die anyway, they might as well do whatever they wanted with it. If its appetites wanted something – eat, drink, and be merry for tomorrow we die! While that is a convenient way to look at life and allow yourself to delve into any sin imaginable, it is not what the Bible teaches. When we answer Christ's call, we don't just get transformed on the inside. We get transformed from the inside out.

Paul challenges the slogan about the appetite saying, "But I will not be mastered by anything." When we do whatever our appetites call for, we are mastered by those appetites.

"I want a Dairy Queen blizzard."

"Well, o.k., body."

"And, while you're at it, get a large one and a double cheeseburger to go with it."

"Ok, body."

Before you know it, you weigh 300 pounds and have become a slave to your body.

"Look at that girl. Check her out. Lust after her."

"Ok, body."

Before you know it, it's no longer enough to look and lust, you have to have, to touch. Soon, you're a slave to your sex drive.

It doesn't matter what it is – sex, things, money, popularity – you can get trapped and enslaved by any of them. If you are a follower of Christ, however, you're not supposed to be a slave to anything but Christ! He has set you free to serve Him and His service is a blessing instead of a curse. Why would you want to allow yourself to be trapped? You have the power of the Holy Spirit living within you. Therefore, tell your body, "You don't need a large Blizzard from the DQ. You can have a mini one next week because you already had ice cream this week." Tell your body, "The Holy Spirit is going to train my eyes away from lust."

After dismissing the Corinthians' slogans, Paul affirms the importance of the body. If you are in Christ, does your body belong to you or to Christ? Of course the answer is Christ. That is because when you choose to follow Christ, you give over everything to Him. He comes to live inside you.

Therefore, whatever *you* do, you cause *Him* to do. Paul says, "Would I take my body, in which Christ dwells, and go to bed with a prostitute?" For many in Corinth, sex with a prostitute was just a fact of life – in fact, it was a religious act! Pagans worshiped the sexual goddess Aphrodite by having sex with the prostitutes at her temple. Sexual immorality was par for the course. Paul's answer is the strongest way to say, "No!" that the Greek language offers. Never! Not a chance! Why? Because of what happens in sex. When two people have sexual intercourse, they become one. God created Eve to complement Adam. The two were made different so that when they came together they became one. Paul even quotes Genesis 2:24, "The two will become one flesh." I take couples in premarital counseling to Genesis 2. God's order for sexuality is clearly given in Genesis 2:23-24:

Step One: Receive the mate God has for you.
Step Two: Leave your parents.
Step Three: Cleave. Be united to your spouse in marriage.
Step Four: Become one flesh through sexual intimacy.

When you mess up the order or jump to 4 without 1, 2, or 3, you unite yourself in spirit with someone with whom you aren't supposed to be united. You will have unholy connections with that person forever; you may have comparison issues in marriage; and you may have other thoughts wandering around in the attic of your mind. But, even more than that, when you unite yourself with someone, you also unite Christ with them. When we engage in sexual immorality, we involve Christ in the act. That is a repulsive thought! Paul asks, "Would I do that?" No way!

Most of us would say, "Well, I'll never be with a prostitute." Well, good. But what about other kinds of sexual immorality? We need to have a repulsive thought about those too. For example, if we showed pornography on the screens in our church sanctuary during worship, every person in the worship center would freak out, anyone involved would get fired, and the church would probably get crushed in the news media. But what's the difference in the church building and your home? Even more – what is the difference in this temple of God and your body as temple of God? Nothing. The same follows for other forms of sexual immorality.

What does Paul tell us to do when it comes to sexual immorality? Run! When the temptation arises, run. Don't stay around. If you stay around, you are likely going to fail morally. Sexual temptation is powerful, so don't mess with it. If you are married and you find yourself thinking a bit too much about a member of the opposite sex, run. How do you run? Distance yourself from that person and spend more time with your own spouse kindling the fire at home. If that pornographic image comes up, run. How do you run? Turn off the computer or your phone, and the next time you get on download a filter! If those homosexual tendencies arise, run. How do you run? Recognize the sin, confess it, and turn from it. You may need to get a biblical counselor to help you through the issues. If things are getting too heated between you and your girlfriend, run. How do you run? Don't put yourself in situations where things can get too heated. Girls, dress modestly. Guys, think, "Would I do this if her dad was in the room?" Never underestimate the power of sexual temptation or overestimate your ability to refuse.[104] Run. Don't even pray about it. Just run!

Why should we flee from sexual immorality? (vv. 18-20)

There are two reasons we must flee from sexual immorality which basically restate what we have already seen.

First, sexual immorality is not consistent with what we are (vv. 18-19a). If you know Christ, you are righteous; therefore, don't live like you are unrighteous. Flee from sexual immorality. The Holy Spirit is in you. Don't bring the Holy Spirit into that sexual immorality.

Second, sexual immorality is not consistent with Whose we are (vv. 19b-20). Our body is the temple of the Lord. When you delve into sexual immorality, you desecrate that temple. If someone came and spray-painted graffiti all over your church sanctuary, every person in the church would think that horrid. If we delve into sexual immorality, we do the same thing to our bodies, and it is just as horrid. Do you know what else it does? It ignores the cost of our redemption.[105] If you have received Christ's gift of salvation, that gift may be free for you, but it wasn't free for Him. You have been bought at a high price. Jesus Christ laid down his life for you. Therefore, Paul says, honor God with your body. The body is the medium through which the Christian may glorify God. How can you glorify God with the same body that you are desecrating daily?

How should we respond to this passage?

1) If you have a child or teenager, you should be praying protection over them. I encourage you to do that out loud with them so they can hear it.
2) If you are dating, make a covenant with your boyfriend or girlfriend to be pure.
3) If you are a grandparent, pray for your family. No one knows the challenges of life more than someone who has lived life.
4) If you are right now involved in sexual immorality, you must repent. Stop excusing the sin. Stop decorating the sin. Stop explaining the sin. Pour your heart out to God, confess the sin, and turn from it.

CHAPTER 18
The Need for Intimacy in Marriage
1 Corinthians 7:1-7

With the seventh chapter of 1 Corinthians, we begin a section of the letter where Paul addresses certain questions the church had sent to him. One of the topics they had asked about was intimacy in marriage.

When I go through premarital counseling with couples, during one of the sessions, we talk about sexual intimacy. During one counseling session many years ago, I told a young couple that their sexual relationship could get better the longer they were married. The bride burst out, "Thank goodness! I always thought people stopped doing it after a while!"

That brings me to the story from a couple in their eighties. After a message on marital intimacy, this couple came to me. The husband said, "My old friends tell me that the sexual part of their life ended years ago. Ours has not. I notice that they're now all dead. I want to live." His wife chimed in with a big smile, "And I want to help him!" He quickly added, "Do you know why I think it's still a part of our life? It's because we did it like God said. She's the only woman I've ever been with. In fact, she's the only woman I've ever kissed. Married lovemaking is more fulfilling than sex of any kind." That's a powerful lesson from a lot of life together through over sixty years of marriage!

Don't listen to the lies of the world. Your sexual relationship can get better the longer you are married. Paul's instruction to the Corinthians helps us see why that needs to be the case and how it can happen.

My study for this chapter was both eye-opening and heartbreaking. I was reminded of the numerous issues that can impact the marriage bed including previous sexual relationships, incest, rape, impotency, physical ailments, hormonal imbalances, and so forth. Being reminded of the numerous deeper issues that can be involved, I admit that I cannot deal with everything related to sexual intimacy in one chapter. Further, some discussions are better held in a counseling room with those couples who need specific help. If you find you have some issues beyond what is addressed in this chapter, please ask your pastor for a reference to a Christian counselor who can help you and your spouse.

Intimacy in marriage is good (vv. 1-2, 7).

Why is it good? Because marriage and sex were created by God.

Paul demonstrates that marriage is a good thing, especially in a society where immorality abounds outside of the marriage covenant. While it can be good for a man not to marry, since there is so much immorality, it is best for a man to have his own wife and a woman her own husband.

There is something unique captured in the idea of "own" wife and "own" husband. Obviously, you have one husband/wife, not more than one; and you have *your* spouse, not someone else's. But "own" also carries the understanding that you have a wife or husband that is uniquely crafted for you. Each of us can say as Adam said of Eve, "Yes! This is what I've been looking for!" If you are married, you should say of your spouse, "This is the one God made for me."

God created marriage and sexuality to go together. In marriage, sexual expression is the repeated reenactment of the covenant made with your spouse at your wedding. Sexual intimacy in marriage is the "reenactment, reaffirmation, and symbolic embodiment of the marriage vow."[106]

When I was in fifth grade, sex education was part of the religion class at my school. The night before the test on that unit, mom was calling out the information. I had everything down – female anatomy, male anatomy, egg, sperm, etc. But when we got through studying, I said, "Mom, our teacher asked today if we all knew how the sperm gets to the egg. My friends all said they did, so I said I did. But I really don't know." Mom called from my room to our den across the hall where Dad was, "Charles, you need to come in here." Mom and Dad then explained "how" it happens. I think I was in shock for most of the conversation because I only remember being grossed out. I then remember Dad saying, "Son, when a husband and wife love each other and come together, it is a beautiful thing." Beautiful? Not to a fifth grader.

My Dad was exactly right, of course. When a husband and wife love each other and come together, it *is* a beautiful thing because they are reenacting and celebrating the covenant they made to one another. They are celebrating that marriage is good and that sexual expression in marriage is good because both were created by God to go together.

Why is intimacy in marriage good? Because it captures everything about love.

Way back in Genesis 2 we have the first people, the first marriage, and the first sexual expression between a married couple. Genesis 2:24-25 reads, "For this reason a man will leave his father and mother and be united to his wife, and they will become one flesh. The man and his wife were both naked, and they felt no shame." There in Genesis 2 we see total commitment, followed by total transparency and total intimacy because of unconditional acceptance. It is a picture of the totality of love.

There is a big difference in "sex" and "love making." In fact, one older couple I know says, "In all our years together, we've never had sex because we make love." Sex is a bodily function. Love-making is what happens in marriage. Christian theology asserts that sexual expression cannot be dismissed as a mere bodily function devoid of meaning. When placed under the parameters of our fundamental commitment to the lordship of Christ and to the spouse He has given us, we have more than sex; we make love.[107] I'm not just trying to use a softer word for sexual intimacy than "sex" when I say "make love." There is a difference! Sex is a selfish act engaged in by two people who are only interested in getting. Love-making is a shared experience by a husband and wife who are experiencing all of love in one relationship in one place.

In English we have one word for love. We use the same word to say, "I love my dog" and "I love my wife." Hopefully, we mean different things when we say that, but no one really knows because we use the same word! The Greek language was more precise. The ancient Greeks had numerous words to express love. Consider how each of these six words for love can be enjoyed in marriage and how they can only collectively be enjoyed in marriage:

Agape – unconditional acceptance
Eros – sexual passion
Philea – deep friendship
Storge – affection
Ludus – playful love
Pragma – longstanding love

Only in marriage can you experience all of these forms of love at the same time. Marriage is good and sexual expression in marriage is good because you get all of love in one place!

Second, intimacy in marriage should be enjoyed by both spouses (vv. 3-4).

Paul speaks here of "duty" and "belonging." In our culture, this could get people riled up! Some woman might say, "I belong to my husband? How dare sex be a duty!" If we notice what Paul is saying, however, we will all find ourselves agreeing. Paul's words were radical in his day, and they are still radical in our day. In his day, when women were the property of their husbands, Paul said, "Husband, you belong to your wife, just as much as she belongs to you. You have a duty to fulfill her just as much as she has a duty to fulfill you." That was radical thinking then. In our selfish day, Paul's words say something a little different to us: "It's not all about you. It's about her too. It's for him too." When we practice what Paul teaches, we find sexual fulfillment in marriage by our giving of ourselves to our mate.

God designed sexual intimacy in marriage to have three purposes. *The first purpose of lovemaking in marriage is procreation.* God told Adam and Eve to be fruitful and multiply. Such procreation happens through marital lovemaking. Not all couples choose to have children or are able to have children. Still, children are one purpose of lovemaking in marriage, but procreation is not the only purpose.

A second purpose for lovemaking in marriage is pleasure. A husband and wife are to enjoy one another – that is biblical and expected by God. Just as you want someone to enjoy the gift you give them, God wants us to enjoy the gift He gave us. God created the bodies of both men and women to enjoy the sexual experience. God even built into women one "sexual structure that has absolutely no other function than to provide sexual delight."[108] Pleasure is what God intended. He created us this way.

The Bible indicates in numerous places that pleasure is a purpose of sexual intimacy in marriage. This is as R rated as we'll get in this chapter – just remember this is from the Bible:

> ***Proverbs 5:18-20*** *May your fountain be blessed, and may you rejoice in the wife of your youth. [19] A loving doe, a graceful deer-- may her breasts satisfy you always, may you ever be captivated by her love. [20] Why be captivated, my son, by an adulteress? Why embrace the bosom of another man's wife?*

How about this from Song of Solomon? The young bride is looking at her husband and describing his body as she enjoys it:

> ***Song of Solomon 5:10-16*** *My lover is radiant and ruddy, outstanding among ten thousand. [11] His head is purest gold; his hair is wavy and black as a raven. [12] His eyes are like doves by the water streams, washed in milk, mounted like jewels. [13] His cheeks are like beds of spice yielding perfume. His lips are like lilies dripping with myrrh. [14] His arms are rods of gold set with chrysolite. His body is like polished ivory decorated with sapphires. [15] His legs are pillars of marble set on bases of pure gold. His appearance is like Lebanon, choice as its cedars. [16] His mouth is sweetness itself; he is altogether lovely. This is my lover, this my friend, O daughters of Jerusalem.*

Now, how about the husband as he looks at and enjoys his bride?

> ***Song of Solomon 7:1-11*** *How beautiful your sandaled feet, O prince's daughter! Your graceful legs are like jewels, the work of a craftsman's hands. [2] Your navel is a rounded goblet that never lacks blended wine. Your waist is a*

mound of wheat encircled by lilies. [3] *Your breasts are like two fawns, twins of a gazelle.* [4] *Your neck is like an ivory tower. Your eyes are the pools of Heshbon by the gate of Bath Rabbim. Your nose is like the tower of Lebanon looking toward Damascus.* [5] *Your head crowns you like Mount Carmel. Your hair is like royal tapestry; the king is held captive by its tresses.* [6] *How beautiful you are and how pleasing, O love, with your delights!* [7] *Your stature is like that of the palm, and your breasts like clusters of fruit.* [8] *I said, "I will climb the palm tree; I will take hold of its fruit." May your breasts be like the clusters of the vine, the fragrance of your breath like apples,* [9] *and your mouth like the best wine.*

And she replies: *"May the wine go straight to my lover, flowing gently over lips and teeth.* [10] *I belong to my lover, and his desire is for me.* [11] *Come, my lover, let us go to the countryside, let us spend the night in the villages."*

Notice the commonality among Proverbs, Song of Solomon, and 1 Corinthians 7. There is total commitment to the other person. You can hear the couple saying:

"You are awesome!"
"No, babe, you are awesome!"
"I want to make you fulfilled!"
"And I want to make you fulfilled!"

People sometimes try to explain marriage as a 50/50 relationship – give 50%, receive 50%. But that's wrong. Marriage is 100% give. What happens when both individuals give 100%? They both receive 100% as well! I'm not great at math but isn't 100% better than 50%? Since God created marriage and sexual intimacy for marriage, perhaps we should listen to Him so we might have the best marriages and the best lovemaking in marriage!

Third, intimacy in marriage protects the marriage (vv. 5-7).

Sexual intimacy is a fire that burns between the husband and the wife. When a fire is contained in the fireplace, it gives light and heat to the home. Marriage serves as the fireplace for the fire of sexual intimacy. There are times when it rages and there are times when it glows, but it is there, giving warmth and light to the home.

What happens when fire gets out of the fireplace? It burns down the home! When the sexual intimacy that is intended only for marriage steps out of the fireplace of the marriage, the home is burned down. Adultery destroys homes. Pornography destroys homes. Any kind of sexual immorality that takes the fire out of the fireplace, destroys the home. Even if the marriage doesn't end in divorce, there is always a burned part of the house that takes considerable time to restore. For example, it takes years to restore trust that is burned by adultery.

The fire must stay in the fireplace, but it also needs to be kept burning there. Paul says, "Do not deprive one another." There are numerous reasons individuals sometimes deprive their spouse. Those reasons could be tiredness, resentment, disinterest, boredom.[109] Each of those reasons is a warning sign. If you're too tired, you need rest so you won't be. If you are harboring resentment, you need to deal with that. If you are disinterested or bored, you need to ask yourself why, and you may need to have a loving and serious conversation with your spouse in the right place at the right time. In other words, you have to rekindle that fire.

The fire that burns in the bedroom is kindled all day every day. Understand this principle: Love making in the bedroom cannot be separated from the love sharing in the rest of the marriage. Your sexual intimacy will only be as good as the rest of your marriage. What happens outside the bedroom has impact on what happens in the bedroom. Work at the rest of your marriage, and the sexual intimacy will grow.

Husbands need to heed this word especially. Sexual intimacy doesn't start the moment you get into bed at night and say, "Hey, come here a minute." It starts the moment you wake up in the morning. It is in how you communicate and how you show appreciation. It's all those little pieces of wood that you put on the fire. You need to figure out how to show her love the way she best receives love. And, wife, you need to figure out the same for him.

My eyes were opened several years ago by Gary Chapman and his five love languages: acts of service, physical touch, words of affirmation, quality time, and gifts.[110] All of these languages communicate love, but we're all built a little different and speak a different language. You need to figure out what love language allows your spouse to most feel love and speak that to him or her. The fire is kindled in marriage as the love tank is filled.

Paul says there may be a time you separate sexually. The purpose is spiritual – for a time of focused prayer. Notice that the time is agreed together, set together, devoted to together, and then ended together. "Together" is important because otherwise Satan can work in even the most harmless of circumstances.

Whenever the fire is burning out, Satan can work to try to pull the fire out of the marriage. I think he works through people innocently at first. No genuine Christian wakes up one morning and says, "I think I'll burn down my home today by committing adultery." Rather, it starts innocently. Someone at work starts meeting a need – maybe without you or them even knowing it. Maybe they take time to listen or give gratitude where it is due. That feels good, and there's nothing wrong with it; but since it doesn't happen at home, the love tank starts getting filled by the wrong person. Soon the spouse starts wanting to be with that person who makes them feel good. An emotional affair develops. Next, comparisons start: "My spouse never . . . , but this person . . . ." The comparisons may just be in their mind or they may manifest themselves in criticisms of the spouse to friends and family. All of this could be happening without the other person at work even knowing it. But, if at the same time, the other person is having similar issues, you have two homes that are about to burn down. The spouse falling into this relationship needs to recognize it, stop it, and flee the potential for sexual immorality. Stop it quickly, and there is no harm done. Recognize what is missing in your own marriage and talk to your spouse about it.

Don't ever think an affair won't happen to you. It can, and it will if you don't work to kindle the fires at home and protect your marriage when you're not at home. Every married person needs to create boundaries for themselves and build walls to protect themselves. I have to do that as a pastor. For example, if I am meeting with a lady even remotely close to my age or younger, my assistant must be in the office next door. If for some reason my assistant isn't there, my office door is open, and I ask the other staff members to walk by my office every few minutes. Further, there is not a single place in my office suite that I cannot be seen through some window (other than my restroom!). If I have to go by a female's house, and I discover no one else is home, I don't go inside. Likewise, my wife has every password to my phone, social media, and email, and often reads through things. We have a Pastor Care Group made up of a handful of deacons which provides accountability and care for me. Why all of this? It's to protect me, my marriage, and our church. But every person reading this book should do similar things depending on your setting and situation in life.

Likewise, each of us should work hard to make sure our spouses fire is kindled by us and not someone else. If you find that your spouse is enjoying something from someone else, ask yourself, "Why?" and start meeting that need yourself – whatever it takes, whatever it costs.

The writer of Hebrews says in Hebrews 13:4, "Marriage should be honored by all, and the marriage bed kept pure, for God will judge the adulterer and all the sexually immoral." My heart's desire is that we will have strong marriages. We need raging fires. Would that all of us who are younger could say in our 80s, "We're still in love, and we're still on fire." Would that all of our older couples would model for our younger couples what it means to be in love and on fire.

CHAPTER 19
What if My Spouse is Lost?
1 Corinthians 7:10-24

Stan was one of the hardest nuts to crack spiritually. He attended our church in Forestburg, Texas, but he didn't always buy what we were selling. A brilliant man who spent his career as an engineer and had an interest in science, Stan enjoyed arguing theological points in Sunday School. Most people got tired of arguing and let Stan be Stan. Everyone that is, except his wife. Anita was determined to see Stan come to Christ. She witnessed to him continually and kept Stan on our church prayer list for salvation. But Stan's shell was hard. He had gotten mad at God for something years before. It became his goal to poke holes in the truth of God's word. We began praying for Stan when we arrived in Forestburg, and Anita never let us forget to pray.

The question that may have come to Paul that led to our text for this chapter was, "Paul, what do I do if my spouse is lost?"

We have to remember that the gospel was new to the people of Corinth. Just a few years before, no one knew of Christ. As the gospel was preached, though, people responded. Often, one spouse would be saved, but the other would not be. The believing spouses wanted to know what to do. Now that a radical change had come to them, should everything else about their life change too? What do you do if your spouse is lost?

This is not a question that ended 2000 years ago. In every church there are couples, like Stan and Anita, in which one spouse is a believer and the other is not. It's a challenging situation. Often there is frustration on the part of both spouses and desperation on the part of the believing spouse. Naturally, the question comes, "What do I do if my spouse is lost?" Paul answers this question with two key principles.

The first principle: Preserve the sanctity of marriage (vv. 10-11).

This is a guiding principle for all marriages: preserve the sanctity of marriage. Wives should not leave their husbands. Husbands should not leave their wives. If they separate, they should remain unmarried or be reconciled to their spouse. The fundamental approach to divorce is – don't. Preserve the sanctity of marriage.

Paul's principle comes from the teachings of Jesus. His teaching parallels the teaching of Jesus recorded in Mark 10:2-12:

> ***Mark 10:2-12*** *Some Pharisees came and tested him by asking, "Is it lawful for a man to divorce his wife?" [3] "What did Moses command you?" he replied. [4] They said, "Moses permitted a man to write a certificate of divorce and send her away." [5] "It was because your hearts were hard that Moses wrote you this law," Jesus replied. [6] "But at the beginning of creation God 'made them male and female.' [7] 'For this reason a man will leave his father and mother and be united to his wife, [8] and the two will become one flesh.' So they are no longer two, but one. [9] Therefore what God has joined together, let man not separate."*

In Matthew 5:31-32, Jesus provided an exception for marital unfaithfulness.

> ***Matthew 5:31-32*** *"It has been said, 'Anyone who divorces his wife must give her a certificate of divorce.' [32] But I tell you that anyone who divorces his wife, except for marital unfaithfulness, causes her to become an adulteress, and anyone who marries the divorced woman commits adultery.*

Why doesn't Paul have the exception? There are a couple of possibilities. First, Paul probably wrote 1 Corinthians before any of the gospels were written. What Paul knew of the sayings of Jesus would have been limited. He apparently knew the same tradition as Mark. Second, perhaps Corinth's rampant problems with immorality would have introduced marital unfaithfulness into so many marriages that to offer exception without the opportunity for pastoral counsel might well have imperiled many good marriages.[111] Therefore, Paul doesn't even mention an exception. Whether we include an exception or not, the foundational biblical principle for any marriage remains, preserve the sanctity of marriage.

Many, if not most, marriages that end in divorce do so because the couple did not seek help early enough. The key to preserving the sanctity of marriage is this: instead of pursuing a divorce, a couple needs to pursue their marriage. Divorce needs to come off the table and the couple go back to these verses and let them be their standard. If a Christian couple will accept the authority of God's teaching and put themselves and their marriage under that authority and walk with God daily, they will see restoration in their marriage. It will take time. It will take work. But they *will* see restoration.

A retired pastor friend of mine shocked me when he shared about a time many years ago when he and his wife went through a difficult season. He said if you looked at his ministry and life on the outside, everything looked like it was great. What people didn't know was that his marriage was falling apart. However, he and his wife were desperate to save their marriage. They prayed hard, sought the help of a counselor, and did the hard work on themselves individually and as a couple. They have now been married over 50 years. It took admitting the problem, getting help, and being desperate before God for transformation to come, but God brought that transformation!

If you are having problems in your marriage, are you desperate to save it? You should be. Losing your spouse should be like losing part of yourself. If you are desperate, do something about it! Don't sit back. Don't hope it will change on its own. Pray hard for God to move. Pray hard for God to work in you. Pray hard for God to work in your spouse. Then go to your spouse with loving concern and do everything you can together to save your marriage. Preserve the sanctity of marriage!

With the general principle established, Paul gets more specific and goes directly to the question, "What if my spouse is an unbeliever?" The situation in Corinth posed challenges. Potentially both spouses had previously been lost. Then one was saved and began following Christ. This situation was a struggle for both spouses.

The question from believing spouses may have been, "Shouldn't the believing partner separate so they will not be unequally yoked?" Some people were telling them, "Just divorce your spouse and marry a

Christian." Others were saying, "Divorce your spouse but don't remarry."

For the unbelieving spouse, the situation was equally frustrating. When their spouse trusted Christ, suddenly everything changed. A modern day story captures the challenges. The true story is told of a brain surgeon who was asked what he found so difficult about his wife's new-found faith in Christ. He stressed two things. First, she was no longer the person with whom he had originally fallen in love and whom he had decided to marry. Second, there was another Man about the house to whom she was all the time referring her every decision and whom she chose to consult for advice. The husband was no longer the man of his own house: Jesus gave the orders and set the pace.[112] With all of these questions bringing frustration to everyone, the people of Corinth likely had sent the question to Paul, "What does a Christian do whose spouse is an unbeliever?"

Back in v. 10, Paul gave the instruction straight from Christ. Here, however, there was no clear teaching of Jesus. Therefore, Paul takes the principle of Jesus he knows (preserve the sanctity of marriage) and applies it to a unique situation:

> ***1 Corinthians 7:12-13*** *To the rest I say this (I, not the Lord): If any brother has a wife who is not a believer and she is willing to live with him, he must not divorce her. [13] And if a woman has a husband who is not a believer and he is willing to live with her, she must not divorce him.*

What do I do if my spouse is an unbeliever?

If your spouse wants to stay with you, stay with them.

> ***1 Corinthians 7:14*** *For the unbelieving husband has been sanctified through his wife, and the unbelieving wife has been sanctified through her believing husband. Otherwise your children would be unclean, but as it is, they are holy.*

This verse indicates the power of Christian witness in the home. The principle seems to come from the Old Testament principle of holiness by association. In Exodus 29:37 we read, "The altar will be most holy, and whatever touches it will be holy." Everything that became associated with the altar became holy. A similar principle is being applied here. True holy living shines such a bright light that everything around it is changed.

The Corinthians were probably wondering, "Isn't the believing spouse defiled by close association with an unbeliever?" Paul says, "No, it's just the other way around. The unbeliever can be won through the continual exposure to the gospel." John Calvin said, "The piety of the one has more effect in sanctifying the marriage than the impiety of the other in polluting it."[113]

Paul goes on to say that if there are children in the home, they too can be transformed by the power of the gospel through the consistent witness of the believing spouse. Paul holds "out the real possibility that the miracle of conversion will eventually bring the family into true oneness in Christ."[114]

There is power in consistent witness. The unbelieving spouse should stand firm on the principle of the sanctity of marriage and let his or her light shine before their spouse and children.

If you are the believing spouse in your home, you have a great responsibility. Let your light shine! Your witness can make a difference. The same idea applies for children and youth who are the only believers in their homes. Let your light shine as well. God can use you to bring your parents to faith in Christ.

If your spouse wants to leave, let them.

What if the unbelieving spouse wants to leave? Paul addresses that situation in the next two verses.

> ***1 Corinthians 7:15-16*** *But if the unbeliever leaves, let him do so. A believing man or woman is not bound in such circumstances; God has called us to live in peace.* [16] *How do you know, wife, whether you will save your husband? Or, how do you know, husband, whether you will save your wife?*

As Paul says in v. 15, "God has called us to live in peace." The Christian spouse should "permit the marriage to dissolve peaceably."[115] In all of Paul's teaching, the unbelieving spouse has the initiative. If they want to stay, you stay. If they want to go, let them go. Why does

Paul give the unbelieving spouse the initiative? Because "the Christian spouse should never take the initiative to end the marriage."[116] As far as it depends on them, the Christian partner upholds the sanctity of marriage and its lifelong permanence. But if the unbelieving spouse wants out, the believing spouse is free.

Divorce in this situation amounted to widowhood for the believer. Presumably a second marriage would not be completely excluded for the believer. Probably each case must stand on its own merits. Sometimes Christian husbands or wives try to push their unbelieving spouse to leave so they might have "scriptural grounds" for divorce. That is not at all what Paul intends. He intends that the Christian spouse preserve the sanctity of marriage. If the unbelieving spouse wants to stay, the Christian spouse should stay. If the unbelieving spouse wants to leave, they should be allowed to leave with peace.

The second principle: Stay where you are (vv. 17-24).

Paul cuts to a core Christian truth: Life status is unimportant; what matters is your status before God. Are you lost or are you saved? If you are lost, you need to be saved. If you are saved, you don't need to rush to change your social, economic, or marital status. Stay where you are.

It is interesting that sometimes when people come to faith in Christ, they want to change their social, economic, or marital status. Perhaps they want to start jumping through religious hoops like those in Corinth who were not circumcised but felt they needed to be. But you don't need to become a Jew to become a Christian. Why jump through those religious hoops? There's no need. What matters is a person's status before God, not his religious status.

Others, when they come to Christ, think Jesus is the pathway to Easy Street. Sometimes the transformation Jesus brings does cause a person to see economic advance in his life because he puts down money burners like drugs and alcohol and becomes a more faithful worker who earns promotions. But the person should not view Jesus as a means to Easy Street. If transformation comes, great. If not, great. What matters is one's status before God not his economic status.

As Paul says in v. 24, each person who comes to faith in Christ is responsible to God, and our first responsibility to God is where we are when He calls us. God may intend to use us right there to reach others. In marriage, he may use the believing spouse to reach the unbelieving one. So what do I do if my spouse is lost? Preserve the sanctity of marriage by staying where you are.

I guess I should tell you the rest of Stan's story. In May of 2005, the doctors told Stan and Anita that Stan was in the early stages of Alzheimer's. In the hours that followed that diagnosis, Anita found a quiet moment with Stan. She said, "Stan, do you know what Alzheimer's is?"

Stan said, "Yes."

She said, "Stan, you have that now." Anita then reminded Stan that while he may continue to live, his great mind was deteriorating. She then focused in on what mattered most. Anita said, "Stan if you are ever going to respond to God in faith, and accept Jesus Christ as your Lord and Savior, you need to do so. We don't know when you will no longer be able to make that decision." Finally, Stan's hard shell cracked and he said, "I want to." That day Anita helped him to pray, and Stan opened his heart to the Lord. The questions no longer mattered. The anger was gone. What mattered was Stan was facing the rest of life and eternity with Christ. When I next saw Stan, he had a new countenance on his face. The change was genuine. That was May.

In August I had the privilege of baptizing Stan in an old-fashioned lake baptism. It is a moment in ministry I will never forget. I had just finished baptizing two young men. Those men along with another man of our church then assisted in walking Stan into the water. Before I even had my feet firmly planted and was ready to baptize Stan, he pinched his nose. I remember thinking, "I wonder how long he can hold his breath? I better hurry!" With great joy we four men baptized Stan. The church rejoiced.

Within a couple of weeks after his baptism, Stan was bedridden. He went to be with Jesus on October 12. He had been a believer less than six months. The day he died, Anita was at peace. She gave thanks to God that Stan had finally come to trust Jesus.

Anita could have given up. Just about everyone else had. But she didn't, and she wouldn't let us. She stayed, and she prayed.

What do you do if your spouse is lost? You stay right where you are and preserve the sanctity of marriage. It may take years, but you stay, you pray, you shine your light, and you watch God work.

CHAPTER 20
A Word for the Single and the Single Again
1 Corinthians 7:8-9, 25-40

Sunday after Sunday, singles walk away from church services wondering, "Is there anything for me?" Since most adults in the church are married, it is easy for singles to feel left out – and rightly so because often they *are* left out. This is unfortunate because singles make up a large section of society. In fact some 15% of adults in our region of Louisiana are single having either never married or are single-again because of a divorce or the death of their spouse. All of us spend a significant part of our life single. We spend typically the first twenty-five years before we marry, and some will spend the last ten to fifteen years single after their spouse dies. Because singleness is such a large part of life, God has something to say about it. In fact, He says that whether the season of singleness lasts for a few years or for your entire life, you should make the most of it.

Who knows? You may end up like Jake and Jessie. Jake was 92, and Jessie was 89 when they found each other and decided to get married. They were so excited. One day they were strolling along discussing their wedding plans, and on the way, they passed a drug store. Jake said, "Let's go in here," and Jessie followed. He walked to the rear of the store and asked, "Are you the pharmacist?"

"Yes, I am."

Jake said, "Well, we're about to get married. Do you sell heart medication?"

The pharmacist said, "Of course we do."

"How about medicine for circulation?"

"All kinds."

"Medicine for rheumatism, scoliosis?"

"Definitely."

"Medicine for memory problems, arthritis, jaundice?"
"Yes, a large variety."
"What about vitamins, sleeping pills, Geritol, antidotes for Parkinson's disease – any of that?"
"Absolutely."
"You sell wheel chairs, walkers, and those scooter chairs?"
"Yes, all speeds and sizes," said the druggist.
"That does it. We'd like to register for our wedding gifts here."[117]

Single person, if you want to get married, there's still hope! But what about the years between now and then? And what if marriage never happens?

Remember that in this section of the letter Paul is responding to concerns the Corinthians had regarding marriage and related matters, such as singleness. The questions regarding singleness may have come to Paul because of his own singleness. We're not sure if Paul had ever been married, but we do know at the time of this writing he was single. Knowing of Paul's singleness, some of the holier-than-thous in Corinth may have wanted Paul to endorse his own preferences. Some may have wanted to uphold singleness as the most holy of lives, even the only holy life. In this passage Paul offers a good word for singles, but he is fair to those who are married as well.

As a single or single-again himself, Paul has a keen perspective on the single-life, and he has a good word for the single and the single again. You know what it is? LIVE!

Now, Paul's idea of living is not as we typically might see singles portrayed on television sit-coms or dramas. However, his vision is full of life and joy.

LIVE! with the right attitude (vv. 8-9, 25-31).

Paul doesn't encourage us to change our status just because we come to Christ. If you are single, it's o.k. to be single and enjoy being single. In these verses, Paul exhorts singles to uphold the sanctity of marriage by remaining pure in their singleness. He says, if you cannot control yourself, it is better to marry than to burn with passion. But if you can control yourself as a single, LIVE!

While Paul doesn't ask us to change our state, he does ask us to change our attitude about things in that state. For singles, that attitude shift begins when we realize that singleness is good. Single ladies, it's o.k. to be "always a bridesmaid and never a bride" (except for some of the bridesmaid dresses you have to grin and wear!). Single men, it's o.k. to enjoy your bachelor pad. No one cares if you pick up your socks or not. Single life is good. Enjoy it.

God calls some people to singlehood. He calls others to marriage. There is freedom to marry, but you do not *have* to marry. While you are single, live with the right attitude realizing that singleness is good.

I read the true story of a 65-year-old single missionary woman who was talking with a group of young women about answered prayer. She explained to the women how she prayed fervently for a husband to share in her missionary ventures. Nevertheless, she had always been single. In response, one young woman asked, "But you never married, so how can you talk about answered prayer?" The missionary smiled and explained, "Somewhere there's a 65-year-old man who has been resisting the will of God for the last 45 years!"[118]

If you are young and single, still being single at 65 may seem horrific to you, but Paul encourages you to change your attitude. Look at your singleness as a good thing. This missionary certainly did. She realized that singleness is good while waiting for her mate, whoever he is, to hear God's call.

We also need to remember that there's more to life than today. Paul lived with the expectation that the end of the world was close at hand. He also realized that in Corinth immorality was all around. Both of these facts contributed to the "present crisis" and "short time" in Corinth. Paul knew that there's more to life than today. Today is a blip in the grand scheme of things. Change your attitude from loathing today to anticipating eternity.

Too often we let our circumstances control our attitude. Our circumstances can greatly limit our perspective by creating blinders. Consequently, they mess up our attitude. In vv. 29-31, Paul shares five common circumstances we face in the world that can create blinders.

First, Paul mentions marriage (v. 29). Singles can get caught up with "Oh, if I were just married!" Paul says, "Don't focus on that." Besides, those who marry will face troubles. As someone has said, it's better to be single and wish you were married than to be married and wish you were single![119]

Second, Paul mentions sorrow (v. 30a). Mourning can really get us in the mulligrubs. Paul says, "There's more to life than today." Live as if you did not mourn! There's more to life than today.

Third, he mentions joy (v. 30b). Don't get consumed by today's joys; they may be gone tomorrow. Be joyful for today but don't get consumed with today. There's more to life than today.

Fourth, Paul mentions what we buy (v. 30c). Sometimes what we buy consumes us – a house, a car, a toy. We want it so much we think we *need* it. Things never satisfy long term. Besides, what you buy today, someone else will have in the future. You'll die and someone will buy your house. You'll trade your car for another. You'll donate that dress to Goodwill. There's more to life than today.

Then Paul reminds us of the things of the world (v. 31). Even this world is passing away. It won't be here forever, so don't focus on it. Change your attitude. Use this world. Enjoy this world. But don't put all your focus on this world.

Do the things of this world control your life by putting blinders on you? Or does Christ control your life by opening up your eyes to the fact that there is more to life than today? Is your perspective only on this world or does it include eternity? You don't have to ignore this world – just don't ignore eternity!

Second, LIVE! with a right devotion (vv. 32-35).

I love the first verse. "I want you to be free from concern." Singles, God says that He wants you to live a care free life! "Whoo hoo! Party on!" Right? Well, not exactly. God wants singles to have a care free life, but He knows that it comes by taking advantage of a tremendous opportunity: singles can get to know God like no one else.

Singles do not have some of the responsibilities that married people have. A married man is concerned about how he can please his wife and how he can better provide for his family. Likewise, a married woman is concerned about how she can please her husband and how she can better care for her children. Singles don't have to worry about that stuff. They don't have to remember, as my wife does, that their husband likes plain bread for tomato sandwiches and toasted bread for bacon and tomato sandwiches. They don't have to worry about leaving the toilet seat up or down or which way the toilet paper roll should be hung (over, of course).

For married people, we need to be concerned about pleasing our spouses. Paul is not saying we shouldn't. He's just admitting that these concerns naturally vie for our attention. A married person has a hard time being totally focused on the Lord because his or her interests are divided (v. 34). The order of priority for the married person is supposed to be God first, spouse second, and children third. I think all of us who are married can agree that it is a daily challenge to maintain some semblance of that priority.

Singles, though, can have a single interest to know God (see vs. 32b & v. 34b). Singles have the unique opportunity to grow in the Lord like no one else can. As you live with a right devotion, there are a couple of things you can do.

Discover God's ability to satisfy. Sometimes singles live such "exciting" lives because they are trying to satisfy a feeling of loneliness. Mother Teresa said, "The most terrible poverty is loneliness and the feeling of being unwanted."[120] Singles often deal with loneliness. The feeling can get greater when you are around your married friends.

I challenge you, singles, to put your focus on God. Get to know Him so that He can satisfy you. Isaiah 55:2-3 has a strong admonition, "Why spend money on what is not bread, and your labor on what does not satisfy? Listen, listen to me, and eat what is good, and your soul will delight in the richest of fare. Give ear and come to me; hear me, that your soul may live." Nothing can satisfy you like the Lord.

Discover God's grace. As a single, you face a lot of temptations. The chief of these may be sexual temptation. Don't kid yourself that this temptation ends once you're married. It doesn't. You need to take time during the season of singleness to learn how to deal with it. God has three powerful words for us regarding temptation:

1. Jesus taught us in the Lord's Prayer to ask to be delivered from temptation (Matthew 6:13).
2. In 1 Corinthians 10:13 Paul reminds us that, "No temptation has seized you except what is common to man. And God is

faithful; he will not let you be tempted beyond what you can bear. But when you are tempted he will also provide a way out so that you can stand up under it."

3. In Titus 2:12 Paul writes, "[God's grace] teaches us to say 'No' to ungodliness and worldly passions, and to live self-controlled, upright, and godly lives in this present age."

In the New Testament God teaches that: (1) we can pray to be free from temptation, (2) we do not have to give into temptation because God always provides a way out, and (3) God's grace can teach us to say "no" to temptation.

Still, God's grace is even greater! He knows that even though we can pray to be set free from temptation, we don't pray that near enough. He knows that even though he provides a way out, we don't always take it. And he knows that even though we've been taught to say "no," too often we say "yes." But God's grace is so great that no matter where you are in life and no matter what you've done, God says, "If you will confess your sins, I am faithful and I am just and I will forgive you of your sins and I will cleanse you from all unrighteousness" (1 John 1:9).

Maybe you've been too care free in your singleness and your life has become dirtied by sin. Or maybe God just isn't anywhere near the center of your life. While the world says, "Just do it and don't worry about God," you're thinking, "This isn't getting me anywhere. I'm not happy. I'm lonely. I want more out of life. I'm supposed to be care free, but I'm worried. I'm scared. I feel used." God is right there with you. He has His hand out ready to pick you up. He is eager to cut the chains that bind you. He has a shower prepared where you can get clean. He has new clothes for you. He wants to make you new. Will you let him?

Third, LIVE! with a right freedom (vv. 36-40)

There are differences in translation of these verses because of some uncertainties regarding some of the words. Some translations, like the NIV, address this to engaged men and women. Others, like the KJV, address this to fathers and their single girls. Regardless of the way you take it, the point is to live with a right freedom.

Fathers, it's o.k. for your daughter to marry. Or men, it's o.k. to marry the girl to whom you are engaged. But if you don't want to marry, that's o.k. too. Within that freedom, live with the right freedom. Freedom does not provide you a license to do anything. Freedom provides you the opportunity to do what is best. If it is best for you to marry, get married. If it is best for you to stay single, stay single. But, as you do so, live with the right freedom. If you live a married life, live the best married life possible. If you are a single, live the best single life possible.

I once found a forum for Christian singles on the internet. The forum no longer exists, but one testimony was pertinent. Single and single agains, may your heart be the same as Kevin's. He writes:

> I'm praying God will lead me where he wants me to go, and will help me learn to trust in Him more than in other people. I admit, as recently as last year I was so angry and frustrated in my single state that I annoyed even myself. I was so consumed by being with a girlfriend, that I even let minor statements from friends and family about my singleness really bother me. Then I remembered something a good friend wrote to me in an e-mail: "God wants 100% of you." The words made so much sense that now I'm enjoying this period of life despite the fact that I'm 32 and have never been married. I'm really letting the fact that God wants *all* of me sink in, and I'm enjoying it. Without my previous single-minded devotion to getting a girlfriend, I'm now freed to pursue other goals. . . . I'm having fun and becoming a balanced Christian single – Christian first, single second.[121]

May our singles have the same focus to LIVE, and may the rest of us help our singles to achieve that goal.

CHAPTER 21
The Weaker Brother Principle
1 Corinthians 8:1-13

When we read a passage about meat sacrificed to idols, we might ask, "What in the world does this have to do with us?" Well, when it comes to meat sacrificed to idols, pretty much nothing! If you sit down at a restaurant tonight, will you be concerned whether your steak was a sacrifice earlier in the day? No. When you sit down to a roast at home, are you concerned that the grocer may have bought it after it was sacrificed at the local pagan temple? Of course not. We don't have to worry about that. The early Christians had such concerns, however. While this issue has little significance for us, it was a big deal for them. Because God's word is timeless, Paul's instruction provides principles we can still use today.

The Corinthian's primary predicament is the same as our predicament. The predicament didn't have to do so much with meat offered to idols as it did with the question of how we can live as the people of God in the midst of a secular culture.

To glean the timeless principles, we must first understand the Corinthians' predicament concerning meat sacrificed to idols. The heathen religions that existed in Corinth had many practices of sacrificing meat to their gods. As that meat was sacrificed, it was dedicated to the god. After it was sacrificed, the meat was to be used to honor the god. That meat was used in various ways to do so:

- Some meat went to the priests of the religion as a means of payment. That wasn't a problem for the Christians in Corinth.
- Some meat was eaten in public feasts in the pagan temples to honor the gods. This both made money for the temples as well

as provided a social gathering place for the city. Many people went there not so much to worship as just to hang out and eat. The problem for Christians came as they were invited to these occasions.

- Some meat was sold in the market place. The funds generated supported the pagan temple. Sometimes the meat was identified as "sacred meat"; sometimes it was not. When a Christian went to the market, he didn't always know what he was buying. Christians did not want to encourage or financially support heathen beliefs.
- Some meat was served at suppers or dinners or given for special occasions like weddings, funerals, graduations, or social gatherings. Like at the market, sometimes the host announced they were having sacred meat, but other times he did not. The Christians faced the problem of determining whether they encouraged heathenism by eating the meat or appeared uncouth and impolite by refusing to eat it.[122]

There was no way for a Christian to escape meat sacrificed to idols. This was a predicament every believer in Corinth faced weekly, if not daily. Therefore, the question came to Paul, "What should we do? How can we live as the people of God in the midst of a pagan culture? Do we buy the meat? Do we eat the meat? Do we go to the places where the meat is served?" To help them handle their predicament, Paul gives them what is often called the weaker brother principle. What is the weaker brother principle? *Do nothing that might cause a weaker brother to stumble.*

To apply the principle, we should start by identifying our weaker brother. A weaker brother is anyone who is newer in the Christian faith than you or who has not yet come to the faith. That could be a friend. It could be a member of your Sunday School class. It could be your child. It could be your child's friends. The weaker brother is anyone who is weaker or newer in the faith than you but knows you are a believer and watches you for a Christian witness.

If you are a follower of Christ – whether you are a child, youth, or adult – remember that everything is example. You are being watched by your friends, your family, those younger than you, . . . everyone!

You might say, "I don't want that pressure." Too bad. If you are a Christian, you have it. If you don't want the pressure of living a consistent witness, you basically want God's grace for your sin but not His lordship over your life. You're telling Jesus, "I'll take your life given for me on the cross, but you can't have my life." There's something selfish about that! If you want to live a true Christian life, you have to be willing to let your life be an example to anyone who watches, and you have to apply the weaker brother principle. *Everything is example. Think about your witness.*

There is another question that comes to mind. We don't have to worry about sacrificed meats, but what are some "meats" of our day to which this principle applies? There are numerous things in our culture that are not necessarily wrong in and of themselves but when we do them as believers we could cause a brother or sister to stumble.

We can start basic with the clothes we choose to wear. There's a reason schools have uniforms or at least a dress code. Clothes can be a stumbling block. Our clothes say a lot about us. The style or logo may identify us with a particular group or belief system. What are we advertising? Maybe we just think the outfit or shirt is "cool", but, when we put it on, that shirt identifies us with something we are not. Also, the tightness or cut of our clothes can become a stumbling block to members of the opposite sex. This is far more a stumbling block for men, but it goes the opposite way as well. *Everything is example. Think about your witness.*

How about the movies or television shows we watch, the music we listen to, the video games we play, or even the books we read? Those can be stumbling blocks to others. For example, the issue is not whether it is right or wrong to watch an R-rated movie, the issue is if a weaker brother or sister sees you coming out of that movie and thinks, "I didn't know they agreed with that kind of language and immoral activity." You don't, but they don't know that. They assume you do by watching you. *Everything is example. Think about your witness.*

There are certain cultural activities that we need to be careful about. In Louisiana, Mardi Gras is one. There's nothing wrong with going to a family friendly parade or even going to a ball, but be sure to always think about your witness. Ladies should think about the dress they wear. One friend was looking at Facebook pictures of Mardi Gras balls and said, "Mardi Gras is like prom for adults. The only difference is the people grew, but the dresses didn't." That's problematic. There is also a lot of alcohol surrounding those events. Be careful about your witness. Think about what you do, what you drink, and the pictures you post. There is no context attached to the picture of you smiling with your arms around someone else's spouse. What's in that glass in that picture? *Everything is example. Think about your witness.*

Another thing we face in Louisiana is the lottery and gambling. I view these as taxes for stupid people. When it comes to these activities, think about your witness. I've heard numerous times, "We just go eat at the casino." A person who sees you there doesn't know that. They will assume you gambled while you were there. Besides that, eating at the casino is supporting the casino, and we don't need to do that. Sometimes your work may have a meeting at a casino. You obviously have no control over that, but you still have to think about your witness by what you do and how you act while you are there. *Everything is example. Think about your witness.*

We also need to be careful with the things we post on social media. There are a lot of things that float around that may be funny, but it may be off color. We can overlook a bad word or so for ourselves, but when we post that picture or statement, we are putting it out there and endorsing it. What does it say to a weaker brother? *Everything is example. Think about your witness.*

We should do nothing that might cause a weaker brother to stumble. *Everything is example. Think about your witness.*

How do we put the weaker brother principle into action?

First, remember that not everyone knows what you know (vv. 1-8).

Faced with the predicament of life in a pagan culture, some of the Corinthians would have said, "But Paul, we know better. We should be able to eat the meat and it not matter." True, but we must be careful. Knowledge can puff us up. It brings pride and conceit. It brings a "holier than thou" attitude. As it does, it divides. Certainly, Paul is not anti-intellectualism. We need to learn the facts of God, but not the facts alone. The facts are the foundation upon which our faith is built. They are the roadway of talk upon which we walk the walk. Obviously, we cannot know God without knowing about God. But Christianity is not only about gaining a mass of knowledge about Jesus Christ; it is primarily about living our lives for Jesus Christ. That's where knowledge meets love. Whereas knowledge can have the tendency to puff us up, love builds us up. When love for the Lord and our fellow man enter the picture, pride and conceit go away. The other person comes to the forefront. No longer does what we know matter; what is best for them matters.

The Corinthian Christians knew that pagan idols were just sticks and stones. There was no god to worship with that meat. There is only one true God. When they saw an idol, they saw a trinket. When they saw the meat, they just saw meat. But the pagans didn't see that. When the pagans saw an idol, they saw a god. When they saw the meat, they saw sacred meat. When they bought or ate the meat, they thought they were honoring the god. Consequently, if they saw a Christian purchasing or eating the meat, they thought the Christian believed what they believed. They didn't know what the Christian knew. It didn't matter that the meat was just meat; to them it was more than meat.

Second, be careful how you exercise your freedom (vv. 9-13).

Christians had freedom to eat the meat because they knew it was just meat, but it wasn't a good idea to eat the meat because of the weaker brother principle. As shared in the last chapter, freedom is not a license to do whatever we want; it is the opportunity to do what is best. In this case, what is best is what helps the weaker brother.

Knowledge told the Christian he could eat the meat without being hurt, but love reminded him that while he might not be hurt, his weaker brother could be. If his weaker brother was hurt, so was he. In fact, did you notice, he even sinned by causing his brother to go deeper into the pagan practice?

We typically want to ask, "Where's the line? When can I eat the meat and when can't I?" When we ask, "When can I?" and "When can't I?", we're asking the wrong question. We should never ask, "How far can I go?" That is our typical question: "How much can I drink? Is it o.k. if I just don't get drunk? How much can I participate in that activity? How far can I go into that cultural phenomenon?" The question always seems to be "how far can I go?", but that is the wrong question.

The right question is, "What are my motivations for wanting to do that in the first place?"[123] I find this question exceedingly helpful. When we ask, "How far can I go?", we'll never get a clear answer. Take alcohol for example. When you ask, "How far can I go?", some people will tell you that you should never drink. Others will tell you social drinking is fine. Still others might go so far as to tell you even getting drunk isn't bad as long as you do it at home and don't get in a car. When you get all those answers, you really get no answer and will end up being frustrated. You will be frustrated because you're asking the wrong question. Instead of asking, "How far can I go?", we should ask, "Why do I want to drink in the first place?" Is it to be accepted? Bad answer. Is it because everyone else is doing it? Bad answer. Is it because I want to escape something? Bad answer. Is it because I want a beer belly? Really bad answer! Often most of our answers are bad answers when we ask the better question. You can apply that question to anything:

> Why do I want to wear this in the first place?
> Why do I want to watch this in the first place?
> Why do I want to buy this in the first place?
> Why do I want to go there in the first place?
> Why do I want to do this in the first place?

The question of motives can go deeper than the question of boundaries and help you more easily answer the question, "Should I?" Most of the time, the answer will be, "Probably not. Because everything is example, and I need to think about my witness."

Now you might say, "If we live like this, we'll never do anything!" Not so. You just won't do the things that could hurt a weaker brother. We struggle between two extremes: permissiveness and legalism. Permissiveness says, "Go for it, your free!" Notice the "free" and disregard for everyone else. Legalism says, "You're a Christian and you know better." Notice the "know" that puffs you up as holier than everyone else. Permissiveness and legalism are both bad extremes. To go to either extreme is to destroy the church. Because the two extremes lead to two dangers:

> Legalism leads to separatism – that prevents the Christian from being salt and light in the world. It pulls Christians out of the public square into their own little subcultural commune. But when that happens, culture can spiral out of control because there is no salt and light in it.
>
> Permissiveness leads to syncretism which blends true faith with the cultural religion. We might say, "When anything goes, everything goes to hell." There is no truth. There is no foundation. There is no direction. When anything goes, everything goes to hell.[124]

Both legalism and permissiveness lead to the same thing – the continual destruction of the world by sin. Are we to pull away through legalism and let the devil have the world? No. Are we to let anything go and let the devil overtake the church? No. Somehow, someway, we have to find balance.

Admittedly, finding balance is hard. It's far easier to embrace one of the extremes than it is to achieve balance. How do we get balance? We put the weaker brother first. When we do that, we avoid the extremes. We ask, "How can we be salt and light in his life?" On the one hand, if we pull away, the weaker brother never sees us again. On the other hand, if we do what he does, the weaker brother never sees the difference in us. We can't be legalistic because we know we need to have influence over the weaker brother. We also can't be permissive because we want to give example for the weaker brother. So what do we do? We stay with him but don't necessarily do what he does. We are careful how we exercise our freedom. Freedom is not about doing "whatever." Freedom is about having the opportunity to do what is best. You don't have to be a prude or rude. You just have to remember: *Everything is example. Think about your witness.*

Paul concludes the chapter in v. 13 by saying that it doesn't matter that I *can*; it matters that the weaker brother *doesn't understand.* If my brother doesn't understand, I will never eat a piece of meat again until he understands.

Every one of us is faced with the question of the weaker brother, some of us almost every day. The question for all of us is, "What matters more – your freedom or your witness?" Does your being able to do whatever you want matter more to you than your brother being able to come to Christ? Always remember: *Everything is example. Think about your witness.*

CHAPTER 22
Caring for Pastors
1 Corinthians 9:1-18

You've probably heard about the facetious prayer of the church deacon, "Lord, you keep our pastor humble, we'll keep him poor." Sadly, some jokes are born out of truth. Comments like that deacon's aren't uncommon, but they aren't always from deacons. I've heard such comments in my years of ministry, but, frankly, I've never heard them from a deacon. Let's give the deacons a break and look at ourselves.

It is a matter of fact that some churches do not adequately take care of their pastors. Other churches simply cannot do as much as they want to.

Dealing with pastoral compensation is an awkward thing to discuss as a pastor. I've never been comfortable talking about compensation. It was awkward when I made $100 a week in college as a part-time youth minister. It was awkward when I went to pastor my first full-time church, and it's still awkward when we have "that" personnel meeting every year around budget time. Have you picked up that it's awkward? Good. Because in addition to awkward budget conversations, most ministers have to deal with the situation of being one of the few people in the church whose salary everyone knows. That leads to all kinds of comments! No matter the size of the church, some people think the minister should make more while others think he makes too much. Some say it's just right, but still others don't even pay attention but typically think the pastor makes more than he does. This goes for other staff ministers as well. Would you want everyone in the church to know what you make and then get to talk about it?

Compensation is an awkward conversation, but it is one that must be addressed. Thankfully, Paul jumps right into the subject of caring for pastors in this passage.

As we enter chapter 9, Paul deals with his freedoms and rights as an apostle. In chapter 8, he talked about the freedoms of believers and taught the weaker brother principle. He encouraged "the more mature readers to exercise their Christian freedom in a responsible way. They were not to insist upon personal rights that would prove to be harmful to the spiritually immature. To do so would be to abandon love as the guiding principle in Christian conduct."[125]

As Paul wrote such instruction, he was conscious of the fact that people would in turn scrutinize his life. He knew there were those who were ready to judge! I suppose every church has them. Sometimes they work in secret behind the scenes through conversations and phone calls. Sometimes they send anonymous letters. Sometimes they write blogs. Generally, the rule of thumb for pastors is we don't read that stuff or listen to it. Leaders should receive genuine constructive criticism but pay no attention to judgmental criticism.

Here, however, Paul goes to battle and offers a defense of his ministry. These people needed correction. Perhaps they felt Paul was profiting handsomely from his missionary work. Can't you hear the conversation in the church parking lot?

> "You know, Jim, Paul has all these churches he's planted. If he gets some compensation from each church, he's doing alright."
>
> "Oh I know, Frank. The man has more money than Pharaoh."

I don't know how the critics worked in Corinth, but somehow Paul knew about them and what they were saying; therefore, he offers a defense of his ministry.

For one, Paul didn't get a little bit from every church. In fact, he says while he could do this, and might even be entitled to it, he had renounced or limited his rights and liberties for the sake of weaker brethren. He briefly mentions marriage and food since he has been dealing with those issues, then he turns to compensation.

Interestingly, he puts the Corinthian church in the role of the weaker brother. It is because of their weakness that he gives up his rights. As we consider the truths on compensation that are shared here and the way Paul sets them aside for a bivocational ministry, Paul is not saying this is how it should be everywhere. He is not saying that every minister should work for free. In fact, quite the contrary. He is saying that this is the approach he has taken in Corinth because of their situation. If you want to claim to be a weak church, you could force your pastor to do what Paul does here, but if you want to be a strong church, you could follow the principles that Paul himself had to set aside in Corinth.

While there is a message to churches in Paul's teaching, there is an underlying message for pastors as well – the gospel is not for hire. If you can be hired, you can be fired. You shouldn't do what you do for money. You should do what you do for the sake of the gospel. That's why Paul could set aside his rights in Corinth. He wasn't for hire. He was simply obedient to Christ.

Nevertheless, in most situations, compensation should be given. A healthy, strong church can follow these principles to make sure that their pastor or pastors who are doing well at discharging the work of the ministry are compensated adequately.

Paul offers three reasons for ministerial compensation. His first reason is composed of several analogies. His second reason is Old Testament law. His third reason is common sense.

Paul begins by offering three analogies: a soldier who serves his nation, a farmer who tends his vineyard, and a shepherd who tends his flock. The soldier is compensated for his service. The army feeds him, houses him, gives him a uniform, and a salary. A farmer who tends his vineyard expects to be able to eat the fruit of that vineyard. He grows it and benefits from the growth. A shepherd tends his flock. He finds his means of support in the flock. He benefits from the flock. He drinks of the milk produced. One old commentary say, "The Christian minister is a soldier, fighting the battles of the Lord and of his Church; a laborer in the vineyard of Christ, planting, watering, pruning, training; a shepherd, watching over the sheep and lambs of his flock, seeking the wandering, correcting the rebellious, leading, feeding, etc."[126] It follows then that a pastor who serves, tends, and shepherds should be provided for and reap from what he has sown.

After giving these three analogies, Paul turns to the Old Testament law. We are no longer under the law, of course, but the law can give guidance as to how things might work on this side of the cross. Deuteronomy commanded that an ox should not be muzzled when it was treading out the grain. Therefore, if the ox needed a bite of the grain, it might take it. Paul indicates that this truth was more for men than it was for the animals. When a plowman plows and a thresher threshes they do so with the expectation that they can share in the harvest. They may not get it all, but they certainly should get something for their labors.

Third, there is common sense. Doesn't it make sense that those who give the greatest portion of their time, energies, and gifts to the service of the church should be supported by the church? If we give valuable spiritual seed, is it too much to ask that we receive back something of less value (material seed)? Some churches realize the benefits they receive, but they don't want to give the equal compensation back: "We're getting a good deal. Look at what all we get for what little we pay." But there are others that say, "Look at all we're getting! As thanksgiving to God for providing these people to our church, we'll take good care of them."

Paul goes on to give another common sense illustration. He says the priests and the Levites of Old Testament days lived on and were compensated from the offerings made at the temple. Shouldn't a similar thing follow for the ministers of the church? In case you're wondering, the answer is yes! Paul says Christ even commands it. Whatever we may think, this is what Christ thinks. If you take these analogies, the law, and some common sense to mind, what are some principles for ministerial support? Allow me to offer three.

Ministerial support should be given cheerfully.

If the minister has served well, compensate him with joy. Grudging support is disobedience to Christ. From the minister's side, it should be received cheerfully.

I failed miserably at receiving compensation cheerfully a few years ago. As our church was preparing the annual budget, we were adding in a new staff position and doing some other increases. The personnel committee recommended a 5% raise for me. When the proposal got to finance, I was concerned about the overall budget number, so I asked that that the number for me be reduced to 3% and everyone else stay as the committee recommended (which was between 3-4%). We made the change. Sometime after the budget was presented, I was visiting at a retirement center with a couple who were long-time members, Grady and Myrtle Welch. Grady was a retired minister. He asked about my salary, and if I was being compensated well. I told him I was and how I had even asked the committee to reduce the raise.

Grady replied, "That's dumb."

His response took me off guard, but his explanation made sense. The main reason was that I didn't just give up that compensation for one year but what that raise would have meant in every year after that – even if other raises were added! What seemed to be a "help" to the church in one year would end up being a "loss" to my family in the long run! "Oh," I said. Most importantly, however, giving up that raise was dumb because I didn't receive the compensation with cheer. If it is given cheerfully, receive it cheerfully. Lesson learned. (Thankfully, our church has long since made up for anything I lost in that year.)

Ministerial support should be sufficient.

The analogies, law, and common-sense point to the fact that the pastor should be able to care for himself and his family.

I once worked with a young minister in our church who was looking at going to pastor his first church. They wanted to move from a part-time to a full-time pastor. As I recall, they were offering my friend a package of around $48,000. That sounded o.k. on the surface because they had a parsonage. The problem was the church provided no ministry expenses reimbursement, no insurance, and no retirement. Everything had to come out of the $48,000. That amount of money goes away quickly when you start breaking it down. Once we took out taxes, insurance, tithe, travel to and from hospitals, ministry expenses, utilities, and some to tuck away for retirement, we ended up with less than $1500 a month for my friend to provide for his family. Good luck with that. He went back to the church and had the awkward conversation with the search committee of asking for just $500 more a month so he could at least end up with $2000 a month. The church decided they couldn't do it. They could generously support a bivocational pastor, but they weren't quite ready for full-time. They would have to make a big step to do that. They were either not able or not willing to make that step.

Ministerial support should be sufficient. Churches should do all they can to provide for their ministers. They should research what is fair and adequate compensation for ministers in their region, their size of church, and based on their church's budget and demographics. Don't just get by in providing for your pastors. Be generous. Sure, we want to do that so they'll stay, but we primarily need to do it so we'll be obedient. I want our church to be one that people know supports their ministers well. (And we are, and our staff if grateful.)

From the minister's side, the minister should be grateful for a church that provides sufficiently. Just about every church could add a perk or pay more in time, but if the compensation is sufficient, then the minister should be grateful.

Paul is clear that ministerial support should be given cheerfully and be sufficient. However, because of the weakness of the Corinthians, Paul says he set aside those rights. There is one more powerful principle for ministers as Paul offers his reasons for setting aside his rights.

Ministers should preach out of compulsion not compensation.

I like hearing our retired ministers talk about their early churches: "I made $50 a week whether I needed it or not. Sometimes we didn't know where the next meal would come, but we'd get home and there'd be corn on our doorstep." Those stories are a reminder that preachers don't preach for compensation; they preach out of a compulsion.

A minister has been trusted with the charge of pastoring his church. Every day he discharges that trust. I've heard many a thankful minister exclaim, "I get paid to do what God called and equipped me to do!" There is joy and fulfillment in that kind of attitude.

First Peter reminds us that pastors should not be greedy for money but should be eager to serve. That's the same idea Paul shares here. In the churches I've served, I've found that, generally, if I was eager to serve, the church was eager to support.

When I began my first pastorate in Forestburg, Texas, Rebecca and I had only been married a couple of years and had no children. Our first night in the parsonage, we felt like we were in a palace, even though it was an older home in need of a good bit of T.L.C. Since I was also finally in a full-time ministry, I was making just over twice what I was making as a part-time minister. We were doing well as far as we could tell. A little over a year into our ministry there, the church leadership came to the conclusion that they could do far better. They immediately gave me a 25% raise! I don't care how much or little you make, 25% is a huge raise! It blew us away, and we were so grateful. Now, I realize some churches would milk that for about ten years saying, "Remember, we gave the preacher that big ole raise back when." But not Forestburg. They gave some sort of raise every year we were there. They practiced scriptural principles effectively. Rebecca and I will always be grateful for their generous support.

Unfortunately, Corinth must have been an exception, so Paul relinquished his rights and offered the gospel free of charge to the weak church. While a minister should be willing to do as Paul, a church should not be like Corinth. A church should be spiritually stronger than that.

Make sure your church supports your ministers as best they can. Make sure your pastors are taken good care of – not just so they'll stay around, but so your church will be obedient to Christ. If you need to, ask to be on the personnel committee. One member at Forestburg used to always say, "I'm on the personnel committee to make sure the pastor gets a raise!" Perhaps that should be you at your church!

CHAPTER 23
Stretching Far to Win More
1 Corinthians 9:19-27

We all face the danger of thinking that everything is about us. That problem may be greater in the Unites States than most countries because of our emphasis on personal freedom and liberty. As believers, however, though we celebrate freedom, scripture reminds us that life is not all about us. Still, when it comes to church life, we often get caught in this mentality. We like what we like and want what we want. We sometimes forget about the people who have yet to be won to faith in Jesus Christ or we think they should be won the same way we were won.

In this passage, Paul reminds us how far we must sometimes stretch to win more people. Sometimes, or maybe a lot of the time, we must get out of our own comfort zone in order to see other people won to Jesus Christ.

Paul practiced what he preached. Let's go on a journey through the book of Acts to see the varied circumstances in which Paul witnessed effectively in a variety of places to a variety of people in a variety of ways.

In Acts 13:14ff Paul and his companions were in Pisidian Antioch. While there, he shared the gospel in a Jewish synagogue. In this mostly Jewish context, Paul shared the gospel by walking through Old Testament history. Paul took his audience through the Egyptian captivity to Samuel to David and finally to Jesus. He addressed the group gathered at the synagogue saying, "Brothers, children of Abraham, and you God-fearing Gentiles, it is to us that this message of salvation has been sent" (Acts 13:26).

Later, in Acts 14:8-18, Paul met a man's need, used that need to gain the crowd's attention, and spoke to the crowd in the open air.

However, then, in Acts 17:16-34, we find Paul in Athens, the cultural center of Greece. Paul took time in Athens to observe what was going on in the city and spend time with the people. Only then did he speak boldly to those who were well-grounded in ancient and contemporary philosophies.

In Acts 22 Paul secured permission from a Roman tribune to make his defense to a Jewish mob that wanted to assassinate him. Then, in Acts 25, Paul found himself in the great audience hall at Caesarea before the impressive company of the Roman procurator Festus, King Agrippa, and Bernice, the military tribune, and prominent civic leaders. Paul shared his testimony, the gospel, and his journey.

In all of these accounts, we see how Paul stretched far to reach more – from a Jewish synagogue to an open-air crowd to the seat of philosophy to the seat of power. He was willing to change and adapt his location and his method so that his message would be heard. This should remind us to refuse to get stuck in one method or one place.

Unfortunately, the church has long struggled with being stuck in methodology. We face the challenge every thirty to forty years as a new generation in the church begins to rise up. The older generation likes their own method, the one that reached them and that is comfortable to them. However, methods have to adjust for new generations. The adjustments come in everything from architecture to programming to organization to dress to worship music.

I chuckle when I read church history and find people arguing over the same stuff people argue about today. For example, we all know how people love to argue about church music. Well, guess what, that isn't new. Someone once wrote a letter decrying the new worship music. It reads:

> There are several reasons for opposing it. One, it's too new. Two, it's often worldly, even blasphemous. The new Christian music is not as pleasant as the more established style. Because there are so many songs, you can't learn them all. It puts too much emphasis on instrumental music rather than Godly lyrics. This new music creates disturbances making people act indecently and disorderly. The preceding generation got along without it. It's a money making scene and some of these new music upstarts are lewd and loose.

Do you know when that letter was written? 1723! It was written by a pastor attacking Isaac Watts, the writer of great hymns like "When I Survey the Wondrous Cross", "Joy to the World", and "O God, Our Help in Ages Past". You know, that *new* music. At least it was new in 1723, and people didn't like it!

It is said that Isaac Watts wrote "We're Marching to Zion" to shame those who left church early because they thought singing hymns as opposed to singing Psalms was frivolous. The second verse is especially telling. It says, "Let those refuse to sing who never knew our God. . . ." You refuse to sing these new songs, fine, you never knew God anyway. Ouch![127]

That was 300 years ago! Poor Isaac Watts should have lived longer. Now people are writing the same kind of letter about somebody else's new music while his is celebrated!

It is rather humorous if you think about it. Fast forward a few years to the music of the 1880s Sunday School Era. That music was looked down on by many because the hymns and testimony songs being written were too personal and not directed toward God. Many thought there was no room for music like that in the church. So, throw out all your Fanny Crosby songs. "Blessed Assurance Jesus is Mine" is too personal!

Jazz influences of the early twentieth century brought out an edict from the Pope that the piano was forbidden in the Catholic Church because of its worldly influences. Still, some people did, and, wouldn't you know it, you let in that jazzy piano and soon after that came the Jesus Movement with drums, guitars, and other instruments. Choruses and praise songs followed close behind.[128] Following it all was what we called "the worship wars" of the 1980s and 1990s.

Do you see how silly all of this arguing over methodology is? Every time there is a shift, people get upset, churches split, and letters are written like that preacher to Isaac Watts 300 years ago. Yet, many of those shifts help advance the gospel and reach a new generation. Similar things go for so many other methodologies from architecture to programs to structure to organization. If you look around your church and all you see is one generation, you may want to check your methodology.

We must remember that much of what we do as "church" is purely cultural. Most of what church members argue about is not even addressed in scripture. Choir robes, stained glass, organs, guitars, hymnals, screens, pews, bylaws, committees – none of that is in scripture. All of it is cultural. At some point in time, someone started doing things a certain way because it reached people of a certain culture at a certain time. Then, that "new" thing became tradition.

Our church is a "First Baptist on Main Street," therefore, it is somewhat traditional in many ways. However, during the hot summer months of Louisiana, our staff goes without ties on Sunday morning. One deacon enjoys picking on us about that. After he quipped about my lack of tie one day, I asked him, "Did Jesus wear a tie?" He replied, "Yes!" He was joking, of course, and we both laughed.

Unfortunately, when it comes to cultural traditions, we don't always laugh. In fact, too often, we argue about change. Why is that? The answer is imple. We argue about change because there is security in what we know. It is in the cultural rigidity that we find our traditions, structures, paths, and phrases. There is nothing wrong with those. It is in the traditions, structures, paths, and phrases that we find peace and comfort and joy. We like "our" particular music because it brings about good memories of days gone by. That's natural, but it doesn't mean different music is wrong. In fact, the music you don't like has the same effect on the people who like it as the music you like does upon you.

We are most comfortable with certain traditions. I am far more comfortable preaching in a more traditional setting like our sanctuary than I am a more contemporary setting without a pulpit. When our church moved into our gym for nine months while our sanctuary was being remodeled, it took me nearly a month to adjust to the casual surroundings. When we had to live stream for many weeks during the COVID-19 pandemic, it took me time to adjust to preaching to a camera with a table instead of a pulpit. But those struggles with change are my own hang-ups, and I'm better for being forced out of my comfort zone. Besides that, I can't find a pulpit in the Bible. Nor do I find most of the things we use in church today. They are cultural and traditional not biblical and foundational.

Clinging to traditions and what we are most comfortable with also involves minimal risk taking. Staying with what we know is safer. Still, we must remember that neither tradition nor cultural comfort is orthodoxy. Though it may feel right, that doesn't mean it is right, the only right, or that everything else is wrong.

Had Paul clung to culture, he would have never gone beyond the Jewish synagogue. He would have stayed right there trying to reach people through Judaism. Thankfully, he didn't do that. Paul wasn't limited. A rigid person might think this is compromise, but it's really evangelism. Jack MacGorman says, "Compromise does not know where to *stand*, and rigidity does not know where to *bend*."[129] Paul knew both where to stand *and* where to bend.

Paul says in v. 22 that he became all things to all people so that by all possible means he might save some. That statement is so helpful. Let's draw out a few principles as we seek to stretch far to win more:

We need to keep all people in mind.

Not everyone is like us. There are people all around us from different races, nationalities, economic levels, backgrounds, and family situations. All of them need to be reached with the gospel.

Not everyone has come to faith. Sometimes we can slip into the attitude of, "They know better;" or "They know where we are." But how is a lost person to know any better? They're lost. Lost people need to be found not left lost! They cannot be expected to find their way on their own.

We need to reach all people by all possible means.

Not everyone will be reached like us. Sometimes we want people to first become like us before we reach them. We want them to look a certain way and dress a certain way, then we can let them come to church or then we can minister to them in our group. Paul didn't do that. He did what he needed to do to reach them where they were or accept them as they were so he might lead them to Jesus.

Not everyone will be reached like us. Some will be reached in the church; some will be reached outside of the church. Some will be reached with one type of program; some will be reached with another. Some will be reached through one type of music; some will be reached by another type of music. Some will be reached through a special event; some will be reached through personal evangelism. Some will be reached through our church; some will be reached by another church. Some will be reached by a traditional church; some will be reached by a church plant. Like in fishing, it takes different bait at different times in different places to reach different people. The strongest churches will be those who work hard to adapt the message in various ways through various methodologies to reach the people in their region. After all, that is your mission field!

Not everyone we try to reach will be reached.

This may be the most encouraging part. Paul said he did all of this that "I might save some." Paul knew that not everyone he tried to reach would respond. Sometimes people reject the gospel. Sometimes we try something, and it doesn't work. It's like going fishing and never getting a bite. It's not necessarily your bait, but it could be. It's not necessarily the place you are fishing, but it could be. Therefore, we go fishing again another day – maybe to a different place with a different bait, and we find success.

Paul's statement in v. 22 is helpful, but everything he has said about reaching people is mediated by v. 23. Our motivation must be nothing other than the advance of the gospel. Sometimes our motivation is simply to grow our church. Growing the church is fine as long as we are primarily advancing the gospel. A growing church is an indicator of advancing the gospel, but not always. Sometimes a growing church is just good at marketing. Think about it like this. McDonald's is widely popular, but do they have the best hamburgers? No, not by long shot. However, McDonalds is a marketing genius. Most of us will go there for one reason or another several times a year. Since we handle the gospel of Jesus Christ, our motivation shouldn't just be to grow our church. It must be to advance the gospel. Naturally, as we advance the gospel, the church will grow – hopefully, like a wildfire as the early church in Acts!

Further, our motivation shouldn't be to just do something different or creative or shocking. There are churches that do that. Maybe God is using them to open new doors, but it seems they often do things simply for shock value. If our motivation is to help advance the gospel, then do something new, different, creative, even shocking. Just stay true to the Bible as you do.

We must do everything we do to advance the good news of Jesus Christ and to see His kingdom grow. Paul says to run hard toward that goal. The Isthmian Games was a sporting event that was held in Corinth every two years, therefore, the people of Corinth understood sports. Using such an illustration is an example of Paul adapting to his audience. Paul notes how an athlete preparing for those games went through a strict training routine. It was grueling, tiring, and hard, but it was not too great a price to pay if victory was achieved. Paul adds, "If an athlete goes through all of that to win a wreath that withers in a day or two, shouldn't Christians train even harder for a victor's wreath that never fades?" We might say, "If athletes train hard for a trophy that eventually just collects dust at the back of the trophy case as it is replaced in importance by newer ones, shouldn't a Christian train and push himself just as hard to receive a onetime trophy kept in heaven for us?" Yes!

We must push hard in ministry with discipline and purpose. We don't run aimlessly or punch the air. We find direction, discipline, and purpose so that we will not be disqualified from that prize kept in heaven for us!

As time marches on, the church will need to adapt to reach new generations. In the first twenty years of my ministry, I watched a lot of things change. Things that were cutting edge twenty years ago are almost laughable now. (Anybody still using an overhead projector in worship?) Things are still changing. Perhaps the greatest advance has been in technology. We are using tools in every worship service today that didn't even exist when I first came to our church twelve years ago. As we continue to reach a smart phone culture and whatever culture is to come after them, we must continually stretch far to win more.

Hold onto your hymnal, Ethel. Download all the Passion and Bethel music, Eric. Most likely neither will be around in the next generation. But that's o.k. as long as the gospel reaches that next generation.

CHAPTER 24
No Complacency or Presumption
1 Corinthians 10:1-33

There are two great dangers that plague believers and the Church. They are dangers that creep in unnoticed and make their home in our individual lives and among us as a corporate body. They then bring erosion to what Christ wants to do in and through us. These two dangers are complacency and presumption.

To help you understand these two problems, let me present them to you with two mental images. Think of complacency as a rocking chair. The idea of complacency is "I'm fine where I am, and I don't want things to change." In a rocking chair, you may make motion, but there is no progress. You may be busy, but there is nothing productive happening.

Think of presumption as a large empty box. When you are presumptuous you just sit and wait on God to fill you up. "Because I believe in God, He will fill me up. I do not have to do anything; He will do it because that's what He is supposed to do." The problem is doing nothing usually gets nothing.

Complacency and presumption are deep spiritual problems which limit our spiritual lives and ruin the church.

How Do We Avoid Complacency and Presumption?

Remember the Example of Israel (vv. 1-12)

Paul takes us back to the time of the Exodus from Egypt when Moses led the Hebrews out of slavery. That generation proved to be rebellious to God, so they did not enter the Promised Land. Notice how Paul repeats the word "all." *All* the Hebrews left Egypt. *All* the

Hebrews passed through the Red Sea. *All* the Hebrews ate the manna from heaven. *All* the Hebrews drank water from the rock. *All* of them. Nevertheless, *not all* of the Hebrews entered the Promised Land. In fact, how many of that generation that originally left Egypt and passed through the Red Sea actually got to enter the Promised Land? Only two, Joshua and Caleb. An entire generation of people was shown God's power every day by His provision for them and His protection of them, but they still did not trust God. Therefore, God was not pleased with them. Consequently, only two of them were allowed to enter the Promised Land. The rest died in the desert. Why was God not pleased? Complacency and presumption.

The Hebrews of the Exodus are the poster people for complacency and presumption. They thought that since God had rescued them, they were immune from anything ever coming against them. They thought that since they were God's people, they had privileges that prevented them from being accountable. They are a classic picture of a people who went through the motions but didn't go anywhere (complacency) and who sat there waiting for God to do the next thing while they did nothing (presumption). They thought they had faith, but they really had nothing.

All of them went through the motions of faith. Their crossing of the Red Sea was like baptism. It was a one-time act of following their leader Moses. Their eating manna from heaven and drinking water from the rock was like our celebration of the Lord's Supper. They were repeated actions. Still, they were just the motions of faith. Every day they presumed God would provide manna. When they needed water, they presumed God would bring it out from a rock for them. In fact, two times we are told of God bringing water from the rock. The first was believed for. The second was presumed. The Lord looked upon Moses' presumption that second time with such seriousness that it is for this particular sin that Moses was refused admission to the Promised Land.[130]

Presumption is dangerous. Complacency is dangerous. The Israelites thought they had faith, but they really had nothing. Because they had nothing, they lost everything.

Let those last two statements settle in for a moment. Everyone went for the ride. Everyone followed along. But God was not pleased with everyone. They thought they had faith, but they really had nothing. All they had was complacency and presumption. Therefore, they lost everything.

They were in a place to see faith at work, but they didn't have true faith. They wanted all the stuff of God instead of all of God Himself. Wanting the stuff is just rocking and box-filling. Desiring all of God Himself is when you get up out of that rocker and kick the box aside.

The Corinthians had a similar problem. Many of them were complacent in their faith and presumed upon God. In fact, they even thought that their baptism and participation in the Lord's Supper made them immune to harmful consequences from idolatrous practices. It is almost like they thought the ordinances of baptism and the Lord's Supper created a magical force field around them. They felt a license to do whatever they wanted and then they expected God to give them whatever they wanted. Because they were doing religious things (complacency), they felt they deserved to be taken care of (presumption).

Going through the motions of baptism doesn't save us; it's following Christ that saves. The bread and cup of the Lord's Supper do not save; it's complete dependence on Christ that saves. You can rock on in religious stuff all day long, all week long, all month long, all year long, your whole life long, but you're still not going to have true faith. God is still not going to be pleased, and you're not going to rock your way into heaven. Complacency is displeasing to God.

Likewise, presuming that because you do religious stuff you deserve protection or blessings displeases God. We deserve nothing. God has already given everything in Jesus Christ for us to be saved. Anything else we receive is lagniappe (that's a 'little something extra' us Louisianians). We can't just want the stuff of God; we must pursue God Himself.

Four Sins of Complacency and Presumption:

Worshiping Idols (v. 7) When we are complacent in our faith and presume upon God, idolatry seeps into our hearts. We can place things in the place of God while all the time equating them with the blessings of God. We can rock away and hold out our box and gain money and say, "God has blessed", when really we are bowing before money as our god. We can rock away and hold out our box and gain prestige and say, "God has blessed", when really we are bowing before our self as our god.

Sexual immorality (v. 8) When we are complacent in our faith and presume upon God, lust and desire can grow. Because we are seeking the stuff of God instead of all of God Himself, sin creeps in. We think we are immune. Our guard drops. Temptation rises, and we give into things we never thought possible.

Putting the Lord to the Test (v. 9) When we are complacent in our faith and presume upon God, every day we test God. "Will He fill my box? Will He give me the God stuff? Will my rocker of religion and tradition be comfortable?" It is dangerous when we put the Lord to the test in these ways! For the Israelites, the snakes came up and killed many of them. Do not put the Lord to the test – unless you like snakes, I guess.

Grumbling (v. 10) Take note that grumbling is placed right alongside sexual immorality and idolatry. Watch out! Grumbling comes when we are rocking away expecting our box to be filled. "We should have stayed in Egypt. Slavery was better!" "This is not how I want my life to go." "This is not how I want church to be." "God should give me better; I've been so good to Him."

Paul calls all four of these things "desiring evil." How dangerous are the sins of complacency and presumption! They cause us to desire evil. Even when we rock away in our Sunday finest holding out our blessings box, we are actually desiring evil. We look like we're doing the churchy thing when actually we're doing the worldly thing in churchy dress. That's why the same sins that spoiled people in the days of Moses wreck churches today.[131]

Many people are complacent just being in the church. They presume that if they go through the motions of faith they must have faith. But faith is not motions; faith is a relationship. Too often in the church we have become slothful, habitual, uninspired – doing what we do often for traditional, cultural, or preferential reasons rather than because it is best. But that is complacency and presumption, and they are dangerous because they are sin. Pride is at the root of all of sin. At the moment you are most comfortable with your rocker and lift your box the highest, that's when you can fall the farthest.

How do we avoid complacency and presumption? Remember the example of Israel and do not follow it! Instead, follow three simple steps when you are faced with the temptation to delve into sin of any kind.

See Temptation for What It Is (v. 13a)

What is sin? Common and run-of-the-mill! Never think that the temptation you face is unique to you. Never think that the trial you face is unique to you. Whatever you face has been faced before. In fact, Paul says, "It is common to mankind." Satan has no new tricks.

Look for the Way of Escape (v. 13b).

The most powerful statement in v. 13 is not so much that there is a way of escape, but it is "God is faithful." The way of escape is a gift to us given by God, but the gift always points back to the Giver. Since God is faithful, when you face a temptation, look around, there is a way of escape.

Sometimes we think there is no way out. That is because sin makes you deaf, dumb, blind, and stupid! If you will look to God, He is faithful. His Spirit will help you not be deaf, dumb, blind, and stupid! The Spirit will help you hear God's voice, know God's plan, see the way out, and take the way out. The Spirit is more powerful than the flesh. Look for the way out. God is faithful. The way out will be there.

Run! (v. 14)

1 Corinthians 10:14 *Therefore, my dear friends, flee from idolatry.*

Never flirt with sin. Flee from sin. If you flirt, you lose. If you run, you win. Get out of there. You may think that it's impossible. You may find yourself deep into a particular sin, and the way out may seem difficult. In that moment, remember that Jesus has walked the same path and faced the same temptations. He knows how much we can endure. He knows the way of escape. He will show you, if you will let Him.

The word translated "way of escape" is almost exactly the same word as "exodus."[132] When we face temptation, we often don't think we can find a way out. The people of Israel didn't think they could get out of Egypt. They were under deep oppression. They faced numerous road blocks. But when they cried out to God, when they looked to Him, He didn't just show them the way out, He *led* them out! God is the God of exodus.

When they came to the Red Sea, they didn't know where to go. The army of Pharaoh was closing in. Again, they looked to God, and He didn't just show them the way out, He *led* them out! He is the God of exodus.

After wandering in the wilderness, the new generation came to the Jordan River. It was time to take the Promised Land. They weren't sure they could, but they looked to God. He didn't just show them the way in, He *led* them in. God led them through the Jordan and into the Promised Land. He is the God of exodus, and He is the God of the entrance.

As the people entered that Promised Land, they found giants and peoples who were stronger than they. The people knew they couldn't take them on their own, so they looked to God. God didn't just show them the way in, He *led* the way in. He is not just the God of the exodus, He is the God of the entrance.

When you come to a place where you are throwing up your hands in despair, when you come to a place where you don't think you can make it or get through, look to Him. He'll not just show you the way out, He will lead you out. He is the God of exodus.

You will be tempted. You will face trials. You will get bewildered. You will think there is no way out. You will feel hopeless. You will get depressed. You will want to do something you shouldn't do. In those times, look to God. He will lead you out. He is the God of exodus.

Be sure the temptress will wink; the bottle will call; the ad will pop up; the pride will rise; the temper will flare; the foul words will come to your tongue. In those times, look to God. He will lead you out. He is the God of exodus. But He will also lead you into a new day because He is the God of the entrance as well.

Please know that this kind of victory will never come from rocking in the chair of complacency. Neither will that kind of victory come from presuming upon God to fill up your box. He is not required to fill up your box just because you do religious stuff. He is not required to fill up your box just because you rock in religious motion. If you presume upon God to fill up your box, your box won't be filled by God. It will be filled by something else. Troubles will fill it. Temptation will fill it. In time, you won't be able to handle that.

But if you have no more to do with complacency or presumption, and you cling to God in a genuine relationship, then you can remember that God is faithful. Isn't that where you want to be? Isn't that what you want to enjoy?[133]

CHAPTER 25
Witness in Worship
1 Corinthians 11:2-16

What kind of witness do you give as you worship each week? As you sing, what does someone else see? Do they see you engaged in worship? Can they tell on your face that you are worshiping? When a message is being delivered do they see you listening with interest?

When different people lead in worship – as the choir sings, as the musicians play, as someone stands to pray, as a soloist sings, as your pastor preaches – what kind of witness do those people provide? Is that individual or group performing or are they worshiping?

The church at Corinth had some issues in their worship services that were harming the church's witness. They had people disrespecting each other at the Lord's Supper, showboating their spiritual gifts, and flaunting their freedoms. Their services were a three ring circus of prideful performance; therefore, Paul addressed the problems.

Earlier in this letter, Paul talked about Christian witness outside the church. He now turns to our witness within the worship services of the church. Obviously, the first century church did not have church buildings as we do, but they did meet in physical spaces. Many churches met in homes or the open courtyards of homes. When believers gathered, wherever they gathered, there were lost people in their midst. Therefore, the gathered church members were witnesses. Paul goes after those who flaunted their personal freedoms to the detriment of others in worship.

First Corinthians 11:2-16 has been misused in a couple of ways. On one hand, it has been caricatured as male chauvinism. On the other hand, it has been used to promote restrictions in female clothing, appearance, and even participation in the church. These are both incorrect uses of the text. Paul is not a male chauvinist who is trying to keep women silent, frumpy, and covered up.

To understand this text properly, we must go back to the original context. We should ask: "Why does Paul give these instructions?" Remember, much of this letter consists of responses to questions the Corinthians had asked of Paul. It seems that a question came to him about what was happening in the worship services. Paul responded with detailed instructions.

The particular trouble Paul addresses was what some women were doing in worship. Some of the women were breaking prevailing customs by participating in public worship with uncovered heads. Now, before you say, "Well, good for them! Break that glass ceiling!" – that's not what was happening here. When it came to head covering, there was not a need for women's liberation.

In the first century world, there was considerable diversity about the wearing of veils among the ethnic groups. Jewish men prayed with their heads covered. Greek men and women prayed with their heads uncovered. Roman men appear to have prayed with their heads uncovered.
Veils were a natural cultural phenomenon among the various groups.

Some of the Christian Corinthian women, however, were trying to blaze their own trail by refusing to wear a veil on their head. To us that is a nonissue, but to a first century person with a Jewish synagogue background, this would have been scandalous conduct.

In the first century world, a woman's hair was a symbol of her sexuality. The Jewish woman of that age grew her hair long and would wear it tightly on the top of her head. She only let her hair down before her husband in private.

Do you remember the story of the woman wiping Jesus' feet with her hair? She outraged the people gathered there when she let down her hair and began wiping His feet. No woman would let down her hair in public!

Put yourself in the worship services of Corinth. These women were letting down their hair in worship as a sign of their freedom, but in so doing, they were causing great difficulty for the men of the church. The men were already not used to women prophesying, and here they were letting down their hair. Was anyone going to hear the prophesy?

No! Everyone in the church was distracted, offended, or shocked. Therefore, the witness in worship was nullified. These women did not care if they edified the church. They simply wanted to exercise their freedom. In so doing, however, they were harming the church's witness. Therefore, Paul has a word for them – STOP! He tells the women they need to keep their heads covered. To support his teaching, Paul appeals to five different things.

First, Paul says women need to keep their heads covered because of the order in creation (v. 3).

Paul uses the word "head" in three different ways:

1) Woman's head – physical head
2) Man's prior creation – first created
3) Christ – head of the church

Paul appeals to the order of creation to show that there must be order in relationships. God the Father is the head of Christ. Christ is the head of the man. The man is the head of his wife. This is simply the order of creation. There must be order; otherwise, there will be chaos.

The women in Corinth likely were aware of Paul's teaching that in Christ there is neither male nor female. Some of the women were trying to equate themselves with men in every way possible. In this explanation, Paul says to them, "Right idea. Wrong application." In any relationship, even a partnership, there must be order.

When Paul speaks of the man as the head, he is not arguing for any lordship of man over woman. Subordination is not to be seen as reflecting inferiority or less worth but rather different functions or roles.[134] The man has a job. The female has a job. Both jobs are vital. They happen in a specific order created by God from the beginning. Even within that order, however, Paul emphasizes partnership. Men and women need each other.

In Genesis, the man was created before the woman. The woman came from the man. Now, every man comes from a woman. Why did God change the order? Why didn't God make us men have babies? He knew we couldn't handle it! Not really. The reason God reversed the order is found at the end of v. 12, "Everything comes from God." God changed the order so we would look back and see that though woman is first now and man was first then, God is first in all things. God must be head of all. God has established the order. His order is best.

Second, women's heads need to be covered because of social customs (vv. 4-6).

In any witness situation, we respect social customs and remember them so as not to do unnecessary harm to our witness. Paul speaks of the social custom of the woman's hair being a sexual symbol. He uses the order of creation as his basis. When a man prays with his head covered, he dishonors his head, which is Christ, because the man has been set free in Christ to go to the throne of grace with confidence. The Christian man does not pray through a priest or idol or anything. He is not in subordination to another human being when he comes before God.[135] In the first century, a man praying with his head uncovered was a radical move, but it didn't bring disgrace and distraction like the woman with an uncovered head.

Since it was such a sexual thing for a woman to let down her hair, when she did this, she created a distraction in worship causing people to look only at her. As she did, she disgraced her "head", meaning her husband. Any husband is disgraced by a wife who flaunts her sexuality before other men. Paul says, "It is just as though her head were shaved." In the culture of the time, an adulterous woman's head would be shaved by her husband. Some pagan temple prostitutes also wore shaved heads.

Notice, Paul does not say these women should not pray or prophesy. Apparently, he has no problem with them doing either. What he speaks against is *how* they are praying and prophesying. Ken Hemphill explains, "If Paul had thought the women should be silent, he wouldn't have wasted time saying what they should do when they do speak."[136]

Third, Paul says the women should keep their heads covered because of the angels (v. 10).

This is pretty hard to understand. Scholars even debate the meaning. A possible meaning is that if the angels are the protectors of the created realm. They would be offended by these actions because they know how the order should be. When the order is not followed, it causes disruption in the spiritual realm.

This obscure kind of statement is a good reminder to us that there is more going on when we meet in worship than just the physical realm. The spirit realm is very much at work as well. We must do all we can to not disrupt what is happening there.

Fourth, Paul says the women should keep their heads covered because of the evidence of nature itself (vv. 13-15)

Paul felt that nature teaches that long hair is degrading to a man but commendable in a woman. The hair serves two purposes. First, it serves to distinguish between the sexes. In a day when clothing was similar for men and women, long hair, even that was pulled up on top of the head, distinguished between a man and a woman. Second, the hair served as a covering. If it was down, it could cover her.

Finally, Paul says the women should keep their heads covered because of the prevailing practice in the churches (v. 16).

Paul basically says, "This is how most churches are doing it these days." There is often wisdom in the general consensus of godly brethren.

Those are the reasons Paul gives for women keeping their heads covered in worship in the first century. Now, what do we do with this? Certainly, the *timely* teachings of Paul for that day are not the same as the *timeless* teachings of Paul for every day. We do not have the same social and religious culture. For us to start making women wear veils in worship would do as much harm to our witness today as the women *not* wearing veils back then! So, what are the timeless principles?

Social conventions should be respected.

"Every culture has its social conventions that define acceptable public conduct. Churches do not advance the cause of Christ by outraging them. When a church [ignores] the prevailing social customs, it offends many of the people to whom it seeks to bear witness. Also, it incurs needless suspicion."[137] If unbelievers attend our services, they should find God honored in every aspect of worship. They should see nothing that would bring reproach upon the gospel or distract them from hearing the gospel. We want to witness in our worship.

Distinctions between men and women should be honored.

God does not intend to abolish the distinction between the sexes. To abolish one would be to say that one is inferior to the other. This is what is so maddening about movements that try to make the sexes equal. To abolish womanhood is to say women are inferior to men. That just is not so. To abolish manhood is to say men are inferior to women. That too just is not so.

Instead, God sees male and female as a perfect partnership. When a woman wants to do everything like a man, she is admitting that she somehow feels inferior to a man as a woman. When a man wants to do everything as a woman, he admits that he is not comfortable in his masculinity. God has created women to be feminine and men to be masculine. Each gender has a unique and important role to fulfill through its own unique and important abilities. We should enjoy our differences and realize our mutual dependence on one another.

Men and women should dress modestly and appropriate for Christian service.

Still today, men and women can become stumbling blocks to other worshipers by what they wear. Anyone who stands before a group must be careful how they dress. Sometimes we need to ask for the opinion of others, and other times we need to be open to the instruction of others when offered in the right spirit. When we dress modestly, we can witness in our worship.

Every worship service must be focused toward mutual edification and conducted with order.

Worship should have order. That does not mean it has to have a printed order, but there must be order. Things should be done in an orderly fashion so as not to create confusion. That is because while a worship service is directed to God, it is for the mutual edification of the worshipers.

If one worshiper stands to sing for their glory instead of the Lord's glory, then worship is not fulfilling its purpose. If a preacher stands to deliver a message to entertain, then he is seeking his own glory and worship is not fulfilling its purpose. In worship everyone should be edified, and God should be glorified. Some people are in front, but they are only there to help prompt worship. They are never the focus of worship. In reality, when we worship, we should not be focused on the choir or the soloist or the preacher or anyone in leadership. We should be focused on God. The point when we gather for corporate worship is not to see the choir or the musicians or the preacher. The point is to see God.

"Every church has the privilege of bearing witness to its faith through public services of worship."[138] Regardless of the songs or hymns selected, the instruments accompanying, whether there is a choir or isn't, whether the preacher wears a suit or skinny jeans, and whether the congregation sits in chairs or pews, worshipers witness. The question is, "What kind of witness do we give?" Of course, you can't really worry about the "we." Perhaps we need to ask the question a different way, "What kind of witness do *you* give?"

Would a lost person attending worship in your church be drawn to the Lord by your worship? Would they look at you and say, "I'm not sure what that person has, but I want it. They're getting something out of this time in this place that I don't understand." Or would they look at you and think, "Jesus must be joyless and boring"? You witness as you worship. What is your witness saying?

A couple who was prayerfully considering becoming a part of our church once shared with me how they felt the Spirit in our services and enjoyed worshiping with us. Their original plan was to visit some other churches, but they kept being drawn back because of the witness of worship in our church. That needs to happen to everyone who comes to our church and your church. How is your witness in worship?

CHAPTER 26
Questions Related to Spiritual Gifts
1 Corinthians 12:1-11

A good, strong chain is a useful tool. Give my dad a chain and his tractor, and he could move anything (well, with some help from me and Mom). With a chain and tractor we cleared stumps, pulled out overgrown bushes, hauled cars, moved cross ties, and more.

A paper chain, however, is pretty much useless. Oh, I know the chains our preschoolers made us were cute, but after one or two years on their Christmas tree, the construction paper rots, the glue breaks down, and the chains are done.

Spiritual gifts are like the links in the good, strong chains my dad used. Every follower of Christ receives one or more spiritual gifts from the Holy Spirit. A spiritual gift is "a skill or ability that enables each Christian to perform a function in the body of Christ with ease and effectiveness."[139] Each spiritual gift that has been developed is like a good, strong link. That link, that spiritual gift, however, is most useful when it is combined with other links to form a strong chain.

Therefore, think of the spiritual gifts in a church like a long, strong, useful chain. The strongest church is a chain of people with strong, developed spiritual gifts. A chain like that is useful. Even though it may grow old and worn through age, like many of my dad's chains, it remains strong and able to do the work.

Those preschool paper chains represent a church that is made up of undeveloped spiritual gifts. While it may be colorful and exciting, it is absolutely useless.

When it comes to knowing and using their spiritual gifts, sometimes people feel more like paper than they do iron in terms of their usefulness in God's kingdom. But let's remind ourselves of something Paul said back in 1 Corinthians 2:9-10:

1 Corinthians 2:9-10 *However, as it is written: "No eye has seen, no ear has heard, no mind has conceived what God has prepared for those who love him" --* [10] *but God has revealed it to us by his Spirit. The Spirit searches all things, even the deep things of God.*

We can never imagine what God has prepared for us! However, He has given us His Spirit to reveal the things He *has* prepared for us. Keep that amazing truth at the forefront of your mind as we enter these next several chapters on spiritual gifts. God intends for no one in the church to be a useless paper link! You are meant to be a strong link, and your church is meant to be a strong and useful chain.

The Church at Corinth was having a big problem with spiritual gifts. Some of the people were celebrating the more sensational gifts to the disparagement of the not-so-dramatic gifts. Particularly, those who had the gift of speaking in tongues, or at least thought they did, were grandstanding their gift and considering themselves more spiritual than others. They had a junior Holy Spirit mentality that said, "I'm more holy than you are." Obviously, this created great division in the church. There was little love shown for one another, but there was much pride and envy displayed. Love builds a church. Pride and envy destroy a church. The problem related to spiritual gifts was so great in Corinth that it takes Paul three chapters to correct it!

Let's work through Paul's instruction in 1 Corinthians 12:1-11 by asking and answering some questions related to spiritual gifts.

Who receives spiritual gifts? (vv. 1-7)

Every believer! This is Paul's first corrective to the Corinthians about spiritual gifts. The people who thought themselves to be super spiritual felt that the possession of showy spiritual gifts was verifiable proof of their advanced spirituality. These people had become spiritual giants in their own eyes. "The word 'to puff up' or 'make arrogant' occurs only seven times in the New Testament and six are found in 1 Corinthians. The word 'boast' is found fifty-three times in the New Testament, and thirty-five of them are in this letter."[140] You can see these were some conceited, boastful people!

Paul shows these "spirituals" that each believer has his or her own special gift, and every gift is special. Your gift does not make you any more holy than someone else in the church. The Spirit is at work in all believers, not just some.

Paul demonstrates his point by saying, "Isn't it obvious that no person who truly trusts Christ and has the Holy Spirit would ever say, 'Jesus be cursed'? Then isn't it also obvious that no one could say, 'Jesus is Lord' except by the Holy Spirit?" That simple, most fundamental confession of salvation is an indicator of the Spirit's work in a believer's life – even the newest and most immature believer.

Paul's instruction reminds us that the experience of salvation is a confession experience not an ecstatic experience. There is power in the basic confession, "Jesus is Lord." That confession does not have to be accompanied by some ecstatic experience. Every believer is a spiritual person, not just those who possess certain types of gifts. When a person confesses Jesus as his or her Lord, that person is given the Holy Spirit and spiritual gifts to accompany God's work through their lives.

Aren't some Christians more effective and active than others? Sure. But "the differences between Christians is not that the Holy Spirit indwells the lives of some and not others. Rather it is that He has freedom and dominion in some and encounters resistance and self-will in others."[141] Every believer has the potential to be useful for God's kingdom. The only reason they aren't is they never allow their gifts to be developed! I concur with Ken Hemphill who says, "The impotence of the average Christian and the average church is directly related to the failure to appropriate the empowering of the Spirit of God."[142]

It is vital that we discover our gifts because they "determine, to a great extent, where we will find purpose and make a meaningful contribution in life"[143] as well as "where we can make the greatest contribution through the church for the cause of Christ."[144] If we all have gifts, and we do, then we should discover them and use them.

Who gives spiritual gifts? (vv. 8-10)

The Spirit of God gives spiritual gifts. The work of the Holy Spirit is vital in a believer's life. You cannot be saved except by the Spirit helping you to confess, "Jesus is Lord." Likewise, you cannot be gifted except by the Spirit giving you the gifts God intends for you to have. "The emphasis is upon endowment, not that which a righteous man earns from God, but what a gracious God bestows upon a saved sinner."[145]

We call them spiritual *gifts* for a reason. They are not spiritual payments or spiritual rewards – they are spiritual *gifts.* All gifts are given; no gift is earned or merited. If it is, it's payment or reward, not a gift! Even more, "to identify the receiving of any gift as the evidence or consequence of total commitment is to inject works into the gospel of grace."[146] We are not saved because of our works. Neither are we gifted because of our works. God gives us gifts for the same reason you give anyone a gift – He loves us.

There's also no use praying, pleading, or waiting on some particular gift. Consider again v. 11. Pay special attention to that last phrase, "just as He determines." God gives the gifts He wants to give to whom He wants to give them. We need simply to ask the Lord to show us what our gift is (or gifts are).

Paul uses two different Greek words that mean "spiritual gifts": *pneumatika*, which means "manifestation of the Spirit," and *charismata*, which means "manifestation of grace." This is a corrective of Paul to the Corinthians. Paul prefers *charismata* to *pneumatika* to emphasize that these are grace-gifts. Spiritual gifts are supernatural manifestations of the grace of God working through the power of the Holy Spirit in the believer's life.

The gift says nothing about the gifted; it says everything about the Giver. If you really want to know your gift and experience your gift to its fullest potential, you need to get to know the Giver.

When I was in junior high, my mom and dad gave me a shotgun. It was my first real gun. Oh, I had a B.B. gun, but that didn't count. That thing didn't kill anything but small birds. Until junior high I used my Dad's old .22 when we went squirrel hunting. I wasn't very successful in the hunts, but I sure went through the bullets! That rifle held 15 rounds, and I unloaded on nearly every squirrel. Daddy probably figured it would cost him less to buy me a shotgun than to keep furnishing me with bullets for the .22! The shotgun was great when I opened it, but what I really needed to do was shoot it. So one day during the Christmas holidays, Daddy and I went out to shoot the gun.

We set up targets, and Daddy helped me learn how to use that shotgun effectively. He helped me know about gun safety, loading and unloading the gun, holding the gun properly, aiming properly, etc. I got to know my gift better by spending time with the giver of that gift. (Oh, and my bullet usage did go way down!)

The same happens with our spiritual gifts. God gives us gifts, but we get the most out of those gifts as we spend time with the Giver.

Are all spiritual gifts the same? (vv. 4-10)

Paul makes clear that all spiritual gifts are not the same. Look at his emphasis on differences:

v. 4 – different kinds of gifts
v. 5 – different kinds of service
v. 6 – different kinds of working

There are many gifts. Paul's list here is not meant to be exhaustive. It is representative. Lists like this appear in several places in scripture. Consider the following chart:

New Testament Lists of Spiritual Gifts		
1 Cor. 12:8-10	*1 Cor. 12:28*	*1 Cor. 12:29-30*
Word of wisdom Word of knowledge Faith Healing Miracles Prophecy Distinguishing spirits Tongues Interpreting Tongues	Apostleship Prophecy Teaching Miracles Healing Helps Administration Tongues	Apostleship Prophecy Teaching Miracles Healing Tongues Interpreting Tongues
Romans 12:6-8	*Ephesians 4:11*	*1 Peter 4:11*
Prophecy Service Teaching Exhorting Giving Leading Showing Mercy	Apostleship Prophecy Evangelism Pastor/Teacher	Speaking Serving

While Paul's list in 1 Corinthians is not exhaustive, neither is it haphazard. It is a safe assumption that this list clearly reflects the gifts most eagerly desired by the spirituals in Corinth.[147]

Paul demonstrates that there are all kinds of gifts. There is not one super gift. There is not even a collection of four or five super gifts. There are varieties of gifts, varieties of services, varieties of workings all given by the same God. He gives the gift of wisdom to one and tongues to another. He gives healing to one and prophecy to another. He mixes it up. You may not have the gift of someone else, and that's o.k. In fact, it's best that way.

Why are spiritual gifts given? (v. 7)

While each gift is different, there is something similar about them: every gift benefits everyone. God gives gifts for the common good.

When a wife is given a small kitchen appliance, like a toaster, by her husband for Christmas, she sarcastically thinks, "Whoopee!" Some ladies would like to go "womp!" on their husband's head! Most wives tell their husbands, "Appliances are not gifts." The reason is, while the gift is useful, it's not just for you. It's not like a pair of earrings or a blouse or even a book. It's an appliance that's going to sit in the kitchen and be used by everyone.

Well, spiritual gifts are a bit like a toaster at Christmas. They are given to you, but they benefit everyone. However, before you start thinking, "Well, great. Just when I was thinking a spiritual gift was something special you go and compare it to a toaster!" Hang on! God does still give the gift to *particular* people for *particular* reasons. The gifts themselves are *uniquely* tailored to the makeup of *each* individual. God is not going to give the spiritual gift equivalent of a coffee maker to a person who hates coffee or a mixer to a person who hates to bake. However, if God has wired up a person to love coffee, He's going to give them a spiritual gift that is the top of the line coffee maker. The gift is uniquely suited to the individual, but it benefits everyone.

Spiritual gifts benefit the entire congregation. Jack MacGorman, one of my beloved seminary professors, explained it this way:

> Spiritual gifts are not personal merit badges to mark the levels of achievement in piety. They are not insignia to distinguish God's elite. They are not rewards or trophies. They are not adornment for our private benefit but rather anointment for our joint service. They are divinely distributed powers that relate all members of the congregation together as a vibrant fellowship. Though bestowal is individual ("To each is given the manifestation of the Spirit"), the benefit is congregational ("for the common good").[148]

God calls His followers to do a lot of things. We are to reach up to God in worship, reach out to others in evangelism, grow deeper in discipleship, grow stronger through fellowship, and reach wider through ministry. Thankfully, we are not left on our own to fulfill these roles. The Holy Spirit provides gifts to equip us. Some in the church are gifted for evangelism. Others are gifted for worship, others for discipleship, and still others for fellowship or ministry. But each one's gifts benefit everyone else. Why are the gifts given? For the common good to accomplish God's purposes.

You can drive by a construction site and be quite impressed with the cranes and bull dozers and the massive structure being raised up. Just outside the work zone you can find a sign that reads, "Men at work." For all that wonder, it's just men at work. But whenever you see a church that is fulfilling its mission, advancing, and growing, you don't see just men at work. You see God at work. "There is no greater excitement than being a part of a fellowship where that is taking place."[149] When the chain is strong, useful and effective work will be accomplished.

CHAPTER 27
Without You the Church is ____________
1 Corinthians 12:12-27

What is a church? Certainly, when we hear that question, one thing that comes to mind is a place. You might think of your own local church or the church in which you grew up. Then, as we think about the place, we can't help but think about the people who meet at that place. Faces come to mind of people we loved or simply remember (like that guy with giant ears who sat in front of our family when I was five). As we think a little more about the question, we remember times when the church ministered to us when we were hurting or encouraged us when we were down or celebrated with us when we were joyful or congratulated us when we achieved. The scrapbook of our mind flips open, and the pages fly by us filled with the laughter and tears we have shared with the people of God.

As the place, people, and ministry of the church fills our mind, we soon realize that the church is more than just a random gathering of people who happen to show up at the same place every Sunday. It is an intricately connected, unified, and integrated people – a people so connected, unified, and integrated that they can be called a body – the Body of Christ. You don't get that from the crowd gathered in a stadium, theatre, hall, or gymnasium. You get that from the crowd gathered as the Church.

Paul gives us this picture of the Church in 1 Corinthians 12:12-27. In a day before anyone had ever heard of the Church being a place because no one had a church building to go to, Paul demonstrated what the Church is, the living and active Body of Christ.

Paul gave this image of the Church to help the Corinthians understand his instruction about spiritual gifts. Specifically, he helps them understand how their various gifts unite to form the living, active

Body of Christ, we call a church. As we journey through this text, we see Paul comparing the church to a body.

Like a body, a church is one unit (vv. 12-13).

If everything was not connected in your body, you'd just be a pile of body parts instead of a living and active body. The same is true in the church. How in the world do 50 or 100 or 500 or 10,000 people become one body? The Holy Spirit. "The variety of members are molded into one body by the action of the Spirit"[150]

The Spirit enables *every* believer in an individual experience to confess "Jesus is Lord," and He dispenses gifts to each individual as He wills. In verse 13, Paul emphasizes that the *one Spirit* has brought *all believers* into a *single* body. The emphasis changes from the work of the Spirit *in* an individual believer to His work of making one Body *from* the individual members.[151] The same Spirit who bestows gifts to each individual then brings all those individuals together into one living and active body. Only the Spirit could do such an amazing thing. Who else can take a bunch of different individuals and help them all be one body together? Only the Spirit of God can. (For anyone else, it would be like herding cats!)

Like a body, a church is made of many parts (vv. 14-20).

There were people in Corinth who thought they had the "best" gift or the "most important" gift. Their haughty attitude caused others in the church to think that their own gift was unimportant. Paul says, "Oh no. The body is made of many parts!"

Those members who are the feet of the church might think themselves less important than the hands. After all, the hands are out front. They shake hands. They high five. They mix. They throw. They pick up. So the foot says, "I'm just a stinky foot. I'm outta here."

Paul says, "Wait!" What happens if the foot leaves? The whole body falls over. The body is stuck in one place! While the foot may not be out front as much, it is vital!

The ears could say, "Have you ever heard anyone say, 'Oh what pretty ears you have! No, men have to pull hair out of us. Kids have to get wax cleaned out of us. Ladies stick things in us to try to make us look better. But everyone says, 'Oh what pretty eyes you have!' The eyes get to see things and direct the vision. We ears are outta here!"

Paul says, "Wait! Ears, you are important! What good is it to see a bird, if you can't hear its song? What good is it to see your family, if you can't hear a conversation with them?" Eyes may be important, but, if the whole body were an eye – well, besides being creepy and you just rolling around everywhere – you couldn't hear! And, if the whole body were an ear, can you imagine the size of ear hairs? The parts are different because the body demands diversity in function for unity in action.[152] Every part is different, but we work together to form a living and active body.

Someone might say, "I want to be an eye!", or another, "I want to be a hand!" To that Paul says, "Take that up with God." The church is sovereignly designed. God is always working to shape the church. Every single part is personally gifted and selected for the body at a particular time.

I have seen it happen over and over again. The church needs to step out in missions, and God gifts and raises up someone who has the passion to lead in that endeavor. The church needs finances, and God blesses it with people who practice biblical stewardship and have the gift of giving. The church needs to develop a media ministry, and God sends people with skills and gifts to do that. Whatever God's vision, God gives a provision to the church in spiritual gifts. God assigns and deploys different people for different tasks.

Can you imagine if the church was just one gigantic finance committee? We'd have well-managed money but never teach the word of God! Or what if we were one big hospitality committee? We'd have great food, but never go out on mission. We need everyone just as God has designed.

Whatever your gift, be thankful for it and enjoy it! It's uniquely suited for you. You have been placed in the body by design and for a purpose. You are exactly who God designed you to be. Without you, the church would be lacking. You have been placed in your local body by design and for a purpose. You are exactly who God designed you to be. Without you, the church would be lacking.

We can't be arguing among ourselves about who is most important. The disciples tried that, remember? One day they were arguing about who was the greatest among them. One said, "I am!" Another said, "No, I am." Jesus stopped, sat down, called these grown men together and said, "If any one of you wants to be first, he must be last of all and servant of all" (Mark 9:35). Pow! He hit them right in the nose!

No matter what your gift, no matter whether you're out front (hands) or down below (feet), whether you're celebrated (eyes) or never celebrated (ears), your role is to serve the whole body as a part of the body.

Like a body, a church's parts are interdependent (vv. 21-26)

Just as one member can't consider itself less important and pull away from the body, so another member can't consider itself more important and push others aside.

A big toe is not all that exciting, but it is important. Just get an ingrown toenail, and you'll know how indispensable that toe is! Or how about a tooth? Get a toothache, and you'll find out how indispensable that tooth is. There are numerous things that our body needs and uses that are covered up and seldom, if ever, celebrated.

There are members in the church that are not out front, but they are needed just as much as the people who are out front. There are people who never step foot on the platform but make a tremendous difference in the life of the church.

Dan Colvin was one of those in our church. Mr. Dan was never on the platform or in the lights, but he greeted preschoolers and children every week with a green peppermint and invited young families to church while he was at McDonalds and other places young families hang out. Mr. Dan also did electrical work around the church and kept our air conditioners running. When he died, we had to get a service contract with a local HVAC company. Let me tell you, when we got the bid for that service contract, we realized just how important Mr. Dan had been! Although the people with the out front gifts may think themselves the most valuable and important, sometimes the opposite is true. We need everybody all the time.

I spent five years of my early ministry as a Music Minister. With the church choir, I emphasized that we needed everybody all the time. Now, like any choir, I had some people who were better singers than others. In one choir, I had a choir member who flat couldn't sing. But that person had the absolute best facial expressions during worship. I needed that person in the choir as a worship leader, so I just kept that choir member away from any microphone and let 'em rip! I probably spent a little more time on that somewhat unseemly member, but they were just as vital as those who sang the solos.

Why do we need everybody all the time? There are two reasons in v. 25. First, we do not want there to be any division. Second, we want to be able to care for one another.

How strange it would be for the body to say, "Finger, we don't want you!" and lop it off. Division in the body creates problems for the body. We know about that in the life of a church, don't we? Churches with division are not living and active. They are dying and lethargic. Division is devastating.

When the body is unified, it is living and active. When it is living and active, it can show equal concern for all the members. I love to see that happen in the church, and I see it all the time. I see it when our members post pictures of a large group of church members supporting a member during surgery. I see it when a loved one dies and the calls, cards, food, and visits are sometime more than the grieving person can even manage! I see it when children Sunday School teachers call on their kids and families to encourage them. I see it when a staff member takes extra time with a person who just needs a little extra touch.

I love to see people's reactions, especially when they are new to the whole church thing. I saw a social media post that celebrated what our church was doing for a family having a baby. They shared how grateful they were for the deacon that called on them and the food that their Sunday School class brought them. Do you know what was even greater? The out front guy (a.k.a., me) was there, but it was the deacons and the Sunday School class that got the billing. I loved it! The church is not the pastor. The church is the entire body of Christ!

As I read those social media posts, I realized that if that family had not committed to our particular body of Christ, that deacon would not have known of their need. If they had not plugged into a Sunday

School class, those people would not have known of that need! It is vital for every believer to connect to a local body of believers. In fact, the New Testament assumes membership in a local congregation. The Bible demonstrates that a Christian without a local church is like an organ without a body, a child without a family, or a sheep without a flock. That is a dangerous situation. An organ without a body will die. A sheep without a flock will get eaten by wolves. A child without a family will die in the streets. You need a church home. Pastor and author Ray Ortlund says, "Every believer must be a member of a local body of Christ. When a person becomes a Christian, he or she is already a member of Christ's true body. He or she then needs to identify with and fit in with a real flesh-and-blood people."[153] If you do not have a church home, find one.

You have a part! If you aren't playing your part then, well, we can finally fill in the blank from the chapter title:

Without you, the church is handicapped.

When all parts work in sync in the human body, the result is amazing. But when one part fails to perform for any reason, the whole body is affected. It cannot be all it is supposed to be. There are no prosthetics for the church. There is no physical or occupational therapy. If an essential part is missing, the church is crippled.

The Church needs you. A local church needs you. Are you doing what God has equipped you to do? And are you doing all He has called you to do?"

CHAPTER 28
Keep the Main Thing
1 Corinthians 12:28-31

In his book *Autopsy of a Deceased Church,* Thom Rainer shares five life stages of pastoral tenure.[154] Every pastor knows something akin to these stages exists, but this is the first place I can recall anyone attempting to chart them out. When I first read Rainer's book, I was beginning year six and stage four at our church. I am now nearly through year eleven and well into stage five. Having been through the first four stages, I can testify that the stages have been spot on, though the years might divide out a little differently.

Stage 1: Year 1: Honeymoon

In this stage, the pastor and church are like newlyweds with a blank state. They hope and believe the best about each other. The first year is generally smooth. Unfortunately, that doesn't last forever. At some point, the honeymoon ends. It's natural. It's fine. At that point, the pastor and church begin the second life-stage.

Stage 2: Years 2-3: Conflicts and Challenges

Like any married couple, the church and pastor will eventually face some conflict and challenges. Both the pastor and church discover that neither of them is perfect (well, at least that the other is not perfect!). The spiritual health of both the pastor and the church will determine the severity of the conflicts. Little things can become big things when spiritual health is low, but little things will remain little things if spiritual health is high. If this is the case, the church and pastor can move past them and grow in ministry.

Stage 3: Years 4 and 5: Crossroads, Part One

Rainer says this period is one of the most critical for the relationship. If the conflict was severe, the pastor will likely be forced out or look for a new place of service on his own. Years four and five are the most common years when a pastor leaves a church. On the other hand, if the pastor and the church manage their relationship well, they can often look forward to some of the best years. I would add that it is not always conflict that brings about a pastor's exit during this season. Sometimes, the success of the early years of a pastor's work in the church gains the attention of another church. The pastor may have opportunities to leave during this season. He will have to decide for himself what is God's will. If it is to continue in the present church, he will get to move onto and enjoy stage four.

Stage 4: Years 6 to 10: Fruit and Harvest

Rainer says during this life stage, a church is likely to experience its best years. The church and pastor now trust each other; the plan is in place; the philosophies are adopted; and the church can move forward and then begin to enter stage five.

Stage 5: Years 11 and beyond: Crossroads, Part Two

Few pastors reach this stage because most pastors are called onto another church within the first ten years of service to a church. In fact, in our church's 110 year history, only two pastors have stayed long enough to see this stage. Crossing the eleven year mark does not mean God will never call the pastor onto a different place of ministry, but it becomes less likely because the pastor's ministry at a church is well established, and, when other church's call, the temptation to leave for "greener pastures" is removed and the true will of God becomes far easier to discern that it was in the early days of ministry at the church.

Still, Rainer calls this a second crossroads because at this point the pastor can take one of two paths – he can be reinvigorated as a leader and get ready to tackle new challenges and cast new vision or he can become resistant to change and complacent. The most successful long-tenured pastors lead their churches to do new things during this stage. They are able to build upon the decade-long track record of success and trust they have built with their people and lead them to even greater things.

As I have now journeyed through all five stages in one church, looking back, I would say the way to keep moving forward as a church comes down to four words: keep the main thing.

Keep the main thing.

If any church is to move forward into a new stage of life, they must keep the main thing the main thing. This passage shows us what the main thing should be.

Paul shares a second gifts list. The first list was given back in vv. 8-10. This second list differs from the first in several distinct ways. For one, Paul begins with a numerical order. He says, "First . . ., second . . ., third . . . ." Paul indicates that these three gifts are paramount and then comes everything else. Then notice something else. The first three gifts mentioned are persons rather than abilities.[155] They are functions or ministers rather than gifts themselves.[156] But then, notice one more thing in comparison to the list in vv. 8-10. The first list enumerated only the prized gifts of the spirituals – the visible 'miraculous' ones. In the second list, Paul pulls the top and the bottom out of the first list and expands the accepted definition of spiritual gifts. He adds leadership abilities and service abilities. He shows again how not everyone has the same gift.[157]

Therefore, we have three things Paul hasn't done before: he gives order, emphasizes people, and emphasizes leadership and service. The emphasis on people instead of abilities, order instead of chaos, and leadership and service over the ecstatic and miraculous is a corrective. The corrective is, "You're not keeping the main thing!" Even while Paul has demonstrated that all gifts are vital just as all parts of the body are vital, he shows that there is one thing that needs to be kept primary.

The Corinthians would like to emphasize certain people with the ecstatic gifts. To the Corinthians, those were the most important people in the church. The more razzle dazzle you had, the more spirituality you had. They liked preachers who could overwhelm them with persuasive words and beautiful rhetoric. They liked church members who could demonstrate spiritual gifts that were unusual and mysterious. They wanted ecstasy in the church. Paul demonstrates, however, that ecstasy does not bring efficacy.

Apparently, the most mundane people in the church were the apostles and leaders! They didn't show off their gifts or rhetorical prowess because they were keeping the main thing. Paul shocks the Corinthians by moving the mundane and plain (the apostles, prophets, and teachers) to the top while moving the ecstatic razzle dazzlers to the bottom. In each of his lists, he mentions tongues last as a corrective to the Corinthians. They were emphasizing the wrong thing! Dr. MacGorman says, "It is a trait of immaturity to magnify the minimal and to minimize the 'magnimal'"[158] By deemphasizing the subordinate things, Paul emphasizes the main thing.

What is that main thing?

What do apostles, prophets, and teachers do? They are responsible for the ministry of the word. Therefore, the main thing is the ministry of the word.

The apostles, prophets, and teachers formed a three-fold ministry of the word.[159] If someone walked into your church and said, "Your pastor, staff, and deacons" you would immediately think of the people who fill those roles. Similarly, when Paul mentioned these types of leaders, the Corinthians would have thought of individual people as well.[160]

Paul is saying, "These guys that you criticize, that you do not respect, that you even disregard – they are the ones charged with helping this church keep the main thing!" They are vital for leading the church. Others in the church who you don't respect because their gifts seem rather pedestrian, like the gifts of administration and service, are just as important as you. You have to keep the main thing. No matter what else is happening in the church, the ministry of the word has to be the main thing.

Most of the Corinthians wanted the emphasis on other things. The temptation to do that is still prevalent today. Some churches apparently still haven't read 1 Corinthians because they place undue emphasis on the ecstatic gifts. Let's not be too hard on them, though. The rest of us can be guilty of a similar sin. Perhaps we emphasize music, children or youth ministry, recreation, or mission trips while deemphasizing the ministry of the word.

The problem that comes in churches today is really the same as appears in Corinth – we emphasize a momentary experience instead of a life-long relationship. The Corinthians emphasized the momentary experience generated from ecstatic gifts. Today, we emphasize a momentary worship experience or a missions experience or a children or youth experience. We think that if a church delivers the right experience(s), it's the place to be. But, sadly, in an experience-driven ministry, tomorrow's experience has to one-up today's experience. At some point, you can no longer do that. Consequently, the church crumbles as people try to find that experience somewhere else – either at another church or maybe even outside the church.

Paul says, "You've got it all wrong. Tongues, yes, they are a gift, but they're not the main thing." We might say that worship, missions, children, and youth experiences are great and needed, but they're not the main thing. The ministry of the word is the main thing.

Why is the ministry of the word the main thing?

In his letter to the Ephesians, Paul describes the armor of God. In all of that armor, there is only one piece that is a weapon – the sword of the Spirit. Unlike the other pieces of armor, Paul clarifies exactly what the sword is by saying, "Which is the word of God." We might deduce, then, that the ministry of the word is the main thing because it is the one ministry that stands out in front of the church and says, "Charge!" It is the one ministry that calls the church to advance.

How does the church advance? The writer of Hebrews says in Hebrews 4:12, "For the word of God is living and active. Sharper than any double-edged sword, it penetrates even to dividing soul and spirit, joints and marrow; it judges the thoughts and attitudes of the heart." The word advances by performing surgery. It helps expose problems in the lives of believers and the need for repentance in the lives of the lost. It has the purposes of edification (building up the saints) and evangelism (bring salvation to the lost). The word reminds us of our purpose to go into all the world and make disciples of all nations, baptizing them, and teaching them. The word is involved in evangelism and disciple making. That's why the word is the main thing.

What ministries constitute the ministry of the word in the church today?

The ministry of the word is primarily carried out in two places: the preaching ministry and the teaching ministry. In many churches those ministries are usually carried out in the pulpit and the small group ministry, such as the Sunday School.

Numerous writers have stated that the preaching ministry is vital for the church. Scottish theologian P.T. Forsyth said, "With its preaching Christianity stands or falls." That statement has haunted me since the first time I read it over ten years ago. The stronger the pulpit, the stronger the church. The weaker the pulpit, the weaker the church. However, perhaps my favorite quote comes from Samuel Davies, a colonial Presbyterian pastor of the 18th century:

> [W]hatever contempt the ministerial office has lain under; however much it has been disgraced, and rendered useless, . . . by the unworthy conduct of such as have thrust themselves into it . . . yet, it is in itself. . . the most noble, benevolent, and useful office in the world!
>
> To be the minister of Jesus Christ, the King of kings, and Lord of lords—is a greater honor than to be the most illustrious monarch upon earth! To save souls from death, is a more heroic exploit—than to rescue enslaved nations from oppression and ruin! To make a multitude of wretched, perishing souls—rich with the unsearchable treasures of Christ—is a more generous charity—than to clothe the naked or feed the hungry! To refine depraved men, and improve into a fitness for the exalted employments and enjoyments of heaven—is a higher pitch of patriotism, than to civilize barbarous nations, by introducing the arts and sciences, and a good form of government among them! To negotiate a peace between God and man, and prevent the terrible consequences of

> the unnatural, unequal war, which has so long been waged between them—is a more benevolent and important service than to negotiate a peace between contending nations—to stop the current of human blood, and heal the deadly wounds of war![161]

The pulpit ministry of the church is vital as a part of keeping the main thing.

Sunday School is also vital in a church. Sunday School has a three-fold purpose of reaching people, teaching people, and ministering to people. Every Sunday School teacher has the same tremendous responsibility as the pastor to rightly handle the word of truth.

It is important that every member be a part of a small group. I've found that those members who are engaged in Sunday School grow deeper in their walk with Christ and are more active in the church thereby being more obedient to Christ by using their spiritual gifts.

Why is the ministry of the word so important?

The enemy wants us to put our sword away. He knows that if he can remove our one offensive weapon, he can destroy the church. He knows there is power in the word. He knows that when the word advances, it grows in power. As Acts 19:20 says, "In this way the word of the Lord spread widely and grew in power."

Satan is ever gunning for those who are charged with the ministry of the word in the churches. It does Satan great pleasure to take down a Sunday School teacher or a pastor. All of us can name pastors of small and large ministries who have fallen for one reason or another. When the story breaks and the pastor's life is analyzed, it becomes evident that he had begun not keeping the main thing.

Pray for your pastor. As one of my friends once said, "We're all just one decision away from stupid." Satan comes against God's servants in various ways. Constantly pray a hedge of protection around your pastor and make sure he keeps the main thing.

If any church is to truly see years of fruit and harvest, it won't be because of some impressive building program. It won't be because they have cutting-edge music, children, and youth ministries. It won't be because they have broad reaching missions. It will be because they are keeping the main thing – the ministry of the word.

CHAPTER 29
If You Really Want What is Best . . .
1 Corinthians 13:1-13

It happens numerous times a year – the flowers, the dresses, the tuxes, the music: a wedding. The pastor stands and says, "Dearly beloved we are gathered here today . . . ."

After the opening remarks and the couple has made their way to the platform, there is often a scripture reading. That reading is usually 1 Corinthians 13:1-13.

This text is often called "the love chapter." Certainly, this is one of the most beautiful pieces of scripture and fitting for the setting of a wedding. Therefore, it may be surprising to learn that this text is more appropriate at an ugly church business meeting than at a beautiful church wedding!

Could you imagine a terrible business meeting with people fuming, sides developing, and then someone stands up and starts reading "the love chapter"? It would be appropriate because, unfortunately, "in all religious controversy, love is an early casualty."[162] I don't understand why that is, but church people can become the most unloving people when controversy develops. Whether the controversy involves a serious theological controversy or a petty carpet color controversy, whenever arguments develop, love goes out the window.

In his little book *I am a Church Member*, Thom Rainer says, "If we could just abide by the principles of the love chapter, we would have completely healthy churches. It would be a revolution."[163] No doubt, living 1 Corinthians 13 would bring revival to many churches. There is far more than sentimentalism packed into this passage.

The original context of the love chapter is the controversy over spiritual gifts in the Church at Corinth. As we have seen, there was a severe conflict between those who thought themselves to be super-spiritual because they possessed the ecstatic gifts and those who possessed the seemingly more mundane gifts. So far, Paul has demonstrated that every gift is important and given by God to benefit the entire body. Further, the church must keep the main thing of the ministry of the word in its proper place.

The way Paul says all of this is important. Paul writes in such a way as to meet the spirituals on their own ground.[164] These church members loved to boast in their wisdom; therefore, Paul pulls out the big guns and displays his own prowess at wisdom teaching by crafting one of the most beautiful passages of wisdom literature in the Bible. The spirituals had attacked Paul because his preaching lacked persuasive words of wisdom. Ironically, Paul now uses persuasive words of wisdom to express his own pointed correction.[165]

Through his beautiful language, Paul shows us that if you really want what is best you need to live love. We can glean three important truths about love from this passage.

Love is necessary (vv. 1-3).

Paul sets up some scenarios. First, he says, "Say I *can* speak in the tongues of both men and angels. That is wonderful. However, if I can do that but don't have love, I'm just a noisy gong or a clanging cymbal."

The pagan worship of Paul's day used gongs and cymbals. It was loud, non-melodious, and pointless. Without love, even the tongues of angels is useless.

Then Paul says, "Or what if I have the gift of prophecy and I can go far beyond anyone. I can understand all mysteries. I possess all knowledge. I have faith that can literally move mountains! Even if I am some kind of super-prophet, if I don't have love, I am – what? Nothing."

No one could understand all mysteries, have all knowledge, and have all faith. But if it were possible to be that type of super-prophet, and you did not exercise these gifts in love, all of that knowledge would be nothing.

Paul continues, "And what if I went radical. What if I sold every last thing I have, gave it to the poor and then died as a martyr for the faith. I mean that is something, right? Not really. Not without love. Without love even total sacrifice is nothing."

Nothing. Nothing. Nothing. Without love. Because love is necessary.

The spirituals said that a truly spiritual person possesses certain gifts. Paul says that a truly spiritual person possesses love. The true test of a spiritual person is not some specific gift, it is love. Everything else grows out of love. Romans 5:5 echoes this point, "And hope does not disappoint us, because God has poured out His love into our hearts by the Holy Spirit, whom He has given us." "Love is the one sure sign of the indwelling presence of the Holy Spirit . . . . For that reason, you will find a remarkable similarity between love in this chapter and the fruit of the Spirit in Galatians 5."[166] The same Spirit who puts love on the inside will cause us to live love on the outside.

It can be tempting to look at what comes out instead of what is at the source. We can be tempted to be wowed by works – either from ourselves or from others. Instead, what we should be looking at is whether or not those works come from a fountain of love. If they do not come from love, then whatever the work – no matter how great it may be – it is nothing. Love is necessary.

Love is active (vv. 4-7).

Paul uses fifteen verbs to demonstrate both what love is and what love is not. We see clearly that love is not feeling; it is doing. Love is not an emotion. It is an action. "As great as 1 Corinthians 13 is, it nowhere provides a definition of love. Instead Paul [describes] some of the things that love does and does not do."[167]

Let's walk through these fifteen verbs and feel the emphasis Paul gives them.[168] We will take the seven positive statements together followed by the eight negative statements.

There are seven things love does:

1. *Love is patient.* A better translations may be, "Love suffers long." Even though it may be strongly provoked, love is slow to anger. It is not short-tempered. It is long-tempered.

2. *Love is kind.* Better, "Love acts kindly." It puts others first. It takes their feelings into account. It honors them.
3. *Love rejoices in the truth.* Love does not rejoice in wickedness or wrongdoing of any kind. However, when truth is shared, proclaimed, and stood for, love rejoices.
4. *Love always protects.* Scholars debated the exact meaning of this verb. However, it can carry the idea of love covering a multitude of sins (1 Peter 4:8) or the idea of taking things on so that the work of the Lord can continue. Whatever the case, love protects. It stands in the gap.
5. *Love always trusts.* It believes all things. "This does not mean that it is gullible . . . for love is intelligent and discerning. But it provides a prevailing attitude of trust."[169] It believes the best of people. MacGorman writes, "To be sure, love will be frustrated at times, as those upon whom it relies set little value upon it. But it is better to believe in others and be deceived by some than to go through life suspicious of all. Besides trust has a way of creating trustworthiness in those who incline to falter."[170]
6. *Love always hopes.* It is easy to fall into despair, but love calls forth hope. First Peter 1:3 reminds us of our hope, "Praise be to the God and Father of our Lord Jesus Christ! In his great mercy he has given us new birth into a living hope through the resurrection of Jesus Christ from the dead."
7. *Love always perseveres.* Love endures all things. The word literally means "remain under." It carries the idea of being under a heavy load. "It is endurance under pressure without collapsing."[171] Love pushes, goes the distance, does whatever it takes.

Next, Paul lists eight things love does not do:

1. *Love does not envy.* Love will not want what others have and pity what one does have.
2. *Love does not boast.* Whereas some might want what others have, others might think they have what others want!
3. *Love does not become prideful.* Knowledge puffs up whereas love builds up. The point is, you still go up, but in a different way!

4. *Love does not behave rudely.* Love understands what is fitting and proper. It is courteous. It is wise.
5. *Love does not seek its own advantage.* How can it when it puts others first? Elsewhere Paul instructs that we are never to seek our own good, but the good of our neighbor (Phil. 2:4).
6. *Love does not become easily angered.* Love does not lose its temper.
7. *Love does not keep a record of wrongs.* This is an accounting term. Don't we like to keep that ledger sometimes of every offense people make against us? Love doesn't do that. When love forgives, it forgets. Once forgiveness is granted, the offense is forgotten.
8. *Love does not rejoice in evil.* Wickedness leads to disaster. Love knows that so love avoids it.

Everything love does, the Corinthians didn't do. Everything love doesn't do; the Corinthians were doing. They were envious of one another. They boasted about their gifts. They were prideful about their gifts. They treated each other rudely at the Lord's Table. They sought to one up one another. They got angry at one another, remembered wrongs, and stirred up trouble. What was worse, they liked it! What a problematic place!

Paul skillfully takes the beautiful words of men's wisdom the Corinthians' loved and crafted a passage we still find beautiful enough to accompany the flowers, music, dresses, and tuxes of weddings – and punches them right in the spiritual stomach!

How easy it is to fall into these traps. How easy it is to practice what love is not instead of what love is in the church, in our marriages, and in our families. We should pause long at this description and say, "God, forgive me for when I have not allowed the Spirit to bring forth true love." If you want to see revival in your life, in your church, in your marriage or in your family, live love.

Love is supreme (vv. 8-13).

The other gifts will come to an end. The spiritual gifts, whether tongues or prophecy or helps or administration or hospitality, are temporary. They are meant to enable the church to function as the

Body of Christ in this time in which we live. Beyond this time, there will no longer be any need for the Holy Spirit to bestow these gifts.[172]

When Jesus returns, prophecies will cease, tongues will be stilled, and knowledge will pass away because on that day prophecies will be realized, everyone will understand one another heart to heart, and knowledge will be perfect. As Paul says, "When the perfect comes, the imperfect disappears." We will be grown up, fully matured. The gifts are partial now, but then everything will be complete. Everything, that is, except love. Because love is full and complete now. If you want what is best, live love. Love is supreme. Everything else will end, but love will last forever.

Some people have taken Paul's teaching to mean that the gifts such as tongues, prophecy, and knowledge ended in the apostolic age. Those who take this position press the tense of the verb to demonstrate that though the Holy Spirit bestowed the gift of tongues on some in the apostolic age, as in Corinth, He has not bestowed it on any others since the end of that age.[173] These interpreters also typically take the statement "when the perfect comes" to refer to the closing of the canon of scripture. Therefore, while they may concede that gifts may have existed past the time of the apostles, these people think the more expressive gifts ended when the canon of scripture was closed.

Many competent scholars takes this view. While I understand their emphasis, I do not hold it. You cannot press one Greek verb that far. Jack MacGorman explained, "To inject canonical considerations into Paul's instruction of the Corinthians is remarkably farfetched."[174] The context suggests that it is the return of Christ that will mark the termination of the charismatic gifts, not something before it. There is nothing to indicate that the gifts ended in the apostolic age or when the canon closed. Until Christ returns, "the sovereign Spirit of God is apt to bestow any and all of them as He sees fit – and fortunately without consulting us."[175]

Some, but certainly not all, who take the cessationist approach do so because they do not have these gifts themselves or are leery of these gifts. Unquestionably, we need to be careful with the more expressive gifts. However, please don't let your lack of having the gift or your fear of the gift limit the work of God in your life or the church's life. The day of God's power has not ceased. God gives the gifts, can give the gifts, and wants to give the gifts when He wants, where He wants, and how He wants.

Some may say, "I do not have that gift." That may be no big deal, and, then again, it may be a big deal. There are two reasons a person may not have certain gifts.[176] First, they may not be close enough to God. Every gift flows out of relationship with God. If your gifts are limited, your relationship with God may be limited. That's a big deal. Second, if they are close to God, they may not need the gift. Perhaps God does not see the need to bestow this gift upon the person. This is not a big deal. God will give us any of the spiritual gifts when He thinks we need them as we walk in fellowship with Him.

Don't fret over trying to get a certain gift. If you want what is best, run after love. Love is greater than all the gifts because it is eternal, and they are temporal. "Even of those graces that shall abide forever – faith, hope, and love – love is the greatest."[177] If you really want what is best, live love.

The next time you are at a wedding, and you get a review in 1 Corinthians 13, ask the Lord to give that couple that kind of love, but even more, ask God to give you that kind of love so that you can have what is best.

CHAPTER 30
The Gift and Purpose You Should Desire
1 Corinthians 14:1-40

When a church gathers for worship, the people should be able to participate in a meaningful way, understand what is happening, be enriched by their experience, and leave having met with God.

Unfortunately, we can get distracted in purpose when it comes to worship. Too often, we worship to make ourselves happy, and, even though we would never state it, we could care less if we make God happy. Such a view of worship is as old as worship itself. We see the problem in the Old Testament. We see it in the New Testament. Certainly, we see it in the Church at Corinth.

Chapter 14 concludes Paul's three chapter corrective on spiritual gifts. Chapter 12 emphasized unity. Chapter 13 emphasized love. Chapter 14 emphasizes purpose. As you live love as a functioning body, make sure a singular purpose is maintained.

When the Corinthians gathered to worship, many of them gathered for themselves. Some of them came to worship and exercised their gifts so people would be amazed, congratulate them, celebrate them, and they could feel good. Paul has a strong corrective to the church in this chapter, "Let me tell you about the gift and purpose you should desire. The gift is prophecy. The purpose is to build up the church."

Continuing to deal with an overemphasis on tongue speaking in Corinth, Paul makes clear that both speaking in tongues and prophecy are valid gifts, but they are by no means of equal purpose in the ministries of the church. Prophecy is to be desired above tongues because prophecy edifies the church.

Paul addresses the issue as one who has both the gifts of prophecy and tongues. Therefore, Paul is able to assess the value and purposes of each of the gifts in the church from the vantage-point of personal experience.[178]

We should desire the gift of prophecy because prophecy benefits the church (vv. 1-19).

Paul compares tongues and prophecy. When a person exercises the gift of tongues, he speaks to God. No human understands him because it is an unidentifiable language. He utters mysteries in the content of his speech. But when a person exercises the gift of prophecy, he speaks to men from God. These men understand and are strengthened, encouraged, and comforted. Therefore, the tongues speaker edifies himself whereas the prophet edifies the church.

Is it necessarily bad that a tongues speaker edifies only himself? No. The individual Christian needs to be enriched in his or her walk with God. A person's spiritual life needs to grow. From a church-wide perspective, however, prophecy is superior to tongues because tongues is more helpful for edifying the entire church body.

Paul isn't against tongues, but neither is Paul saying that everyone in the church should speak in tongues. If you pull this one part of a verse out of context, you might think that. But we do not do biblical interpretation by pulling and picking. We take things in context. If we read the entire context of chapters 12-14, there is no way Paul is appealing for everyone to speak in tongues. For one, Paul makes clear in this chapter that no one has all the gifts nor is there one gift that all possess. Further, Paul does far more to settle down the tongues speakers than he does to stir them to action. [179] Paul would rather the people prophesy because that is intelligible.

Using three illustrations, Paul explains how the gift of tongues fails to edify the entire church (vv. 7-11). Paul's explanation sounds something like this:

> What if I were to pick up a harp or a flute and just start playing. I can strum that harp. I can make that flute squeak, but if I do not play a tune with distinction of notes, it's just noise. No one gets anything out of it. It can't help them relax or worship or anything.

> If someone asks, "What did he play?" The listener will say, "A bunch of useless noise."
>
> And what if an army needs to call its forces to attention, but the bugle player can't play. The army won't hear the clear call. If they don't hear the distinct notes they need, they will not respond. They could be run over and defeated!
>
> Or consider the spoken languages of the world – there are some 6,500. Each one has its meaning. But what if I go to Russia and attend a church service conducted in Russian but I don't speak Russian. The people around me may nod with understanding, laugh, or even weep. But all I will hear is noise because I do not understand Russian. I will not nod, laugh, or weep. I will leave empty, having gotten nothing out of the service.

With these illustrations Paul explains how speaking in tongues contributes nothing to the rest of the congregation gathered for public worship. Therefore, Paul encourages the pursuit of prophecy.

Someone might rightly ask, "What if I have the gift of tongues? Can I use it appropriately?" Paul's answer is, "Yes" (vv. 13-17). If someone has the gift of tongues, they need to pray for the ability to interpret. If they can interpret, they could share an edifying word. The ability to interpret still does not elevate tongues to the level of prophecy, but at least the church can understand. However, the speaker should speak only the intelligible meaning to the church.

Don't we want everyone in worship to be edified and not just some individuals? Don't we want the Lord to be glorified and not merely ourselves? Yes, yes, a thousand times yes! We want everyone to come to worship, to hear, to understand, and to say, "Amen! I agree! So be it!" We do not want them to come only to be confused, and say, "What in the world was that!?"

Paul continues with a statement that would have made the tongue speakers say, "Wait? What?!"

> ***1 Corinthians 14:18-19*** *I thank God that I speak in tongues more than all of you.* [19] *But in the church I would rather speak five intelligible words to instruct others than ten thousand words in a tongue.*

That statement would have caused the tongues speakers in Corinth to look at each other and say, "Paul speaks in tongues? We've never seen him do that!"

Paul says, "Newsflash, folks. I do! You don't know about my tongue speaking because I don't flaunt it. In the church, I speak intelligible words because that is what instructs and builds up the church." The gift each of us should desire is prophecy because it benefits the church.

We should desire the gift of prophecy because prophecy reaches people with the gospel (vv. 20-25).

Paul sets up a scenario of two churches. At the first church everyone is speaking in tongues. No one can understand anyone else. Into that worship service someone who is interested in the faith comes. What is going to be their reaction? "Let's get out of here! These people are crazy!" Consequently, you could potentially lose the opportunity to share the gospel!

At the second church the people are prophesying. Into this church walks the same person who is interested in the faith. Immediately, he hears words he understands. He can hear the same truth from everyone and be convinced of his need for the gospel. When that happens, he will fall down and say, "God is among you!"

How different the reactions of the two scenes! One says, "I've got to get out of here!" The other says, "I've got to stay here!"

The super-spirituals thought it would be the other way around. They thought if everyone was speaking in tongues and someone came in, the person would be amazed, and say, "God is here!" Paul says, "No, it's the other way around. What you think will win people, runs them away. What you think is too plain, draws people in."

The super-spirituals may have preferred tongues to prophecy for another reason they may not even have realized. If all they did was come to church and speak in tongues and never hear a word of prophecy, they could have a service of religious ecstasy and go home saying, "What a great service. We're so spiritual and holy!" But if the word of prophecy was spoken, they might find themselves being corrected, rebuked, or instructed in some way and find out that they weren't so holy after all! Since that would hurt, they avoided prophecy.

In this passage we see the power that a worship service has for evangelism. Notice what happens to the person who comes into the service where prophecy is prominent. First, he is convicted by the witness of all. Everywhere he looks he sees and hears people who are passionate about their God and His word. Second, the secrets or hidden things of his heart are exposed. The Holy Spirit is free to lay open the truth of his life. No one can see themselves as they really are until they get close to the reflective glory of the Lord. Then they say, "Woe is me." Third, convinced of his sin, he is convicted of his sin and falls on his face before God in worship. Having seen consistent witness and heard truth and having been touched by the Spirit, he worships God. Fourth, he joins in the worship, "God is in this place!" From unbelief to conviction to confession to worship – all in one service.[180]

Isn't that the worship for which we aim? Where someone can come in, look around, listen up, and be transformed by the power of God's word that is proclaimed in our words and in our lives?

We should desire the gift of prophecy because order is important in worship (vv. 26-40).

Paul describes a worship service to which everyone comes with something to share and do. They all have gifts that need to be used. They all have things to contribute, and they all should be and need to be contributed. There is one reminder: not everyone can do everything at once. That would be chaos.

Do you know that sound just before a symphony concert when everyone is warming up? You hear runs of notes and portions of the symphony to be played. A flute plays some notes in one key. An oboe plays something else in another. A violin plays something even different. It's a cacophony of sound. I actually like listening to it, and, if it is a familiar piece, challenging myself to pick out different parts of the score. However, that cacophony is only good for those few minutes before the concert begins. If the whole concert was like that, it would be a mess. There has to be order.

In our church there is what I call "the holy buzz" before worship starts. The holy buzz is that time when everyone is talking and greeting one another. I love that sound! Sometimes the holy buzz is so loud, I get caught on the other side of the sanctuary from my seat as the music starts! That exciting time of joy of everyone being together is wonderful, but the whole worship service can't be like that. There has to be order.

Not everyone can do everything at once. That would be chaos. Therefore, Paul gives instruction to provide order in worship. We won't deal with this in detail, but let's notice the orderly guidelines Paul provides.

Paul focuses on three problem areas in the Corinthian's worship: tongues, prophecy, and women. He deals with the tongues speakers first. Next, he moves to those prophesying. Finally, he deals with the women. Remember that there was a problem in that church with what the women were doing, so Paul is extra careful in calling for the women to have a limited role in that particular church. Much of Paul's instruction is based on the practice of the Jewish synagogue at the time. After dealing with these three problem areas in worship, Paul makes a final appeal, encouraging those who are truly spiritual discerning to take his words as from the Lord.

Notice how Paul summarizes his argument:

> ***1 Corinthians 14:39-40*** *Therefore, my brothers, be eager to prophesy, and do not forbid speaking in tongues.* [40] *But everything should be done in a fitting and orderly way.*

People should desire the gift of prophecy in worship because it builds up the church. The saints can be edified and the sinners can be evangelized. However, tongues should not be forbidden. Everything should be done in an orderly way.

Order is important to corporate worship. We enter, worship, and leave. Even in that, there is order. Worship is a conversation with God. A meaningful conversation requires order to be understood. You can't just say random words to someone and expect to carry on a conversation! Neither can you both speak at the same time. Like a good conversation with a friend, a service of worship should take on a certain order of good communication as we communicate with God and our fellow man. If everyone does whatever he wants, things get confusing fast. You can also start worshiping just to benefit yourself, glorify yourself, and feel good yourself. But that's not the point of worship. Furthermore, focusing on you does not make God happy.

Worship should glorify God and build up the church. When we leave corporate worship, we should be so full of the Lord that through the remaining days of the week, the world will be revolutionized.

CHAPTER 31
The Simple Gospel
1 Corinthians 15:1-11

My maternal grandma often wondered about random things. She once asked me, "Stew, when did cake mixes come about?" We were trying to figure it out until I said, "Wait a second!" I pulled out my phone and did a quick internet search. We discovered someone started experimenting with cake mix back in the 1930s, but mixes really caught on in the post-war era with all those housewives like my grandma who wanted to cook meals but needed to do it simpler.

Because our world and schedules are often complex, people want things simpler. Simplicity has been part of the success of Google and Apple. They endeavor for their platforms to be clear, clean, and simple.

For all the simple innovations we experience, can I let you in on something? God is the true author of simple. Oh, don't get me wrong; He can do complex – just look at the world, the human body, an insect, the ocean, the planets, and more. But God also does simple – and perhaps one of the simplest things is at the core of our faith: the Gospel.

News is simple headlines, intriguing sound bites, and captivating images. News is now, relevant, and needed. The Good News is that way too! The Gospel has always been a simple headline with intriguing sound bites and captivating images. Though it is 2000 years old, it is still now, relevant, and needed!

In 1 Corinthians 15:1-11, Paul begins a new section of his letter on the resurrection. Here Paul talks about the resurrection of Christ, the resurrection of the dead, and the resurrection of the body.

What is resurrection? It is "a creative act of God whereby the bodies of dead people are raised to life." It is the ultimate miracle, the reversal of everything we know to be normal.

Resurrection is a big deal for Christians. In fact, it is the central and distinct affirmation of the Christian faith. It is *central* because without the resurrection, we have no faith. It is *distinct* because no other religion has any such teaching.[181] First Corinthians 15 is "the fullest and most important treatment in the Bible on the doctrine of the resurrection of the dead."[182] For that reason it has been called one of the ten greatest chapters of the Bible.[183]

Why did Paul need to write this chapter to the Church at Corinth? For the same reason he had to write most of what he did to that church – they had problems! One of their problems had to do with the resurrection. We have to skip down to v. 12 to see the problem stated:

> ***1 Corinthians 15:12*** *But if it is preached that Christ has been raised from the dead, how can some of you say that there is no resurrection of the dead?*

Though it had been preached to them that Jesus Christ was raised from the dead, some people in Corinth were saying there was no resurrection. Due to a lack of information, we cannot be certain as to the exact nature of their denial. Some Corinthians may have not believed the body could be raised. Others may have thought they had already experienced a spiritual resurrection. Some may have even thought Paul was speaking about two different gods (Jesus and Anastasis – the Greek word for resurrection).[184] Whatever their reasoning, it was wrong. Therefore, Paul sought to refute their denial of the resurrection in this lengthy chapter.[185]

Paul begins with a simple restatement of the gospel to establish the certainty of the resurrection. In vv. 1-11, Paul declares several important truths about the simple gospel.

The simple gospel saves (vv. 1-2).

Paul reminds the people of the process they have been through regarding the simple gospel. First, Paul had preached it to them. The word for "preach" here is a word meaning "to herald or announce." It is like a person saying, "Hear ye! Hear ye! I have good news to tell." Paul had announced the good news to them. They had not received the message second hand, and they had not been given a wrong message. He had preached the right gospel to them himself during his year and a half stay with them during his second missionary journey.

Second, the Corinthians had received the gospel. The word we translate "receive" means "to accept a tradition as it is handed to you from a teacher." Paul had passed on the simple gospel, and the Corinthians had readily accepted it in its entirety.[186]

Third, the Corinthians had taken a stand upon the gospel. The tense of the verb is such that it means they stood firm upon it. So Paul reminds them that they heard the simple gospel, received it, and stood firm upon it. Don't miss Paul's implication, "If you deny the resurrection, you deny the very thing upon which you are now standing! If you take the resurrection out of your faith, you have no faith."

Fourth, this gospel had saved them. There is power in this simple gospel. It was "by this gospel" they were saved. Or, more correctly, being saved, because there is continuous action in the Greek suggesting progressive growth in grace. Then Paul adds a condition, "If you hold firmly to the word I preached to you," true faith will continue.

Received – looks to the past.
Stand – looks at the present.
Saved – looks to the future .

In reminding the Corinthians of what had happened to them, Paul reminds them that this simple gospel saves. In fact, it had saved them! Paul had preached it, they had received it, stood upon it, and were saved by it! The simple gospel is the power of salvation for anyone who believes.

The simple gospel is clear (vv. 3-8).

This may be the earliest existing account of the resurrection of Jesus Christ. Paul wrote this letter within 20-30 years of the event itself. That's not long at all. That's like me telling you about my senior year of high school. For today's high school students, that's ancient history, but for most of us, that wasn't long ago.

In this early account of the resurrection, Paul shares four simple facts of the gospel. These four simple facts make up Paul's four-point gospel sermon. First, Christ died for our sins according to the scriptures. Paul doesn't just say Christ died. He reminds us why Jesus died – for our sins. That death was according to the scriptures. In referring to the scriptures, Paul means the Old Testament. Does the Old Testament really say that much about Christ dying for our sins? Well, consider these passages:

> ***Genesis 3:15*** *And I will put enmity between you and the woman, and between your offspring and hers; he will crush your head, and you will strike his heel."*
>
> ***Isaiah 53:5*** *But he was pierced for our transgressions, he was crushed for our iniquities; the punishment that brought us peace was upon him, and by his wounds we are healed.*
>
> ***Zechariah 12:10*** *And I will pour out on the house of David and the inhabitants of Jerusalem a spirit of grace and supplication. They will look on me, the one they have pierced, and they will mourn for him as one mourns for an only child, and grieve bitterly for him as one grieves for a firstborn son.*

Consider also the entire sacrificial system that continually and consistently pointed to the need for an ultimate blood sacrifice to cover sin. Why was blood sacrifice needed? Because death is in sin, but life is in blood. Therefore, the most precious thing of life is needed to cover death. When Jesus died, the blood of the greatest life was spilled over all the sins of all the world, the greatest death.

Second, Christ was buried. Paul probably includes this often not included detail to affirm the death. He was so dead he had to be buried.

Now, if Jesus had stayed in the tomb, we would have no reason to be talking about Him. A dead and buried Jesus is nothing – no matter what else He said or did. But, thankfully, there's more to the story. Third, Christ was raised according to the scriptures. While Christ's death as the ultimate sacrifice was prophesied, that wasn't all that was prophesied. The scriptures also told of this triumph of resurrection:

> ***Isaiah 53:10*** *Yet it was the LORD's will to crush him and cause him to suffer, and though the LORD makes his life a guilt offering, he will see his offspring and prolong his days, and the will of the LORD will prosper in his hand.*

> ***Psalm 16:9-11*** *Therefore my heart is glad and my tongue rejoices; my body also will rest secure, [10] because you will not abandon me to the grave, nor will you let your Holy One see decay. [11] You have made known to me the path of life; you will fill me with joy in your presence, with eternal pleasures at your right hand.*

We do not serve a dead man. We serve a living Lord. "In that very body, transformed indeed and adjusted to its eternal form of existence, Jesus emerged from the tomb never to die again."[187] And still there was more! Jesus wasn't just raised and then gone. He let people know He was alive!

Fourth, Christ appeared to numerous witnesses. Jesus appeared to Peter and the apostles. He appeared to 500 disciples, most of whom in Paul's time, at the moment he was writing the letter, were still living! They were telling their children and grandchildren and great-grandchildren about that event. Amazing! Each of these people to whom Jesus appeared believed, received the good news, stood on the good news, and were saved because of the good news!

The simple gospel changes you (vv. 9-11).

> ***1 Corinthians 15:9-11*** *For I am the least of the apostles and do not even deserve to be called an apostle, because I persecuted the church of God. [10] But by the grace of God I am what I am, and his grace to me was not without effect. No, I worked harder than all of them--yet not I, but the grace of God that was with me. [11] Whether, then, it was I or they, this is what we preach, and this is what you believed.*

Before he met Jesus, Paul (Saul) hated Jesus and Christians. He was a terrorist against believers – throwing them in jail, killing them, doing whatever it took to stop this religious sect from gaining any momentum – until one day on the road to Damascus. While Saul was on his way to do more of the same, the resurrected Jesus appeared and radically changed Saul's life. "Why do you persecute me?" Jesus asked. Jesus got Saul's attention, and the change began. Saul became Paul. The persecutor became the proclaimer. The murdered became the life giver. The imprisoner became the releaser.

The simple gospel changes. The one who doesn't believe is transformed into the one who does. The one who can't understand becomes the one who explains.

The gospel changes a person because of grace. Grace is when God gives you what you do not deserve. Because of your sin, you deserve death, but God gives you life when you receive the simple gospel. Paul received that life through grace, and he couldn't get over the change it brought in him!

God's grace is so rich and so far reaching. It is also so desperately needed. Romans 3:23 says that all have sinned and fall short of the glory of God. All of us fit into the sinner category. Even though many of us are good people, we still sin and fall short of the glory of God. Therefore, even the best of us still need God's grace.

If you were to stand before God and He were to ask you, "Why should I let you into heaven?" An answer of, "I lived a good life" won't cut it. The only thing that will cut it is if you can stand before God and say, "I have been radically changed by the simple gospel. I am a sinner saved by grace. I have repented of my sins and placed my complete and total faith in Jesus Christ as my Savior. I have followed him as Lord. I know He died for my sins on the cross. He was buried. He was raised, and He has now come into my life. I receive that gospel, stand upon that gospel, and am saved by that gospel." Then with that simple affirmation of the simple gospel, God will say, "Welcome home, my child."

Simple is powerful. Water is simple. Pure water doesn't have a taste. It doesn't have a smell. It doesn't have any color. It is about as simple as you can get. But without water you die.

Friend, the gospel is simple. But without it you die, not just a physical death but a spiritual eternal death. The simple gospel is the power of salvation for anyone who believes – will you believe?

CHAPTER 32
The Consequences of Denying the Resurrection[188]
1 Corinthians 15:12-19

What if the resurrection is not true? What if the apostles just made up the resurrection? What if the cross is true, but the resurrection is not?

Have you ever asked those questions? It's o.k. to do so. It's o.k. to wonder. There were people in Corinth wondering about the truth of the resurrection. Some were confused by the truth. Some were denying the truth. Some just had a hard time believing the truth. Even though Paul had stated the gospel simply and clearly, sometimes the simplest things are the hardest to believe. In this passage, Paul says, "Let's grant that there is no resurrection. What are the ramifications of that?"

If there is no resurrection of the dead, not even Christ has been raised (vv. 12-13).

Though they had been taught about the resurrection of the dead, some people were saying it could not be. First, the resurrection was incredible. It was hard to believe. They had seen dead people. You don't come back from that. Second, it was improbable. It was unlikely. How would a dead person be raised to life? Third, it was impossible. It could not happen. There's no way a dead person can be raised to life. Since the resurrection of the dead seems incredible, improbable, and impossible, people were saying, "There is no resurrection of the dead."

But if there is no resurrection of the dead, we have a problem. Things quickly start to unravel. For, if there is no resurrection, then Jesus could not have been raised. "If dead men don't rise, then Jesus is still dead."[189] If there is no resurrection of the dead, then that most significant resurrection of the dead could not have happened. The two go together since the one is the first fruits of the other. Jesus' resurrection paved the way for future resurrections. The resurrection was not a test case but the event that makes all else possible.

If Jesus has not been raised, His body is somewhere on the earth hidden away. That was the lie the chief priests and elders circulated among the people after Jesus' resurrection. But what if it *is* true? Then you have a big problem that spirals out of control.

If Christ is not raised, our preaching is pointless (vv. 14-16).

The word translated "useless" means "hollow, empty, meaningless, void of all truth, reality, and power."[190] If Christ has not been raised, then what I spend hours each week preparing to do every Sunday is useless and pointless.

Preaching can be partially defined as the oral proclamation of God's truth revealed in scripture. If there is no truth revealed in scripture, then preaching is the oral proclamation of what? If it isn't truth then it has to be a lie. In fact, it must be the grandest lie in history.

If Jesus Christ is not raised, then every Christian preacher is a false witness. For 2000 years preachers have stood before millions of trusting, well-meaning people and lied about the foundation of the faith! If the resurrection is not true, we have a big problem!

If Christ is not raised, our faith is worthless and there is no forgiveness of sin (v. 17).

If there is no resurrection, Christ is not raised. If Christ is not raised, He is still dead somewhere. If He is still dead somewhere, then the whole foundation of our preaching is a pointless lie. And, if the foundation of our preaching is a pointless lie, all those millions of trusting, well-meaning people who have heard this pointless lie for 2000 years have a faith that is worthless. That means there is no forgiveness of sin.

The word we translate "worthless" means "lacking in results." There's nothing to show for it. Therefore, there is no forgiveness of sins. No matter what anyone has ever told you about being able to be forgiven of your sins, forget it. You still bear every sin you ever committed. You're not forgiven, and you cannot be forgiven. Oh, Jesus may have died on the cross, but, without the resurrection, Jesus is just another dead good man. He may be worthy of a plaque or a statue but nothing more. If Jesus Christ is not raised, He didn't accomplish anything for anybody past His own life. His death was worthless and had no redemptive power. We are still in an awful fix, falling short of the glory of God because of our sins and facing death as the wages of our sin with no hope in sight.

If Christ is not raised, there is no hope that our loved ones will be raised (v. 18).

"Fallen asleep" is a euphemism for death. To fall asleep in Christ is to die believing in Him. However, if Christ has not been raised, there is no redemption. We will stand before the judgment seat of God on our own. There will be no advocate. No one will take our place. We will be guilty, and, therefore, we will be condemned. For eternity, heaven will be empty except for God and the angels, and hell will be full of every human who has ever lived. There will be no hope in death. Death will have victory, sin will have triumphed, and Satan will be king.

When I pray for a person who is about to step into glory or pray with a family after the death of a loved one or as I preach the funeral message for those people, the only reason I can possibly offer any hope to the family is because I know that my Redeemer lives, and that in the end He will stand upon the earth (Job 19:25). If that is not true, then every time I face a funeral, I face "death without hope"[191] I couldn't take funerals if there was no hope. None of us could take the losses in our lives if there was no hope of seeing our loved ones again in heaven because of their faith and our faith in Jesus Christ. But, if Christ is not raised, then there is no hope that our loved ones will be raised either. (Isn't this chapter encouraging? Don't give up, keep reading!)

If Christ is not raised, this world is it, and we are deceived (v. 19).

If Christ is not raised, then this world is all there is, and we are deceived. That is a pity. The doubters are correct, "Look at those silly

Christians believing a lie. Can you believe they put all that energy into stuff that doesn't matter? They spend billions of dollars a year to continue telling people a lie!"

If all we have is this life, we're in bad shape. We have renounced this world for the world to come only to find out that there is no world to come. We have "sacrifice without meaning."[192]

Certainly, then, we should be pitied. We are wasting our time, effort, and resources. Instead, we should just eat, drink, and be merry for tomorrow we die. Do whatever. Throw the concept of sin out the door. Throw morality to the street. Think, do, and say what you want. Put the missions money towards parties. Turn the church buildings into night clubs. Warm the poor of the world with burning Bibles, hymnals, and Sunday School literature. Be deceived no more!

Let a world like that sink in for a moment. The consequences of denying the resurrection are enormous. By not believing just one thing, everything else falls apart.

Of course, we believe that the resurrection *is* true. We believe that there was a day 2000 years ago when God raised Jesus from the dead. On that first resurrection Sunday, the stone was rolled away, and Jesus walked out of the tomb triumphant. We believe that He then appeared to hundreds of people to affirm and confirm His resurrection. We believe that the apostles, who had struggled with belief before the resurrection, were absolutely convinced after the resurrection. We believe they traveled around their known world preaching the simple gospel because they had been changed by the power of that gospel. They believed the gospel so much that they left their former lives to dedicate themselves completely to sharing this good news. They believed it so much that they were willing to face death for the truth of the resurrection!

Those apostles and disciples taught other believers. Many of them faced persecution and death for their faith. Yet, still more continued to believe! One person who believed told another person who believed who told another person who believed. Preachers were called by God. Missionaries were called by God. Consequently, millions of people believed the truth of the gospel all the way to me writing this chapter and you reading it.

I, of course, believe the exact opposite of everything we've seen in this passage. I believe:

- This world is not all there is. In fact, this world is just a blip on the timeline of eternity.
- There is hope for our loved ones to be raised and for us too. Therefore, there is hope and joy and victory every time we gather for a funeral.
- Our faith is valuable, and we can be forgiven of our sins because Jesus Christ has the power of salvation. If we confess our sins, He is faithful and just and will forgive us our sins and cleanse us from all unrighteousness.
- All preaching has power because it comes forth with the power of the Holy Spirit.
- Jesus Christ has been raised. He's alive! Death has been defeated. Satan has been conquered. Jesus Christ is the King of Kings and the Lord of Lords!

I believe all of that. Do you believe?

When I say "believe," I mean do you stake everything you have on the Lord? For some reason, when we consider faith, it is easy to put it off until tomorrow. Even though we sense the Spirit tugging on our hearts, even though we know we need to commit our lives to Christ, we tend to put it off. Perhaps you have put off faith so long that you've nearly forgotten you need Jesus in your life. Your heart is growing hard, and your eternity is growing darker. Friend, without Jesus you face life without the guidance and purposes He wants to provide. You carry around the burden of your sins. You face every day without the power of the Holy Spirit, and you will spend eternity in a real, horrible hell forever separate from God. If you choose to be separated from Him here, you also choose to be separated from Him there. If you continue to deny Christ, you lose everything for eternity.

However, if you will believe, you gain everything. Won't you say for the first time, "Lord, I know I am a sinner. I cannot bear to carry my sin on my own. Even though I am a pretty good person compared to a lot of others, compared to Your holy perfection, I am the vilest of sinners. I need the life of your blood to cover the death of my sin. I want abundant life now and eternal life in heaven. I want Jesus. I need Jesus. I receive Jesus."

What will make you finally take care of business with God? What will make you finally put everything else aside and focus on Him? What will make you get the priorities of your life in the correct order? What will it take?

I believe it will simply take you listening to the Holy Spirit speaking to you. Lost friend, as He reveals to you your need for salvation, or, Christian friend, as He reveals to you the misplaced priorities in your life, listen to Him. Don't deny Him. Don't quench Him. Obey Him. Follow Him. Have your life forever changed by Him!

CHAPTER 33
The Greatest Victory
1 Corinthians 15:20-34

It was impossible. At least that's what everyone thought. There was no possible way for barely trained, poorly armed, and loosely organized colonists to take on the experienced, equipped, and massive army and navy of their rulers. It certainly seemed impossible when the first shots rang out and even in many battles along the way. However, when the forces faced one another at Yorktown in July of 1781, the climax of the American Revolution was reached. The American colonies were victorious over the British. While other battles may have been larger and more dramatic, no battle in history has been more influential. From the days following their victory at Yorktown, Americans have steadily gained power and influence up to our present role as the most powerful country in history.[193] Yorktown was the greatest victory, and it had long-lasting consequences. The greatest victories are like that – they change things. You might even say they change everything.

In 1 Corinthians 15:20-34 we encounter another victory that changed everything. However, this victory didn't just change everything for one nation, it changed everything for all nations for all eternity. The victory we are talking about is, of course, the resurrection of Jesus Christ. The resurrection was the greatest victory to ever occur.

The resurrection is the greatest victory in history because it affirms that Christ is raised (vv. 20-22).

When Adam and Eve sinned in the Garden of Eden, they opened wide the doorway for sin to come into God's perfect world. From then on, sin has affected every generation of humanity. If the situation had been left there, life would be hopeless and our inheritance worthless. If the will was read, the news would be bad.

"What did grandma and grandpa leave us?"

Death.

"What do we get from mom and dad?"

Death.

Because of Adam's sin, every man and woman inherits death. There are no exceptions. All have sinned and in Adam all die.

Thankfully, God loved us enough not to leave it that way. Because Christ has been raised, we too can be raised. Because Christ is alive, we too can have life.

Here's the wonderful news: just as Adam as the first man ushered in humanity; so Christ ushers in a new humanity (v. 22). Paul celebrates this idea in 2 Corinthians 5:17, "If anyone is in Christ, he is a new creation; the old has gone, the new has come!" You and I can have a brand new identity in Christ! We who are dead in sin can be made alive again! Though we will still die a physical death, we have the hope of eternal life and the resurrection of the body. Because Jesus was born, lived, died, and was resurrected as man, He has opened the way for humanity to also be raised from the dead.

Paul gives us a word picture to help us understand this truth in v. 22. He says Christ's resurrection is the "firstfruits." When the Jews celebrated the Feast of Firstfruits, they would take the first sheaf of grain and bring it to the Lord as an offering. In bringing that sheaf, they were saying, "God, I'm giving you the first sheaf of grain. In giving to you first, I give to you all."

Jesus' resurrection is the firstfruits. When He was raised, God made possible the resurrection of all other men. Christ's resurrection was the first. The resurrection of those who know Him will be the last.

The resurrection is the greatest victory in history because it reminds us that Christ is victor (vv. 24-27).

Christ's resurrection was the first step in His complete triumph over evil. His second coming will be the final step. In these days between, the enemies of God are still battling on earth. The primary way they do it is through our fear of death and dying. If most of us are honest, death scares us to death.

That is why the enemy holds death over us. He knows that when a loved one dies, it rips at our heart. He knows that when we hear the doctor say, "You have cancer," the fear of death immediately comes to our mind. He knows that as we walk by the casket of a friend, we can't help but think, "One day that will be me." The enemy loves to see fear, worry, and dread come upon us. Therefore, Paul reminds us that the last enemy to be destroyed is death. It will be last, but it will be destroyed. In fact, the victory is so certain we can say the enemy of death *has been* defeated. The process of destruction was begun with the resurrection of Jesus Christ. Vaughan and Lea write:

> With His resurrection the decisive battle was won and ultimate victory was assured. All that remains is the 'mopping up' work. At the coming of Christ His people will be raised, all opposition to the rule of God will be abolished, and the kingdom will be delivered up to the Father.[194]

Christ *will be* the victor because He *is* the victor.

How does a person know he is the victor? Their enemy is defeated, of course! You are victorious in war when the enemy surrenders. You are victorious in a sport when the game ends, and you have more points than your opponent. You are victorious in an election when the election returns come in, and you have more votes than your opponents. You are victorious in a battle with cancer when the oncologist says, "All clear." You know you are the victor when the enemy is defeated.

We know Jesus Christ is the Victor because He has defeated the enemy! Death raises the white flag of surrender. Death looks at the score and knows it's over. Death sees the returns and discovers it has lost. And death hears the Master of the Universe say, "All clear." If you have lost a loved one, this is victorious news! If you have walked by the casket of a friend, this is victorious news! If you have received that diagnosis and are uncertain of what tomorrow brings, this is victorious news! You can say, "Death, you're through. Grave, you're done." Consider Paul's celebratory declaration in vv. 54-57:

1 Corinthians 15:54-57 *When the perishable has been clothed with the imperishable, and the mortal with immortality, then the saying that is written will come true: "Death has been swallowed up in victory."* [55] *"Where, O death, is your victory? Where, O death, is your sting?"* [56] *The sting of death is sin, and the power of sin is the law.* [57] *But thanks be to God! He gives us the victory through our Lord Jesus Christ.*

The resurrection is the greatest victory in history because it points to God the Father's exaltation (v. 28).

Paul quotes from Psalm 8, which describes both the greatness and the smallness of man while also describing how God is over man and man is over creation.

Psalm 8:1-9 *O LORD, our Lord, how majestic is your name in all the earth! You have set your glory above the heavens.* [2] *From the lips of children and infants you have ordained praise because of your enemies, to silence the foe and the avenger.* [3] *When I consider your heavens, the work of your fingers, the moon and the stars, which you have set in place,* [4] *what is man that you are mindful of him, the son of man that you care for him?* [5] *You made him a little lower than the heavenly beings and crowned him with glory and honor.* [6] *You made him ruler over the works of your hands; you put everything under his feet:* [7] *all flocks and herds, and the beasts of the field,* [8] *the birds of the air, and the fish of the sea, all that swim the paths of the seas.* [9] *O LORD, our Lord, how majestic is your name in all the earth!*

There is supposed to be order. Right now, however, creation is in chaos because of sin. Christ will bring this chaos under submission. Once Christ has overcome every enemy of God and of man, He will hand the sovereignty to God the Father. God will then be "all in all" or "everything to everyone." God will have "unchallenged supremacy."[195] Those who have opposed Him will receive their choice of hell, and those who have loved Him will enjoy the glories of heaven.

There will be perfection in heaven. Perfect order. Perfect allegiance. Perfect glory of God. That perfection that we anticipate in heaven is directly connected to the empty tomb. Because Jesus has been raised, He can complete His work and bring exaltation to God the Father.

The resurrection is the greatest victory in history because it gives us hope (vv. 29-34).

The resurrection gives us hope in death (v. 29). The baptizing for the dead was apparently a practice as familiar to the Corinthians as it is puzzling to us. More than thirty theories about what this means have been proposed by scholars. While no interpretation is without its problems, Vaughan and Lea understand the passage "as referring to persons, who bereaved of loved ones who were believers, turned to Christ in the hope of a blessed reunion – as in the case of a son led to Christ by his dying mother's appeal, 'Meet me in heaven!'"[196] If there is no resurrection, then such a statement is meaningless. However, if the resurrection did occur, then such a statement and the son's turning to Christ in repentance and faith imparts beautiful hope in a moment of greatest suffering of loss. Whenever we stand beside the casket of a loved one, if they knew Christ and we know Christ, we have hope because of the resurrection. Death is defeated and everything has changed.

That hope continues into times of persecution (vv. 30-32). Paul had risked his life for the sake of the gospel. The resurrection gave him hope in times of persecution. His confidence is found in Romans 8:

> **Romans 8:35-39** *Who shall separate us from the love of Christ? Shall trouble or hardship or persecution or famine or nakedness or danger or sword? [36]As it is written: "For your sake we face death all day long; we are considered as sheep to be slaughtered."[37]No, in all these things we are more than conquerors through him who loved us. [38]For I am convinced that neither death nor life, neither angels nor demons, neither the present nor the future, nor any powers, [39]neither height nor depth, nor anything else in all creation, will be able to separate us from the love of God that is in Christ Jesus our Lord.*

Such hope comes only from the resurrection.

Our hope continues in repentance (vv. 33-34). The ultimate victory opens up a way for your personal victory. Paul makes it plain in v. 34, doesn't he? He says, "Just stop it!" Stop lusting. Stop worrying. Stop being unforgiving. Stop cheating. Stop harboring anger. Just stop it! Now, that's easy to say, but hard to do on your own. Still, the resurrection gives you hope to have victory over sin. Isn't stopping the sin the first step in repenting of that sin? Sure it is. Stop the sin. Then, confess it, "Lord, I am sorry for that sin." Next, repent of the sin by turning away from that sin. Then, every moment from that moment, walk in victory. The victory of the resurrection can give us victory over sin. The resurrection provides us the hope of repentance – knowing that if we confess our sin, Jesus Christ is faithful and just and will forgive us our sin and cleanse us from all unrighteousness. Because we know Jesus is alive, we do not face temptation alone. He always provides a way of escape.

The greatest victories change everything. The Resurrection of Jesus Christ changed everything, but, most importantly, has it changed you?

The Battle of Yorktown changed everything for the American colonies. In a sense, it also changed everything for the entire world as the rise of the United States changed world history. A person living outside of the United States doesn't get the greatest effect of this change, though. A person in Mexico even two feet from the border, doesn't get the greatest effect because he or she is not an American. They have not pledged their allegiance to this nation. They do not live here. However, to those of us who have pledged allegiance to this nation and live here, we enjoy the privileges of citizenship in the land of the free and the home of the brave. We know what it means to be American. We have been forever changed by it.

In a similar but far more important way, the victory of the resurrection of Jesus Christ changed everything for everyone in the world. Still, the greatest effect is not made in a person's life until he or she says, "Jesus is *my* Lord." Until a person repents of his sins and claims the salvation offered by Jesus Christ, he stands outside the personal effects of the resurrection. But if he will take the step to become a citizen of God's people, then he can experience the change the resurrection is meant to bring to his life.

The impact of the resurrection doesn't end at salvation, though. Believers need to enjoy their citizenship. They need to live it out as active members of a local church. They need to share the good news with those who intersect their lives. If the resurrection has truly changed a person, it should move them to action.

CHAPTER 34
The Body of a Champion
1 Corinthians 15:35-58

What if you could have the body of a champion? Even more, what if you could have that body without ever going to the gym or lifting a single weight? What if to have that body you didn't have to drink wheatgrass shakes or eat cardboard? Wouldn't that be great?

In 1 Corinthians 15:35-58, Paul tells us that anyone who knows Jesus Christ will one day have the body of a champion! No, sorry, it won't be a body that would land you on the cover of *Sports Illustrated*, but it is a body that will be the result of a championship.

With all his talk about the resurrection, Paul figured someone might ask the questions of vv. 35 and 36.

> ***1 Corinthians 15:35-36a*** *But someone may ask, "How are the dead raised? With what kind of body will they come?" [36]How foolish!*

The first question, "How are the dead raised?" implies that the resurrection is impossible. The second, "With what kind of body will they come?" implies that the resurrection is inconceivable.[197] While these questions may seem perfectly logical to some people, they are foolish to a person who believes in the resurrection.

Is the resurrected body even possible? (vv. 36-38)

Sure it is! We see a similar mystery happen when we plant seeds. Whenever you plant a seed, the first thing it does is die. The process of fermentation is what triggers new life. Similarly, our bodies will die, be placed in a grave, and then be raised, just as a seed dies and produces a plant that is far more glorious than the seed.[198]

How a seed transitions from seed to plant is quite amazing. Think about it. If a person who was totally ignorant of farming watched a farmer plant seeds in the spring, he might ask, "What do you expect to get from that?" The farmer could reply, "From these yellow seeds, I will get corn. From these black seeds, I'll get watermelons. From these round seeds, I'll get okra. From this white seed, I'll get peas." The person who doesn't understand farming could say, "There's no way. These seeds are hard as rocks! They are dead. There's not even life inside it. These will not grow!" The farmer would look at the person like he was crazy and say, "Of course they will!"[199]

Sure enough, soon the seed comes to life and a sprout of green breaks the surface of the earth. The phrase "come to life" is passive. That implies that the seed does not germinate and grow itself, rather it is acted upon by an outside agent. Who is that agent? God. Once a seed comes to life, amazingly, it takes the form of the plant it should and begins to bear the fruit it is intended to produce.

Paul reminds us "you do not plant the body that will be." Just as the burial of the seed is the beginning of a transition to a higher form of life so "death is a transition to a higher form of life."[200] What is planted is similar but different from what grows. It is greater as well.

Similarly, the body that will be raised is similar but different from what is buried. It is a part of what is buried but it is also greater than what was buried. The same God who gives the body of a stately live oak to a tiny acorn or a blooming magnolia to a tiny red seed can give us a resurrected body. Our body on earth is just the beginning.

Is the resurrection conceivable? (vv. 39-49)

Can we comprehend what this body will be like? Yes! The resurrected body will be a gloriously different body (vv. 39-46). God makes a variety of different bodies (v. 39-41). Each creature in the world has a body uniquely suited for its environment. Humans have one kind of body. It serves us well as people who dwell in shelters and can clothe ourselves. But what about animals? God has given the various species different kinds of bodies exactly suited for their environments. What about birds? Likewise, they have bodies especially designed to help them soar and dwell as they do. But they too are different from fish, who are equipped with bodies shaped for swimming and covered with scales to protect them and help them glide through the water. None of that is by accident. It was all on purpose. In fact, we read in Genesis 1 how God created each creature according to its kind.

God is capable of making a vast array of bodies. Still, Paul takes us to another level in vv. 40-41. Just as there are differences among the various bodies on earth, there are differences between terrestrial and celestial bodies. Perhaps Paul is talking about angels being different than humans. But certainly he is saying that the sun is different from the moon. One star has more splendor than another as some merely reflect light while others are sources of light. Nevertheless, each one was made by God in a particular way because God is perfectly capable of making a wide variety of bodies. This body we have now is one body. The one a believer will have at the resurrection is another. None of this is by accident. All of it was done purposefully by God.

Not only will the resurrected body be different, it will be gloriously different (vv. 42-46). Weakness is the hallmark of our present bodies. That keeps the funeral homes in business. There are 2.4 million funerals in the United States every year. Our earthly bodies break down, wear out, and die. This will not be the case for our resurrected body. Whereas the present body is subject to disease, death, and decay, the body that is raised will be imperishable.[201] There will be no more sickness, pain, or death. There will be no hospitals or funeral homes in heaven because the resurrected body won't need them.

The weaknesses that we succumb to now will be gone. That is hard to imagine. Just because it is hard to imagine, doesn't mean it isn't going to happen. Surely such a God who has created such a variety of bodies suitable for so many environs will not be hard pressed to provide "suitable bodies for all who share in his eternal order."[202] The resurrected body will be gloriously different.

Further, this resurrected body will be like Christ's resurrected body – perfected (vv. 47-49). The first man, Adam, was a man of dust. God formed him from the dust of the earth. Our relationship to Adam gives us our physical body. The second Adam, Jesus Christ, came from heaven. From our relationship to Him we will have a spiritual body.[203]

So, as Paul says in v. 49, "just as we have borne the likeness of the earthly man, so shall we bear the likeness of the man from heaven."

What will the resurrected body be like? Think about the body of the risen Lord. Before His resurrection, Jesus had a body like ours. He grew tired. He grew hungry. He could only move so fast. He had to use doors. However, after His resurrection, He had a real but different body. It was a perfected body. It was like the body before, but different. It was of the same kind but greater. While He could do the normal things we can do, His body also had other-worldly properties. His body was more like something out of science fiction! He could pass through solid walls. He could suddenly appear out of nowhere. He could even beam up to heaven in bodily form. Jesus' resurrected body could do things we cannot do now. Yet, this is apparently the kind of body we will have in eternity.

The New Testament is clear that our body will be changed as it is perfected. Our body is sown in death and decay, but it will be raised to be imperishable. It is buried as a thing of no use, but it will be raised in honor. It is planted as something seemingly dead, but it will be raised in power.

As you can imagine, there are some perks to this! The bodies of resurrected Christians will be "permanently and eternally perfect. You will never look in a mirror and notice wrinkles or a receding hairline. . . . You won't be susceptible to injury, disease, or allergies. There will be none of those things in heaven. There will only be absolute, imperishable perfection."[204] That doesn't necessarily mean we'll have the perfect earthly body for which we always wished or worked. You still won't make *People Magazine's* list of fifty most beautiful people. It does mean, however, that you will have the perfected glorious body God intended. Since there will be no sin, there will be no vanity or pride or lust or jealousy. Therefore, we will be perfectly happy with the body we have.

We can hardly imagine what the resurrected body will be like because the only bodies we've ever known have been weak, diseased remnants of the bodies God intended for humans. No amount of Botox, collagen, implants, lipo, nips, or tucks can reverse what happens to our body. One day, though, this earthly seed will give forth to a beautiful tree. You will have the body of a champion!

Remember, though, the only way you get a body like Christ's in the resurrection is if you know Him as your Lord and Savior now. The more like Jesus you become here, the more like Jesus you will be there.

Is the resurrection necessary? (vv. 50-58)

Absolutely! First, it is necessary to enter eternity (vv. 50-53). Since the eternal order is not of flesh and blood, all believers must undergo a change. Those who died prior to Christ's return will be resurrected. Those who survive until His coming will be transformed.

Second, the resurrection is necessary to defeat death (vv. 54-56). For now, death seems to triumph. But just you wait! One day death will be "swallowed up", and that victory will be complete and final. What a great day that will be! I've presided over some 200 funerals in my ministry. That's a lot of death – and that's just the funerals at which I've personally ministered. There have been hundreds more deaths connected to our congregation and other people I know. One day, though, there will be no more death. I often tell the guys at the funeral homes that they have a recession proof business. People will always die. However, there is coming a day when the funeral homes will go out of business for lack of business. What a day that will be! Thanks be to God! He gives us the victory through our Lord Jesus Christ!

Third, the resurrection is necessary to encourage us (vv. 57-58). The "sting of death" depicts death like a venomous snake inflicting fatal wounds. If death wasn't creepy enough, this word picture is horrifying. Without Jesus, we die in sin and are separated from God for eternity. Get the picture of v. 57 where Jesus removes the sting! If we will repent of our sin and come to Him, He will remove the sting of sin. Jesus crushes the head of that old serpent of sin that keeps striking at us (Gen. 3:15). No wonder Paul has such a burst of praise in v. 57!

The resurrection will be the ultimate championship, and the accompanying resurrected body will be the ultimate championship body. We go nuts when our team scores a touchdown, makes a basket, or hits a homerun. We need to get far more excited when we talk about the ultimate victory that Christ has won for us and the body He will give to those Who die in Him! Victory is assured. The championship title is guaranteed!

CHAPTER 35
Principles for Strong Giving
1 Corinthians 16:1-4

After all the exciting, stand up and shout stuff about the resurrection, Paul shifts gears to talk about money. Chapter 16 begins, "Now about the collection for God's people."

We might think, "Really, Paul? You've been talking about this awesome concept of the resurrection and then you shift to talk about something as mundane as an offering?"

It doesn't seem to fit, does it? Well, maybe it does. In fact, the difference between chapters 15 and 16 may be a good illustration about how our faith operates. Every glimpse we get of what is coming tomorrow, encourages us to be faithful to the commitments and responsibilities of today. That faithfulness flows even to the way we use our resources to support God's work.

Therefore, while this may seem like an odd transition to us, Paul put this discussion right where he wanted it. He's winding down the letter, so a reminder about a collection needs to be towards the end. At the same time, the justification for the collection has just been given. After hearing about all God has done, is doing, and will do, the Corinthians should be motivated to support continued ministry. So should we.

In this section Paul is answering another one of the Corinthian's questions. Before we consider Paul's answer, we need to understand what brought about this question from the Corinthians. The church has asked Paul about several things – marriage, food sacrificed to idols, spiritual gifts – and we can see why they may have asked these questions. But why did they ask about a collection?

The Corinthians were seeking understanding regarding a collection for their fellow believers in Jerusalem. The Church in Jerusalem may have become impoverished due to famine or persecution or both. During an early visit to Jerusalem, Paul had eagerly agreed to help the poor in the city (Gal. 2:1-10). As Paul ministered in other areas, he led the Gentile churches that he planted to contribute funds for the needy at Jerusalem. Here he encourages the Corinthians to do the same.[205] As Paul instructs how this collection should be given, we find timeless principles concerning any giving done by Christ-followers.

Our giving benefits God's people (v. 1).

When you and I give our tithes and offerings, our giving does not benefit some nebulous entity. It doesn't even benefit a mere budget. Our giving benefits the people of God. When we give, we say we are giving to God, and that statement is accurate. But God has so designed things that those gifts we give directly benefit His people.

The situation for the Corinthians' offering was specific: there was a need in Jerusalem. This collection was like special missions offerings that may be held in today's churches. This offering would be used to benefit God's people in Jerusalem.

Of course, in actuality, all of our giving benefits God's people. There are two groups of God's people: those who currently know Him and those who do not yet know Him. Those who currently know Him are those who have been transformed by the power of the gospel. Those who do not yet know Him are those who have yet to hear or be transformed by the gospel. Both types of people live in every city, state, and nation in the world. Our giving benefits all of these people.

When we give our offering through our church, we should picture our resources being directed to people. We should see our gifts going to a missionary establishing a church in another country. We should see our gifts helping our denomination's disaster relief team minister to storm victims. We should see our gifts feeding the hungry, clothing the naked, and giving fresh water to a village. We should see our gifts providing homes for orphans. We should see our giving helping people who do not yet know Jesus to do so through missions, evangelism, and ministry.

Likewise, when we give, we should picture our resources also benefiting God's people who do know Him. Some of our giving provides church facilities which are our center for ministry. Our giving benefits us with materials to use, with staff to champion our ministries, and with ministry organizations in which to be involved. Our giving benefits us with musicians and instruments and other tools for worship. Our giving touches babies, preschoolers, children, youth, college students, adults, and senior adults. Our ministries of worship, discipleship, and fellowship all benefit the people of God.

Everything I've mentioned and more happens when you give through your church. Through your own church's ministries and through the work of your church's denominational and missional partners, you minister to the people of God – both those who already know Him and who do not yet know Him. Our giving benefits God's people.

We should all participate in giving (v. 2).

Paul says this offering involved "each one of you." Every person in the congregation should have a part. No one is exempt. The poor should give; the rich should give; and everyone in-between should give.

The poorer in the church can have a hard time because they might say, "I can't possibly give anything." If that is you, I encourage you to tell God your predicament. Ask Him to show you how to switch around priorities and even provide extra income. Trust Him, and watch Him work. Since God calls you to tithe, He will provide for your other needs.

I read of a woman named Nancy, a single mother with young children. Her ex-husband sent her only a small amount of grocery money every week – so small it couldn't even feed one person, much less her family of four. Nevertheless, Nancy decided to begin giving to God from her grocery money and trust Him to provide. Shortly after, she got a job with a cookbook company. The company paid Nancy to go grocery shopping and prepare meals so they could take photographs for their cookbooks. When they were done taking pictures, Nancy could keep the food she had purchased and prepared. Nancy learned that even if you're poor, you still need to learn to give from whatever you have.[206] Trust God to provide.

The rich should give as well. Jesus warned, however, that it is hard for the wealthy to give from their abundance. Truth be told, most people reading this book fit into the wealthy category. Jesus taught, and many of us have experienced, that the more we have, the harder we find it to give as we should. Sometimes we even decrease our giving, thinking, "I don't need to give that much." Don't fall into that trap. As God has provided for you, provide for His kingdom's work.

When we do not participate in giving, we miss out. For one, we miss out on the joy of obedience. Doesn't it feel better to walk in obedience than in disobedience? Sure it does! That's because, second, if we do not give, we miss out on the blessings that follow obedience in giving. Rewards follow obedience! Only punishment follows disobedience. You learned that as a kid! Further, third, when we do not give, we say, "I'll take but never give." How tragic it is to be ministered to, but never make sure others are ministered to. That's totally selfish and totally wrong. Do not miss out on the joy of giving!

Our giving should be systematic (v. 2).

Our giving should be done consistently and regularly. For the early church, the first day of the week, Sunday, had become the day of corporate worship. Therefore, Sunday was the day to set aside a portion of the income – every week to prepare for the offering.

The timeless principle is that there should be a regularity to our giving. You need to establish the habit that when you are paid, however you are paid – by the job, weekly, bi-weekly, monthly – that the first thing you do is give back to God. If your paycheck is direct deposited and you do not get that regular reminder of being paid by holding your check, it would be wise for you to set up an automatic payment of your tithe to your church so you do not forget to be faithful to give back to the Lord.

Systematic giving is necessary because it thanks God for His systematic provision. Would you like to be paid whenever someone thought about it or with whatever they had that day? In one church I served, we had a volunteer treasurer. I was paid once a month. From time to time, our treasurer would forget to pay me on pay day. A week or two would go by with still no paycheck. Finally, the treasurer would come in and say, "Sorry this is late!" I was ever so glad when we made some changes that helped the paycheck come systematically! When we give systematically, we say, "Thank you God for your systematic provision!"

Systematic giving also demonstrates faith. When you give to the Lord, you are saying, "God, I don't know what's ahead, but you do. Help me make ends meet. Help me even increase my wealth so I can bless others." If you give to God first, you free Him to make the rest work. If you wait to give when something is left, you'll never have enough.

Further, systematic giving helps the church be effective. The ongoing operation of the church's ministry requires ongoing support for faithful believers. There are a lot of people who benefit from the ministries of your church – everyone from your staff to the ministries you support locally to the missions partners you have in your region and around the world. The resources need to be there to meet those needs. Your church has to plan a budget. Herky-jerky giving breeds herky-jerky ministry, and that is a pain for everyone. Systematic giving facilitates systematic ministry.

God desires for things to be done decently and in order, not in chaos and uncertainty. We should give systematically.

Our giving should be proportionate to our income (v. 2).

Paul says our giving should be "in keeping with our income." The inevitable question, then, is how much is "in keeping with my income"? What should that amount be? The amount we give should be based on three things.

First, our giving should meet a standard. The tithe is a minimum standard. The first tithe described in the Bible was given by Abraham to Melchizedek the High Priest. Abraham gave a tenth of everything he had to Melchizedek. The Old Testament law later established the tithe. Though we are not under the law, we still should tithe. If 10% was the standard under the law, don't you think it should be a minimum standard under grace?

If you are not yet tithing, you might find 10% difficult. If you are already spending 100% of your income (and many people spend more than 100%), you'll find it hard to jump into giving 10%. Therefore, you need to be systematic about developing a plan for obedience to God. For example, you might try giving 1% for a couple of months and make some adjustments in your spending elsewhere to accommodate. Then work up to 2%, then to 3%, and so forth. Have a goal to reach 10% in a year or at most two years as you adjust your priorities to be faithful to God. You may have to cut out something, sell something, or cancel something to make this happen, but I guarantee you that you will not miss it, and you will be blessed by your obedience!

Second, we should give out of sacrifice. Getting to and giving 10% requires sacrifice. Going beyond 10% does as well. Sacrifice is a good thing. In 2 Samuel 24:24 King David said, "I will not sacrifice to the Lord my God burnt offerings that cost me nothing." It should cost you something to give. Do you really want to offer God leftovers?

Let me offer you a warning. When you look around at your friends who do not give, it may seem like they have more than you do. You may be tempted to think, "Well, if I kept everything I gave to the Lord, I could do extra things or have extra stuff too!" But notice that I said, they "seem" to have more than you do. Remember that things aren't always as they seem. I would rather God's guaranteed blessing and provision because I tithe than a million dollars in the bank without God. God's provision and blessing can stretch and protect what I have whereas life can suck that million away in moments.

Ask yourself an important question: is life all about you? Is life all about you, your toys, and your experiences? Or is life also about that family sitting in front of you at church or that senior adult sitting behind you? Is life also about that missionary in the Philippines or that orphan in Chicago or that new believer at the new church your church is helping sponsor?

Does that family who doesn't give but gets to go on that extra get-away really have more than you if you tithe? Does the extra $500 a month of their bigger mortgage for their bigger house really compare to all that happens when you give $500 to the Lord? Let me help you out: no, it does not. Those of us who tithe are far more blessed, and we are often surprised at how God takes that 90% and stretches it! Sometimes we even end up with a get-a-way or a new house ourselves!

Third, we should give out of expectation. God honors our giving by returning blessings to us when we give.

2 Corinthians 9:6 *Remember this: Whoever sows sparingly will also reap sparingly, and whoever sows generously will also reap generously.*

Luke 6:38 *Give, and it will be given to you. A good measure, pressed down, shaken together and running over, will be poured into your lap. For with the measure you use, it will be measured to you."*

Here's a thought, when you decide how much to give, decide how much on which you would like a return! Then give with expectation. I was challenged with this principle many years ago. I asked a pastor about whether I should tithe on the gross or the net. Without pause he said, "Which amount do you want God to bless?" The choice was easy! I don't want a net blessing; I want a gross blessing! Ever since then, I have tithed on the gross, and Rebecca and I have continued that practice throughout our marriage. We now give more than a tithe and many years ago decided to tithe on what our church pays for our health insurance and retirement because we want God to bless our health and that retirement account!

Our giving should be voluntary (v. 2).

Under the Jewish system, a temple tax was levied on every male twenty years of age and over. In contrast, Paul says Christian giving isn't compulsory, it is voluntary. Can you imagine the church asking every member for a copy of their W2 and then sending out a monthly bill? The accompanying letter would read something like this:

Dear Paul and Jane,

Based on your income, you owe $1000 this month for the ongoing ministry of our church.

Blessings,
First Church of Takesville

I don't know about you, but if I received a letter like that, I'd change churches. That's crazy! Christian giving isn't compulsory, it's voluntary.

I listen to Christian radio and occasionally public radio. Several times a year these stations hold their share-a-thon, pledge-a-thon, or, as my friend calls it, "beg-a-thon." These stations pull out every kind of method to motivate people to give. While I am not a fan of beg-a-thon season, sometimes I listen just to see what kind of oddball thing the radio personalities will say to encourage people to give. Aren't you glad God gave a plan where we don't have to do that in the church? I sure am because, as a pastor, I'd have to be the one begging! Giving in the church isn't begged for, it is voluntary.

Nobody in the church is going to make you give. Nobody is going to beg you to give. Christians do not give because we are forced to. We do not give because we are guilted. We give because we want to. We give voluntarily and joyfully. Paul says in 2 Corinthians 9:7, "Each man should give what he has decided in his heart to give, not reluctantly or under compulsion, for God loves a cheerful giver." Give joyfully and voluntarily. God loves that!

Our giving should be administered wisely (v. 3-4).

If we talk about giving, we should also talk about what should happen once that money is given. Paul did not handle the money himself nor did he appoint those who would handle the money. This policy protected Paul as well as the people's gifts. There has to be wise administration and accountability because the money we give is a sacred trust.

Churches should have responsible financial procedures. Even the smallest of churches can have good practices in place. Have you ever wondered, "What happens to the money I give to the church?" While I do not know exactly what happens in your church, let me tell you briefly how it is handled in our church:

- Sunday's offering is secured until Monday morning.
- On Monday morning, Sunday's offering is combined with other offerings that have come in during the previous week. A

counting committee counts the offering. In order to keep gifts confidential, we have four committees that rotate a month at a time. Not everyone on the counting committee sees everything so no one can know how much or how little someone gives.

- The money is deposited and gifts are recorded by our financial secretary. She is the only person in the church who regularly sees what people give or has access to what people give. She keeps everything confidential. The only thing she lets me know is when an individual or family gives for the first time or for the first time in a long time. However, I am not told the amount. This allows me to encourage first time givers with a personal note.
- The annual budget then guides how we spend what we give. Staff members and ministry leaders manage the budgetary lines for which they are responsible. Our associate pastor keeps a careful watch on every line item. The finance committee helps make decisions on large and nonbudgeted expenses. Each month, the finance committee reviews the budget report as do the deacons and then the church.

There must be wise administration and accountability of the finances given for God's work. The money we give is a sacred trust.

Over all that we see in this passage is a simple truth: "The work of God is to be done by the people of God giving according to the will of God."[207] God wants ministry to His people to happen. He has given us a simple way to help that happen and promises to provide for us and bless us when we are obedient to be sure that happens.

However, when you get right down to it, we give not for blessings or provision. We give because God has given. Have you ever just stopped and thought about that? We give simply because God has given and continues to give. I'm sure you've heard the statement, "You can't out give God." Well, you can't! Not only does God give, but everything He made, gives.

God made the sun – it gives.
God made the moon – it gives.
God made the stars – they give.

God made the air – it gives.
God make the clouds – they give.
God made the earth – it gives.
God made the sea – it gives.
God made the rivers – they give.
God made the trees – they give.
God made the flowers – they give.
God made the animals – they give.
And
God made you
Do you give?

CHAPTER 36
Listening in on a Pastor's Heart
1 Corinthians 16:5-24

I'll admit that when I come to the conclusion of an epistle, I sometimes find myself shutting down mentally. The end of the epistles can sound like 2000 year old personal reflections that have no meaning today: this person says, "Hi"; this person is coming; I'm coming; keep up the good work; Amen. Sigh, yawn.

However, when we slow down and think about what we're reading, we find something helpful. The way a person closes a letter is important. "Sincerely" or "Yours Truly" are formal and used for business letters. "Regards" is a little softer. "Your friend" is warm. "Love" means there is a strong relationship of friend or family. If your fiancée went off to a semester of college in another state and sent you a letter that closed out "Sincerely" instead of "Love", you'd be worried! The way a person closes a letter is important.

Therefore, we might ask, "How does Paul close this letter?" We know this letter was written to a church that was having problems. There were divisions, bad theology, and even some people who didn't think Paul was all that great! So, how did Paul choose to close out the letter? He did so as a loving pastor.

As we read the closing, we are hearing Paul's heart for these people. In this closing, we get an opportunity to listen in on this pastor's heart. We notice some things about this pastor's heart that I hope is true of my heart and any pastor's heart for his church.

Desire for Genuine Relationships (vv. 5-9)

On the surface, this looks like mundane travel plans, but look closer. Read this as a person who knows Paul, loves Paul, and wants to see Paul. What do you notice? Paul is coming! That's good news. Don't you want to see your friend?

But notice something more. Paul doesn't want to stop by for a quick visit. He wants to stay awhile, in fact, maybe even for a whole season. Paul didn't want to pop in for coffee, he wanted to spend quality and quantity time with the Corinthians. This tells us that Paul loved these people and had a desire for genuine relationships with them.

Pastors need genuine relationships. They need people they can enjoy being with, relax with, and share struggles with. Many pastors have a desire for genuine relationships but have a hard time developing them. Part of the struggle is schedule related. Part of it is people aren't really sure they want the pastor as a friend. Other times, though, the pastor is guarded because he doesn't want to be hurt either by the Lord moving him and then him leaving his friends. Still other times a pastor may have been hurt by friends in a church and is therefore wary of making friends again. Nevertheless, for all the things working against them, pastors need genuine relationships.

We hear Paul's heart here, "I want to enjoy some time with you, serving alongside you. I want genuine relationships not a distant pulpit to pew kind of relationship."

The only thing that can delay him pouring into that relationship is his passion to preach the gospel (vv. 8-9). There is an open door for good work in Ephesus. Paul felt compelled to stay for the time being. Pastor's feel the pull to effective ministry. Where there is great opportunity, we feel the obligation to serve. Notice, that obligation to serve comes even in the face of opposition. The passion to preach overrides the discouragement from opposition.

Support for the Ministry of Others (vv. 10-12)

Paul did not only think about his own ministry. He thought about the ministry of others. Paul speaks first of his son in the ministry, Timothy. It seems there may have been some uneasiness about Timothy's visit to Corinth. We know from Paul's letters to Timothy that the young man could be timid. Young ministers have to grow and learn. They may be gun shy on some things and overly zealous in other things. They will make mistakes. Timothy was heading to Corinth where some people did not respect Paul. If they didn't respect Paul, there was no way they were going to respect the preacher boy Timothy!

I wonder if Timothy had said to Paul, "I'm not so sure about this." But Paul replied, "Don't worry, you'll be fine." Then Paul writes to the Corinthians, "See to it that Timothy has nothing to fear while he is with you. He is serving the Lord just as I am." In other words, "Don't mess with my boy!" Paul stood behind Timothy to give him support and encouragement.

Next, Paul mentions Apollos. Remember, Apollos was the eloquent preacher that a group in Corinth absolutely adored. There is nothing to indicate that there was any ill-will between Apollos and Paul. In fact, Paul cordially calls him "my brother." Apparently, the Corinthians had asked Paul to see if Apollos might come visit again. Paul encouraged him to go, but Apollos was "quite unwilling to go." What's up with that? Apparently, Apollos knew of the strife that was happening in the church. He knew the sides were dividing over leaders. He knew the Apollos group would love to have their *preacherama* back again. So he probably said something like, "Paul, I love those people, but there is no way I'm going back there now. The last thing they need is for the pot of division to be stirred." Apollos planned to go when he had opportunity, which would need to be after Paul's letter arrived and the divisive issues were addressed!

When we see Paul asking for fair treatment for Timothy and conveying a message from Apollos, we see Paul supporting the ministry of others. These two guys were co-laborers, and Paul supported them. He was willing to stand alongside Timothy as a young, inexperienced minister. He was willing to stand behind Apollos and support his decision for how best to proceed with Corinth. Even though some favored Apollos over Paul, Paul still supported Apollos.

Pastors need to support the ministry of others. Younger ministers need the support of seasoned ministers. All ministers need the support of their fellow ministers. But I think we can make another application – all three of these men were working with the same church. Though they weren't the staff of the Church at Corinth, I think the application can be for a staff of ministers and the support staff. A pastor needs to support the ministry of his staff, and a staff needs to support the ministry of their pastor.

I once heard a mega-church pastor spout off something like, "You guys in smaller churches think it'd be great to have a big staff. Well, having a big staff is like having a bunch of kids. They're always fighting and whining." His statement jarred me. I thought, "What a rotten attitude – what kind of email did he just read?" Then I thought, "What if that comment gets back to his staff? How are they going to feel?" A staff needs to know that their pastor supports them as competent professionals not that he thinks they're a bunch of whining kids! The younger ones need to know that their pastor will be forgiving, helpful, and encouraging. The seasoned ones need to know their pastor respects their expertise and wisdom and desires their very best.

I've served as a Youth Minister, Minister of Music, and Associate Pastor under three different pastors. Two of those pastors were a joy with whom to work. One was a challenge *for* whom to work. Notice the difference in my language ("with" and "for"). I never want our staff to feel like they work "for" me. I believe in the people on our church's staff. I not only believe in them, I love them. We are a team. We serve the Lord together.

Passion for the Church to be Faithful (vv. 13-16)

These verses serve almost as an overview of major points in the letter. While such imperatives are common in the conclusion of Paul's letters, these seem particularly connected to the Corinthian's situation. There are six challenges. Each challenge shows Paul's passion for the church to be faithful. He wants them to be faithful to be a strong church that follows the true gospel as he had shared with them.

They need to be on their *guard* because Christ is coming back and the enemy is at work. They need to *stand firm* in the faith because there are those who are trying to teach a different gospel. They need to be strong and men and women of *courage* because there is doctrinal error among them as well as those who are living contrary to the moral teachings of the faith. They are to do everything in *love* because love covers and underlies everything else. If you do not have love as a church, you are nothing. True love in the church fixes problems in the church. They are to *submit* to devoted servants because those type of people form the bedrock of a strong church. Paul wanted the

Corinthian Church to be faithful and strong. He wanted them to fix their problems and move forward in advancing the kingdom of God. That is a pastor's heart.

It is a pastor's greatest desire to see the church he pastors become all it can be. That is not for self-congratulation but for advancement of the kingdom. Pastors want to see people growing in their faith. That's what helps a pastor keep going. Every pastor wants the church to be faithful. A pastor even hopes those churches he used to pastor will grow stronger in future years. It is heartbreaking when he hears of problems in a former church. We sense that from Paul. I've experienced it firsthand. When one of my previous churches split a few years after I had left there, it broke my heart.

Gratitude for Servant Leaders (vv. 17-18)

Stephanus, Fortunatus, and Achaicus likely brought to Paul the letter from Corinth to which he gave answer in this letter. Moreover, they probably carried 1 Corinthians to the church.[208] From them Paul received affection from the Corinthian church and through them he could send back advice for the situation at the church. These men had taken time to travel to Paul for the benefit of their church and had encouraged Paul during their stay. Paul was grateful.

Every pastor is grateful for the servant leaders in the church. Those who give of themselves to the life and work of the kingdom of God through the local church are especially treasured by the pastor. Whether they be people who serve behind the scenes or out in front, they are valuable because without them the church would not function. The people who take time to teach, plan, coordinate, cook, fix things, minister to the hospitalized and homebound, welcome new members, secure the campus, and so forth are vital. While technically I guess every member of the church should be a servant leader, the fact is usually only about 20% are. Those 20% do 80% of the ministry work in the church. A pastor has gratitude for those people and is always working to have more people join their ranks. Some of a pastor's greatest encouragements are when he hears that ministry has happened without the initiative of the staff and when people take on a ministry project and run with it. That is servant leadership.

Realization that we are Part of Something Great (vv. 19-20)

Aquila and Priscilla were beloved by many in the congregation. They were what we would call "charter members" of the church. In Acts 18, which tells the story of Paul's evangelization of Corinth, we find that Paul met Aquila and Priscilla in Corinth and that they helped found the church. The couple left Corinth with Paul and had gone to Ephesus. Evidently, they were still there, and a new church was meeting in their home. This news gave the Corinthians a realization that they now had reach in another part of the world! The Church at Corinth was not the only church in the world. There were many others – all of them young churches that needed the support of one another. They needed to know, "We are part of something great and far beyond us that God is doing new in our world today."

Every church needs that same realization to help them fulfill the great commission. One thing I most enjoy about our church is our connection with work outside of us. That comes locally through our Main Street Church and Mission and our collaboration with our sister churches. It comes on a state-wide basis as we host events for and participate in ministry through our denomination. It comes as we help plant new churches in areas of our state without an evangelical witness (yes, those exist in Louisiana!). It also comes in the many connections we have enjoyed with missionaries through the years who stay in our missionary residence. All of those personal connections are reminders that we are part of something far greater than us.

Paul knew that what he was doing was bigger than him and bigger than the Corinthian Church. It was a God-sized movement that was changing the world. When your heart's passion has that realization, you are greatly encouraged.

Right Placed Love for Christ and His People (vv. 21-24)

Paul typically dictated his letters to an amanuensis but would take the pen himself towards the end of the letter to record his personal farewell in his own hand and provide authentication of the letter.

Paul's admonition in v. 22 was one final charge aimed at the troublemakers in Corinth, but it reminds us that love for Christ must be central for us. The whole reason we do what we do as a church is because of Christ and out of our love for him. We serve and witness with urgency because our cry is "Our Lord Come!" That translates the Aramaic expression *Maranatha*! This word expresses one of the deepest convictions of the church – Jesus is coming back! Paul and the early Church had an eager longing to see Christ return. Do we?

If we would allow the Lord's grace to truly settle upon us and if we would realize the amazing thing that grace has done, I think we would have a longing to not only see Jesus return but make sure as many people know Him as possible before He does! Paul's prayer for grace to cover all the Corinthians extended to even or especially those who had caused him the greatest problems and put up the fiercest opposition.[209]

We should have such love that extends to everyone. A pastor wants to see that love extended from himself to the congregation and from one member of the congregation to another. Love should abound in the Church of Jesus Christ.

My love to all of you in Christ Jesus. Amen. Paul signs off, rolls up the scroll, and sends it to Corinth. What would they do with the message when they received it? How would they respond? Paul didn't know at that moment. All he knew was he loved these people and wanted God's best for them. That is a pastor's heart for his church family.

CONCLUSION

The Church at Corinth may have been a mess up, but because some key leaders reached out to Paul for help, they were able to get fixed up and begin growing stronger. These leaders listed out the problems in the church and asked good questions. Paul answered with biblical wisdom and godly advice. The leaders then tackled the challenging issues and worked to bring together a divided church. Thus, the church grew stronger.

My prayer is that every church will grow stronger. Any church can grow stronger than it is today – no matter how bad or good things are. The key to that growth is prayerfully seeking godly wisdom and heeding the lessons of this epistle to the Corinthians.

If your church is experiencing some mess ups, please get help from a trusted advisor. This is why church consultants and denominational strategists exist! Well-respected pastors can also be valuable resources. Seek out godly wisdom. The cause of Christ is too important for church leaders and members to sit back and allow status quo to continue, conflict to grow, members to drift away, and the church to spiral downward. When theological, ethical, moral, and other problems come up in the church, we must work prayerfully and diligently to fix them. We must seek wisdom and apply that wisdom we receive to the situation.

If your church is not experiencing any mess ups, be grateful! Give thanks to God. But don't grow complacent! You can always grow stronger! In watching churches throughout my ministry, I've learned something – even the strongest churches can stagnate. I've seen churches that were the fastest growing and most innovative flatten out and begin to decline. Though these churches were household names twenty years ago, mention them today, and people ask, "What church is that?" They may still be large, but they have grown stagnant and complacent. If something doesn't change, it won't be long until the decline is noticeable and the building is for sale.

I've also seen churches that simply never stopped growing and being effective. While their growth may not have been a rocket to the top, they have steadily and consistently grown. What has been the difference? These growing churches have never become complacent. They always wanted to grow stronger – spiritually, relationally, theologically, and just about any –ly you can think of that applies to a church! That is my prayer for our church, and I hope that is your prayer for your church.

To God be the glory as we all seek to grow stronger.

NOTES

[1] David Prior, *The Message of Corinthians,* The Bible Speaks Today (Inter-Varsity, 1985), 21.
[2] A. C. Thiselton, *The First Epistle to the Corinthians: A Commentary on the Greek Text,* New International Greek Testament Commentary (Grand Rapids: W.B. Eerdmans, 2000), 74.
[3]H. D. M. Spence-Jones, Ed, *1 Corinthians,* The Pulpit Commentary (London; New York: Funk & Wagnalls Company), 2.
[4] Derek Prime, *Opening Up 1 Corinthians,* Opening Up Commentary (Leominister: Day One Publications, 1909), 15.
[5] Ralph W. Neighbour, Jr., *The Seven Last Words of the Church* (Nashville: Broadman, 1973).
[6] Prior, 23.
[7] Ibid.
[8]Gordon Fee, *The First Epistle to the Corinthians*, The New International Commentary on the New Testament (Grand Rapids: Eerdmans, 1987), 38.
[9] Prior, 24.
[10] Fanny Crosby, "All the Way My Savior Leads Me" (1875). Public domain.
[11] J. W. MacGorman, *Romans, 1 Corinthians*, Layman's Bible Book Commentary (Nashville: Broadman Press, 1980), 103.
[12] Prior, 33.
[13] Ibid.
[14] Ibid.
[15] Ibid., 34.
[16] Jack MacGorman, *Romans, 1 Corinthians*, Layman's Bible Book Commentary (Broadman, 1980), 104.
[17] Ibid., 103.
[18] Ibid., 102.
[19] Curtis Vaughan and Thomas Lea, *1 Corinthians*, Founders Study Guide Commentary (Founders Press, 2002), 29.
[20] Ibid., 30.
[21] Ibid., 29.
[22] MacGorman, 104.

[23] Fee, 67.
[24] Prior, 45.
[25] Quoted in Fee, 81. Most commentaries mention at least a portion of this quote.
[26] Vaughan and Lea, 31.
[27] Barclay, 24.
[28] MacGorman, 106.
[29] Prior, 46.
[30] Maia Szalavitz, "Philip Seymour Hoffman Didn't Have to Die." *Time* (3 February 2014), https://time.com/3652/philip-seymour-hoffman-didnt-have-to-die (accessed 12 February 2014).
[31] Barclay, 25.
[32] MacGorman, 106.
[33] Ibid., 106.
[34] H.C. Brown, Jr., *A Quest for Reformation in Preaching* (Nashville: Broadman, 1968), p. 16-21.
[35] Ronald Osborn, *Folly of God: The Rise of Christian Preaching* (St. Louis: Chalice, 1999), 272.
[36] Sidney Greidanus, *The Modern Preacher and the Ancient* Text, (Inter-Varsity, 1988), 332.
[37] Ibid., 332.
[38] We might visualize this as three concentric circles around the death, resurrection, and exaltation of Christ. The first circle is the preaching of the gospel [*kerygma*], "which interprets these events with a view to bringing people to faith in Christ. The second circle is the theological expansion of the first. Its purpose is to lead a new believer into a fuller apprehension of what God has accomplished through Christ Jesus. The outside circle is the ethical expansion of the other two. It lays hold on this new relationship of [a person] to God and brings it into focus for practical daily living." But it all goes back to the cross. From Robert Mounce but shared in H.C. Brown, Jr., et al, *Steps to the Sermon* (Nashville: Broadman and Holman, 1996), 18.
[39] Osborn, 284.
[40] Ibid., 285.
[41] David Larsen, *The Company of the Preachers* (Grand Rapids: Kregel, 1998), 61.
[42] Wayne McDill, *The Moment of Truth* (Nashville: Broadman and Holman, 1999). 11.
[43] MacGorman, 106.

[44] David Allen, *Text Driven Preaching* (Nashville: Broadman and Holman Academic, 2010), 264.
[45] McDill, 11.
[46] Osborn, 311.
[47] Vaughan and Lea, 32.
[48] Fee, 100.
[49] Prior, 51.
[50] Ibid.
[51] Ibid.
[52] Fee, 106-107.
[53] Prior, 50.
[54] MacGorman, 107.
[55] Jimmy Draper, *Foundations of Biblical Faith* (Nashville: Broadman, 1979), 32.
[56] John MacArthur, *The Foolishness of God* (Panorama City: Word of Grace, 1984), 61.
[57] Daniel Iverson, "Spirit of the Living God" (1926). Public domain.
[58] Vaughan and Lea, 38.
[59] T.W. Hunt, *The Mind of Christ* (Nashville: LifeWay, 1994), 12-18.
[60] Barclay, 32.
[61] Fee, 123.
[62] This anecdote is similar to one written by the comedian Emo Philips.
[63] William Barclay, *The Letters to the Corinthians* (Edinburgh: St. Andrew, 1957), 34.
[64] Ibid.
[65] Fee, 123.
[66] Ibid., 121.
[67] Prior, 58.
[68] Ibid., 57.
[69] MacGorman, 108.
[70] Ibid.
[71] Ibid., 109.
[72] Prior, 60.
[73] James W. Bryant and Mac Brunson, *The New Guidebook for Pastors* (Nashville: B&H, 2007), 203.
[74] Jan Waterman, "The Deception of Perception", http://www.themindfulword.org/2012/perception-deception-illusion-true/#v1VmkGs2Mctht053.99 (accessed 2 April 2014).

[75] Barclay, 38.
[76] MacGorman, 110.
[77] Barclay, 39.
[78] Ibid., 40.
[79] Gerald Stone, *God's Front Porch* (Denton: Tattersall, 1997), 1.
[80] Paul Powell, *Shepherding the Sheep in Small Churches* (Annuity Board, 1995), 32.
[81] Ibid.
[82] Ibid., 33.
[83] Vaughan and Lea, 47.
[84] Ibid., 48.
[85] Ibid., 51.
[86] Stone, 129.
[87] Vaughan and Lea, 52.
[88] Ibid., 53.
[89] Ibid.
[90] Prior, 68.
[91] MacGorman, 113.
[92] Ibid.
[93] Ibid.
[94] Ibid., 114.
[95] Ibid.
[96] Findley Edge, *A Quest for Vitality in Religion* (Nashville: Broadman, 1963), 223-225.
[97] MacGorman, 115.
[98] Prior, 79.
[99] MacGorman, 116.
[100] Barclay.
[101] Vaughan and Lea, 62-63.
[102] MacGorman, 115.
[103] Ibid., 117.
[104] Ibid., 119.
[105] Ibid.
[106] Stanley Grenz, *Sexual Ethics* (Westminster John Knox, 1990), 82.
[107] Ibid., 80-81.
[108] Ibid., 86.
[109] Prior, 116.
[110] Gary Chapman, *The Five Love Languages* (Chicago: Northfield, 1992).

[111] Prior., 123-124.
[112] Ibid., 125.
[113] Vaughan and Lea, 75.
[114] Prior, 127.
[115] MacGorman, 122.
[116] Prior, 128.
[117] Charles Swindoll, *Wit and Wisdom: Chuck's Homespun Prescriptions for Love and Marriage*, "Jake and Jessie," Compact-disc (Plano, TX: Insight for Living, 2004).
[118] http://www.beliefnet.com/Love-Family/Relationships/Dating/Dating-Week/What-Churches-Should-Do-For-Singles.aspx#KHLspyXmhZsJXt5Z.99. Accessed 1 July 2020.
[119] Ibid.
[120] Raymond McHenry, *The Best of In Other Words* (Houston, TX, Raymond McHenry, 1996), 156.
[121] Originally available at http://www.christianitytoday.com/singles/newsletter/mind50713.html. Accessed 13 July 2014.
[122] I am indebted to Leon Hyatt for this background provide in his unpublished sermon notes.
[123] Hemphill notes from 1 Corinthians.
[124] Hyatt, unpublished notes.
[125] MacGorman, 126.
[126] Spence-Jones, 303.
[127] http://blog.ncbaptist.org/renewingworship/2011/02/09/worship-wars/
[128] http://blog.ncbaptist.org/renewingworship/2011/02/09/worship-wars/
[129] MacGorman, 125.
[130] Prior, 167.
[131] Ibid., 169.
[132] Ibid., 171.
[133] Much of the remainder of Chapter 10 goes with Chapter 8. I included much of the teaching from this section in the chapter dealing with meat sacrificed to idols. The concluding verses of Chapter 10 give us some general guidelines for living as a Christian community. We are neither Jewish nor Greek; we are a different group, the Church of God. Paul is not

concerned with barriers or stumbling-blocks. Instead, he provides five ground-rules for living together in Christ.

1. Do all to the glory of God (v. 31) – not to establish my freedom, not to grow my church, not to show my spirituality – simply for the glory of God. Above everything we do in our individual lives and as a church is "for the glory of God."
2. Try to please all men in everything (v. 33) – not claiming my rights, but providing an open door for continued witness. Not burning bridges or slamming doors, but propping the door open for an ongoing, unending witness until such time as that person trusts Christ.
3. Seek the good of many (v. 33) – not my benefit or fulfillment. Our fulfillment should come from seeing others trust Christ.
4. Seek that many may be saved (v. 33) – not being preoccupied with my personal salvation.
5. Be imitators of Christ (11:1) – not boosting my reputation.

[134] Vaughan and Lea, 111.
[135] Ibid., 112.
[136] Hemphill class notes.
[137] MacGorman, 133.
[138] Ibid., 132.
[139] Swindoll, *He Gave Gifts*, 3.
[140] Ken Hemphill, *Mirror Mirror on the Wall: Discovering Your True Self through Spiritual Gifts* (B&H, 1992), 36.
[141] Jack MacGorman, *The Gifts of the Spirit* (Broadman, 1974), 30.
[142] Hemphill, *Mirror*, 49.
[143] Ibid., *Mirror*, 47.
[144] Ibid.
[145] MacGorman, *Gifts*, 28.
[146] Ibid., *Gifts*, 30.
[147] Hemphill, *Mirror*, 55.
[148] MacGorman, *Gifts*, 32.
[149] Ibid., *Gifts*, 29.
[150] Hemphill, *Mirror*, 57.
[151] Ibid., 57-58.
[152] Ibid., *Mirror*, 59.
[153] Ray Ortlund, *Three Priorities for a Strong Local Church* (Dallas: Word, 1988), 58.

[154] Rainer, *Autopsy of a Deceased Church* (Nashville: B&H, 2014), 58-60.
[155] Hemphill, *Mirror*, 66.
[156] MacGorman, *Gifts*, 53.
[157] Hemphill, *Mirror*.
[158] MacGorman, *Gifts*, 55.
[159] Don't read too much into the order of the entire list. Paul's point is not so much to create a hierarchy of offices (apostles, prophets, teachers) as it is to emphasize the priority of a certain ministry – the ministry of the word.
[160] Hemphill, *Mirror*, 66.
[161] Samuel Davies, *Sermons*, vol. 3, Sermon LXXVIII: "The Office of Bishop a Good Work," 558.
[162] MacGorman, 139.
[163] Thom Rainer, *I am a Church Member* (Nashville: B&H, 2013), 13.
[164] Hemphill, *Mirror*, 70.
[165] Ibid., 71.
[166] Ibid.
[167] MacGorman, *Gifts*, 62.
[168] Translations and some explanation from Ibid., 64ff.
[169] Ibid., 66.
[170] Ibid.
[171] Ibid., 67.
[172] Ibid.,74.
[173] Ibid., 75.
[174] Ibid., 141.
[175] Ibid., 75.
[176] I am indebted to my friend, Leon Hyatt, for these thoughts.
[177] MacGorman, *Gifts*, 73.
[178] Ibid., 83.
[179] Ibid., *86*.
[180] Ibid., 104.
[181] Vaughan and Lea, 150.
[182] Ibid.
[183] J. Vernon McGee, *First Corinthians* (Nashville: Thomas Nelson, 1991), 170.
[184] Prior256.
[185] MacGorman, 144.
[186] Vaughan and Lea, 152.
[187] Ibid.,151.

[188] The main points for this chapter are adapted from Ken Hemphill's class notes.
[189] MacGorman, 263.
[190] Vaughan and Lea, 154.
[191] MacGorman, 145.
[192] Ibid.
[193] Adapted from Michael Lanning, "The Top Ten Battles of All Time." The History Place - Top Ten Battles of All Time, n.d. http://www.historyplace.com/worldhistory/topten. Accessed 1 July 2020.
[194] Vaughan and Lea, 156.
[195] Ibid., 157.
[196] Ibid., 158.
[197] MacGorman, 147.
[198] MacArthur, *The Glory of Heaven* (Wheaton: Crossway, 1996), 132.
[199] Vaughan and Lea, 159.
[200] MacGorman, 147.
[201] Vaughan and Lea, 160.
[202] MacGorman, 147.
[203] Ibid.
[204] MacArthur, 133.
[205] The contributions of these Gentile churches served at least "three purposes: (1) an acknowledgement by the Gentile churches of the spiritual debt owed to the Jerusalem church; (2) an obvious demonstration of the genuineness of faith of the Gentile Christians; (3) a method of linking Jewish and Gentile Christians more closely together." Vaughan and Lea, 166.
[206] http://givewithjoy.org/true_stories.htm. Accessed 1 July 2020.
[207] Sutherland and Nowery, *The 33 Laws of Stewardship* (Camarillo: NewSource, 2003), 70.
[208] MacGorman, 150.
[209] Prior, 285.

YOU MAY ALSO ENJOY

***The Privilege of Worship* (*Westbow, 2016*)**

There is no such thing as a worship war. We aren't fighting over worship; we're fighting over preferences. For centuries, churches have been fighting preference wars over worship methodologies. Whether it was singing psalms or hymns, using screens or hymnals, playing organs or guitars, or using a choir or praise team, if there has been a method to fight over, we've gone to battle. Unfortunately, the only things we've gained from our warring are church splits, declining rolls, and frustrated members. Is that what we most desire from our worship?

What would happen in our churches if we went to war *for* worship or *in* worship instead of going to war *over* worship? What if we got so serious about worship that we put our preferences aside and focused on engaging God? Worship is not about songs and sermons anyway. Worship is about a privileged conversation with God!

Discover how you and your church can get serious about worship as you delve into the heart of worship. Study who is involved in worship, what you can expect from worship, and how you can get the most out of worship.

If we want to see God do great things in our churches and bring awakening to our nation, we must get serious about worship. Let's stop fighting over methodologies and return to the core of worship. Take some time to explore the privilege of worship.

FOCUS POINT Devotionals

To receive Pastor's Stewart's daily devotional, *FOCUS POINT*, email info@fbcpineville.net and request to be added. You may also follow him on Facebook or Instagram.

Made in USA - North Chelmsford, MA
1310408_9798649881982
04.05.2022 0853